Reclaiming Marx's "Capital"

Raya Dunayevskaya Series in Marxism and Humanism

Series Editors: Kevin B. Anderson, Purdue University
Olga Domanski, News and Letters Committees
Peter Hudis, News and Letters Committees

The Power of Negativity: Selected Writings on the Dialectic in Hegel and Marx
by Raya Dunayevskaya, Edited and Introduced by Peter Hudis and Kevin B.
Anderson
Philosophy and Revolution: From Hegel to Sartre and from Marx to Mao
by Raya Dunayevskaya
*Helen Macfarlane: A Feminist, Revolutionary Journalist, and Philosopher in Mid-
Nineteenth-Century England*
by David Black
Karl Marx and the Future of the Human
by Cyril Smith
Reclaiming Marx's "Capital": A Refutation of the Myth of Inconsistency
by Andrew Kliman

Reclaiming Marx's "Capital"

A Refutation of the Myth of Inconsistency

Andrew Kliman

LEXINGTON BOOKS

A division of
ROWMAN & LITTLEFIELD PUBLISHERS, INC.
Lanham • Boulder • New York • Toronto • Plymouth, UK

LEXINGTON BOOKS

A division of Rowman & Littlefield Publishers, Inc.
A wholly owned subsidiary of The Rowman & Littlefield Publishing Group, Inc.
4501 Forbes Boulevard, Suite 200
Lanham, MD 20706

Estover Road
Plymouth PL6 7PY
United Kingdom

British Library Cataloguing in Publication Information Available

Library of Congress Cataloging-in-Publication Data

Kliman, Andrew, 1955-
  Reclaiming Marx's Capital : a refutation of the myth of inconsistency / Andrew Kliman.
      p. cm. -- (Raya Dunayevskaya series in Marxism and humanism)
  ISBN-13: 978-0-7391-1851-1 (cloth : alk. paper)
  ISBN-10: 0-7391-1851-X (cloth : alk. paper)
  ISBN-13: 978-0-7391-1852-8 (pbk. : alk. paper)
  ISBN-10: 0-7391-1852-8 (pbk. : alk. paper)
  1. Labor theory of value. 2. Marx, Karl, 1818-1883. Kapital. I. Title.
  HB206.K55 2007
  335.4'12--dc22   2006028377

Printed in the United States of America

♾™ The paper used in this publication meets the minimum requirements of American
National Standard for Information Sciences—Permanence of Paper for Printed Library
Materials, ANSI/NISO Z39.48–1992.

For Anne

Contents

List of Tables and Figures

List of Abbreviations

FMT	Fundamental Marxian Theorem
GDP	Gross Domestic Product
LTFRP	Law of the Tendential Fall in the Rate of Profit
LTP	Labor Theory of Price
MELT	Monetary Expression of Labor-Time
NI	New Interpretation
NIPA	National Income and Product Accounts
PNP	Price of the Net Product
PSE	Principle of Scientific Exegesis
SSSI	Simultaneous Single-System Interpretation
TSSI	Temporal Single-System Interpretation

Preface

The economists have changed Marx, in various ways; the point is to interpret him—correctly.

This book seeks to reclaim Marx's *Capital* from the century-old myth of internal inconsistency. Since internally inconsistent arguments cannot possibly be right, efforts to return to and further develop Marx's critique of political economy, in its original form, cannot succeed so long as this myth persists. The myth serves as the principal justification for the suppression and "correction" of Marx's theories of value, profit, and economic crisis. It also facilitates the splintering of what was, originally, a political-economic-philosophical totality into a variety of mutually indifferent Marxian projects.

Logical considerations compel none of this. As this book shows, Marx's theories need not be interpreted in a way that renders them internally inconsistent. An alternative interpretation developed during the last quarter-century—the temporal single-system interpretation (TSSI)—eliminates all of the apparent inconsistencies. The very existence of the TSSI carries with it two important consequences. First, the allegations of inconsistency are unproved. Second, they are implausible. When one interpretation makes the text make sense, while others fail to do so because they create avoidable inconsistencies within the text, it is not plausible that the latter interpretations are correct. Thus the charges of inconsistency, founded on these interpretations, are implausible as well.

None of this implies that Marx's theoretical conclusions are necessarily correct. It does imply, however, that empirical investigation is needed in order to determine whether they are correct or not. There is no justification for disqualifying his theories *a priori*, on logical grounds.

In recent years, Marx's critics have found it increasingly difficult to defend the allegations of inconsistency against the TSSI critique. Thus they generally try to avoid this issue altogether. Instead, they now prefer to debate the pros and cons of Marx's work and of alternative approaches to Marxian economic analysis. In other contexts, these are of course important and interesting topics, but to discuss them here and now is to fall into a diversionary trap, at the very moment when correction of the record has become a real possibility. I will be glad to discuss these topics with Marx's critics once the record has been set straight and they have done their part to help set it straight. This book, however, purposely refrains from offering a positive case for Marx's ideas or for Marxian economic analysis informed by the TSSI.

Yet why should readers support the book's effort to reclaim *Capital* if they are provided with no positive reasons for it? My answer is that this book seeks to reclaim *Capital* in a very specific sense; it seeks to show that the charges of inconsistency are unproved and implausible. If it succeeds in this task, then everyone who favors integrity in intellectual discourse and opposes suppression, whether or not they favor Marx's ideas, will support the effort to set the record straight.

The personal journey that culminated in my writing of this book began twenty years ago, when I was studying economics at the University of Utah. Ted McGlone, a friend and fellow Ph.D. student studying for a comprehensive exam, asked me to explain why Marx's account of the transformation of values into prices of production was internally inconsistent. He had listened to our professors' explanations, but still didn't understand what was wrong with Marx's account. I faithfully repeated what he and I had been taught—"Marx forgot to transform the input prices." McGlone asked why Marx needed to transform the input prices. I found that I could not satisfactorily explain why. So I urged him to just accept the fact—after all, everyone agreed that Marx had made an error, including *Marxist* economists such as our professors—and I noted that it didn't make any difference, because the error had since been corrected.

"Ah, but I was so much older then / I'm younger than that now."

McGlone persisted in his questioning during the next few weeks. My inability to defend the allegation of inconsistency persisted as well, finally impelling me to re-examine the primary source—Bortkiewicz's (1952) proof of Marx's internal inconsistency.[1] After some study, I detected what I thought might be an error. I sat down and, within an hour, produced a refutation of Bortkiewicz's proof (see section 8.5 below). Over the next few days, McGlone and I, working out the implications of this refutation, discovered what came to be known as the TSSI—or rather, rediscovered it, since a few other researchers had independently discovered it some years earlier.

This proved to be a life-altering experience. It taught me to think for myself, to question authority and to demand rational demonstrations instead of relying on intuition. As I continued to explore the implications of the TSSI, I found that it also eliminates the other alleged inconsistencies in Marx's theories, and that, contrary to what his critics claim, their "corrections" do not replicate his theoretical results by different means. I became even more convinced of the need to question authority and to demand that claims be demonstrated rationally.

Of course, many people who have encountered the internal inconsistency charges have lacked the background in mathematics and economics needed to evaluate the charges for themselves, or even to fully understand the issues. This problem has been aggravated—intentionally or not—by the excessively abstruse, jargon-filled, and mathematical manner in which Marx's critics have typically presented their case. In light of these obstacles to understanding, many non-specialists have simply chosen to take the experts' conclusions on faith. Others have turned their backs on debates that they experience as technical and trifling. Unfortunately, this latter response also allows the experts' conclusions to go unchallenged.

For these reasons, I have put a great deal of effort into writing this book in as non-technical and non-mathematical a manner as I can. The result, I believe, is the most accessible full-length treatment of the controversy over Marx's value theory to date, as well as the most accessible extended presentation of the TSSI. Chapters 2 and 3 contain some introductory material on Marx's theory, different interpretations of it, and the history of the value theory controversy. I have used numerical examples instead of algebra whenever possible. In the very few places in which I have used algebra, the reader can "read around it," or skip it. Even readers without *any* prior background or mathematics beyond arithmetic will be able to understand everything of importance if they are willing to read the book slowly and carefully.

I am honored that this book is part of the Raya Dunayevskaya Series on Marxism and Humanism. My effort to overturn the myth of internal inconsistency, so that *Capital* can be reclaimed as a totality, is inspired by Dunayevskaya's (1991) theorization of Marx's Marxism as constituting a totality and her perspective of returning to it as such. As I have tried to understand and come to grips with Marxian economists' refusal to acquit Marx of inconsistency, which initially surprised me greatly, I have also benefited enormously from Dunayevskaya's understanding of dialectical development. Grappling with a similar (but deadlier) process of "internal differentiation"—the emergence of Stalinist counter-revolution from within revolutionary Marxism—she identified ceaseless internal differentiation and self-movement as the key to Hegel's philosophical system. "Hegel as the philosopher of absolute negativity never . . . lets us forget *divisions* of the 'One,' not even where that is the Idea" (Dunayevskaya 2003: 42, emphasis in original). Inasmuch as her *oeuvres* are founded in part upon Marx's theories of value and the falling rate of profit, I hope that my defense of these theories' internal consistency repays a small part of my debt to Dunayevskaya's thought.

The ideas in this book emerged through years of extensive collaboration and dialogue with other proponents of the TSSI, especially Alan Freeman. In many cases, I have long since forgotten whether it was Freeman or I, or someone else, who came up with a particular idea or formulation. Thus, I cannot take full *credit* for this book; it undoubtedly draws upon the works and thoughts of other TSSI theorists in a great many places where they are not cited explicitly. I am deeply grateful to them; in a sense, they are the book's co-authors. Nonetheless, I must take full *responsibility* for the views expressed herein, and for any errors I may have made. Even with respect to the interpretation of the quantitative dimension of Marx's value theory, there are differences among proponents of the TSSI.

I would like to thank Guglielmo Carchedi, Anne Jaffe, Tom Jeannot, Nick Potts, and the editors of the Raya Dunayevskaya Series—all of whom offered extensive, extremely helpful comments on the entire manuscript of this book— and Josh Howard and Eli Messinger, who read and commented on specific chapters. I am grateful to Rob Garnett—for discussions that led me to explain, in chapter 1, how this book contributes to the movement for pluralism in econom- ics; to Roslyn Bologh—for alerting me to Sørensen's critique of Marx and urg- ing me to respond to it, which I also do in chapter 1; and to Keith Gibbard—for bringing Stigler's "principle of scientific exegesis," discussed in chapter 4, to my attention.

I wish to thank Pace University for granting me sabbatical leave in the 2003–2004 academic year, during which I wrote much of this book, and for sub- sequent release time, which I used to complete it. I also wish to thank Joseph C. Parry, my editor at Lexington Books, for his valuable advice and support. Much of this book was written in seclusion, at the home of Barbara Barnes and Eli Messinger, and then at the home of Raymond and Sara Ford; I am very grateful to all of them for offering me refuge from daily life.

Although everything in this book has been written specifically for it, I have drawn upon previously published works of mine in several places. I thank the following journals and publishers for allowing me such use of these works:

Beiträge zur Marx-Engels Forschung (Neue Folge) published my "Deter- mination of Value in Marx and in Bortkiewiczian Theory," drawn upon in chap- ter 6, in its 1999 volume. It also published my "Hermeneutics and the Value Theory Controversy: Lessons from Mainstream Historians of Economic Thought," drawn upon in chapter 4, in its 2004 volume.

Capital and Class published my "Simultaneous Valuation vs. the Exploita- tion Theory of Profit" in issue 73 (Spring 2001). It also published my "Replicat- ing Marx: A Reply to Mohun" (co-authored with Alan Freeman), in issue 88 (Spring 2006). Both papers are drawn upon in chapter 10.

The Centro Studi Trasformazioni Economico-Sociali (CESTES) published my "Se è corretto, non correggetelo," drawn upon in chapter 5, in *Proteo* 2001-2 (Sept. 2001), available at www.proteo.rdbcub.it/article.php3?id_article=139. The same paper was republished, along with an English translation ("If It Ain't Broke, Don't Correct It"), by the Laboratorio per la Critique Sociale, in *Un Vecchio Falso Problema/An Old Myth* (2002), edited by Luciano Vasapollo.

Edward Elgar, Ltd. published my "A Value-theoretic Critique of the Oki-shio Theorem," drawn upon in section 7.2.3 and elsewhere, as chapter 10 of *Marx and Non-equilibrium Economics* (1996), edited by Alan Freeman and Guglielmo Carchedi.

Elsevier B. V. published my "Rejoinder to Duncan Foley and David Laibman" (co-authored with Alan Freeman), parts of which are quoted in section 7.3.3 and drawn upon in section 7.5.3, in *Research in Political Economy*, vol. 18 (2001). It also published my "Spurious Value-Price Correlations: Some Additional Evidence and Arguments," drawn upon in chapter 11, in *Research in Political Economy*, vol. 21 (2004).

Oxford University Press published my "The Law of Value and Laws of Statistics: Sectoral Values and Prices in the U.S. Economy, 1977-1997" in the *Cambridge Journal of Economics*, vol. 26, no. 3 (May 2002). It also published my "Reply to Cockshott and Cottrell" in the *Cambridge Journal of Economics*, vol. 29, no. 2 (March 2005). Both papers are drawn upon in chapter 11.

Political Economy published my "Internal Inconsistencies of the Physical Quantities Approach," drawn upon in sections 5.6 and 5.7, in issue 4 (Spring 1999).

Taylor & Francis, Inc. published my "A Temporal Single-system Interpretation of Marx's Value Theory" (co-authored with Ted McGlone), drawn upon in section 8.5, in *Review of Political Economy*, vol. 11, no. 1 (Jan. 1999). It also published my "Screpanti vs. Marx on Exploitation," drawn upon in section 4.2, in *Review of Political Economy*, vol. 18, no. 2 (April 2006).

The lyrics quoted on page xiv are from Bob Dylan's "My Back Pages." Copyright © 1964 by Warner Bros. Inc. Copyright renewed 1992 by Special Rider Music. All Rights Reserved. International copyright secured. Reprinted by permission.

I have dedicated this book to Anne. I could not have written this book without her intellectual, professional, and personal support. She assisted me in my sometimes obsessive working-through of ideas and endured my absences. Her feedback has consistently been instrumental in helping to turn inchoate notions into intelligible ideas. We have fought the fight against suppression side by side. It is she to whom I owe the greatest debt.

New York City, March 2006

Note

1. Throughout this book, I cite the edition of the work I have used. In the bibliography, I also indicate the date when the work was first published (in the original language) and the years in which Marx's unpublished manuscripts were written.

Chapter 1

Introduction: The Question
of Internal Inconsistency

"[E]xperts" frequently do not know what they are talking about and "scholarly opinion", more often than not, is but uninformed gossip. . . . General acceptance does not decide a case—arguments do. —Paul Feyerabend[1]

1.1 The Lion and the Statue

One of Aesop's fables, "The Lion and the Statue," is the story of an argument between a man and a lion over which species is stronger. Eventually the man takes the lion to the public gardens and points to a statue of Hercules strangling a lion. "This proves," the man exclaims, "that humans are the stronger species!" "No," the lion replies, "it proves nothing, since a man made the statue. If lions could make statues, Hercules would be lying under the lion's paw."

Dozens of accounts have told us that rigorous mathematical demonstrations—often coming from the Marxist camp itself—have proved that Marx's theories of value, profit, and economic crisis are riddled with logical inconsistencies and errors, and that these proofs have withstood the test of time. It is therefore necessary either to reject or correct his work. Those who refuse to accept that such inconsistency has been proved have "done much damage to the intellectual credentials of Marxian political economy" (Howard and King 1992: xiii).

The main thesis of this book is that Marx has been "proved" internally inconsistent in the same way that the superior strength of humans is "proved" by the statue of Hercules strangling a lion: one side of the argument controls the principal means of communication. In fact, the internal inconsistency allegations are implausible as well as unproved, because there exists an interpretation of Marx's value theory that removes the apparent inconsistencies.

1

On the standard interpretation, Marx had a *simultaneist* and *dual-system* theory:

- inputs and outputs are valued simultaneously, so input and output prices are necessarily equal, and
- there are two separate systems of values and prices.

According to the *temporal single-system* interpretation (TSSI) of Marx's theory, however:

- valuation is temporal, so input and output prices can differ, and
- values and prices, though quite distinct, are determined interdependently.

Once these two simple modifications are made, *all* of the alleged inconsistencies in the quantitative dimension of Marx's value theory are eliminated.

These results have been established during a quarter-century of TSSI research. Yet our side has not been able to erect statues in the public gardens, so to speak, and thus the myth of internal inconsistency is almost as ubiquitous as before. But it is time for the hammer and chisel to be handed over to the lions.

1.2 What This Book Is (and Isn't) About

The specific way in which this book seeks to reclaim Marx's *Capital* requires some explanation. It will be helpful to first say what the book is not about. Although it contains some relevant background material, it is not a primer on *Capital* or Marx's value theory. Its purpose is not to provide an overarching interpretation of *Capital*—the TSSI is simply an interpretation of two quite limited aspects of Marx's value theory. It does not promote a particular view of *Capital's* significance for us today or even defend it on the ground that it remains significant. (I do believe that *Capital* remains significant—I would not have written this book if I thought otherwise—and I have reasons for this belief, but the way in which this book tries to reclaim it is quite different.) I do not claim that Marx's value theory and his associated theories of profit and crisis are "fundamentally correct," much less correct in every respect, nor do I argue in the present work that they are substantively or methodologically superior to the alternatives. Similarly, my goal is not to promote the TSSI over other interpretations of Marx's theory as an approach to economic understanding and analysis.

I am well aware, moreover, that the issues I discuss here are not the main themes of *Capital* or even of Marx's value theory. That value and price are determined temporally and interdependently is certainly not what Marx's value theory is "really about." My intention is not to privilege these aspects of his theory over others, nor even to argue that they are important in some broad sense. Similarly, the reason why this book focuses on the "quantitative" dimension of Marx's value theory rather than its "qualitative" dimension is not that I regard the former as more important. (I regard the two dimensions as necessary parts of an inseparable whole, within which the "qualitative" dimension is the more important one.)

So what *does* this book seek to do? Its aim is to reclaim Marx's *Capital* from the myth that his value theory has been proven internally inconsistent. It argues that the conclusions Marx deduced on the basis of his value theory are logically valid. I assess the standard interpretation of Marx's value theory, the TSSI, and other interpretations only in terms of their relative success in making Marx's own theory make sense, not as theoretical approaches in their own right. In short, this book is purely and simply about the question of internal inconsistency.

It is important not to confuse logical validity with truth. Logically valid arguments can have false conclusions (if they begin from false premises). Critics of the TSSI often seem to be confused about this. For example, Veneziani (2004: 97, emphasis in original; cf. Laibman 2004) recently asserted that "the literal truth of *all* [of] Marx's propositions is claimed" by proponents of the TSSI, even though we have frequently made clear that "We have never said that Marx's contested insights are necessarily true . . . . We simply say the claims that his value theory is *necessarily wrong*, because it is logically invalid, are false" (Freeman and Kliman 2000: 260, emphasis in original).

1.3 The Importance of the Internal Inconsistency Question

The main reason why I consider the question of internal inconsistency so important—important enough to devote a whole book to it—is precisely that Marx's value theory would be *necessarily wrong* if it were internally inconsistent. Internally inconsistent theories may be appealing, intuitively plausible and even obvious, and consistent with all available empirical evidence—but they cannot be right. It is necessary to reject them or correct them. Thus the alleged proofs of inconsistency trump all other considerations, disqualifying Marx's theory at the starting gate. By doing so, they provide the principal justification for the suppression of this theory as well as the suppression of, and the denial of resources needed to carry out, present-day research based upon it. This greatly inhibits its further development. So does the very charge of inconsistency. What person of intellectual integrity would want to join a research program founded on (what she believes to be) a theory that is internally inconsistent and therefore false? The reclamation of *Capital* from the myth of inconsistency is therefore an absolutely necessary and vital precondition to any efforts to reclaim it in more ambitious ways.[2]

Another reason why I consider the question of internal inconsistency so important is that the whole of the century-long controversy over Marx's value theory has fundamentally been about this one question. Only incidentally and derivatively has it been a debate about the *meaning and significance* of his work. His critics' primary, conscious, and avowed aims have been to discredit the *logic* of his arguments—thereby disqualifying his theory, in its original form, from further consideration—and then to correct his supposed logical errors. The different schools that have arisen in and around Marxian economics since the 1970s (Sraffianism, the New Interpretation, value-form analysis, and so on) are in essence just different ways of correcting or circumventing these supposed errors and working out the consequences.

These facts are often insufficiently appreciated. It is sometimes suggested, for instance, that there are many things wrong with the way in which Marx's critics have understood and modeled his value theory.[3] The specific problems that the TSSI focuses upon—simultaneous valuation and the severing of values and prices into two systems—are not even the most important problems. However, the question is "Important for what purpose?" The critics' models are attempts to disqualify Marx's value theory on logical grounds and to correct its errors. Their purpose is not to provide a descriptively rich, comprehensive account of the original theory. Accordingly, the purpose of the TSSI is different as well. It seeks to overturn the findings of inconsistency, and the narrow issues upon which it focuses are important for this purpose. Indeed, they are the only important issues; the jettisoning of simultaneism and the dual-system interpretation is both necessary and sufficient to acquit Marx of the internal inconsistency charges.

A similar failure to appreciate the centrality and import of the question of internal inconsistency arises in connection with the so-called "transformation problem," the alleged inconsistency in Marx's account of the relationship between values and prices of production. Many Marxists (and some non-Marxists) have tried to dismiss the issue by arguing that Marx's critics have missed the point he wanted to make; he was not really interested in explaining prices. But it is this dismissal that misses the point. The critics are not concerned with what Marx wanted to say. *They are trying to prevent what he did say from continuing to be said*, on the ground that it is logically invalid. And if it is indeed invalid, a better understanding of what Marx was really getting at does not make it any more valid. Questions of meaning and intent are relevant only insofar as they directly alter our understanding of the actual logic of the arguments.[4]

Those who would downplay the question of internal inconsistency also seem not to appreciate that there is little point in discussing many of the topics they prefer to discuss unless Marx can be acquitted of the errors with which he is charged. Since an internally inconsistent theory simply cannot be right, it is worth studying and discussing, if at all, only as a historical artifact and source of inspiration for a *better* theory. It is certainly a waste of time to devote scarce research time to employing it in empirical analysis.

Would-be defenders of Marx who try to minimize the importance of the question of internal inconsistency often seem unaware that they are repeating a key theme of his critics. The latter frequently claim that his inconsistencies and errors are ultimately insignificant, because they have corrected these inconsistencies and errors in a manner that substantiates *Capital's* essential theoretical conclusions.[5] One of the present book's principal aims is to show that this claim is false. Contrary to what Marx's critics often claim, for instance, their "corrections" of his theory contradict his conclusions that technological progress can cause the rate of profit to fall and that the exploitation of workers is the exclusive source of profit (see chapters 7 and 10 below).

In sum, there is really no way of getting around the logical issues; they need to be confronted head-on. And given that the alleged proofs of inconsistency serve a suppressive function, evasion of the logical issues is certainly not in the interests of those who seek to develop Marx's work.

Because I believe that the allegations of internal inconsistency need to be taken seriously and that logical consistency is truly important, this book will at times examine various purported refutations of the allegations that unfortunately do not pass muster. In some cases, their flaws reflect a failure to treat the issues and the arguments of Marx's critics with the required seriousness.[6] This not only does the critics a disservice, but also makes it much harder for genuine refutations to get a hearing. We have here a case of the boy who cried wolf—or the man who cried lion. Having become accustomed to false alarms, no one pays attention when the lion really does subdue the man.

1.4 The Influence of the Internal Inconsistency Allegations

The question of internal inconsistency is also important because the alleged proofs of inconsistency are ubiquitous and influential. As the following recent examples show, their influence extends far beyond the small circle of radical and Marxist economists, into the rest of economics, other disciplines, radical thought outside of academia, and public opinion generally.

In 1995, the leading journal of the history of economic thought published a symposium on Marx. Anthony Brewer's (1995: 140) lead paper argued that, even "in Marx's own terms . . . *Capital* must be counted a magnificent failure." As his principal supporting evidence, Brewer rehashed the allegations of logical error in Marx's value theory and law of the tendential fall in the rate of profit. "If both fail, as they do, not much is left" (Brewer 1995: 140). Marx's economic writings are of historical interest only. Papers that refuse to accept this conclusion and instead attempt to "resuscitate Marx's ideas . . . should not be published in journals devoted to the [history of economics]" (Brewer 1995: 141).

Nine eminent economists and historians of economics, some quite sympathetic to Marx, were invited to respond. They typically took issue with the last four words of Brewer's conclusion that "[i]f both fail, as they do, not much is left," yet all of them implicitly or explicitly endorsed the first part. It would seem that even if Marx is not exactly a dead dog, we have to accept the fact that two of his internal organs have permanently stopped functioning.

John Cassidy's (1997) widely discussed essay, "The Return of Karl Marx," was published in a 1997 issue of *The New Yorker,* a magazine that appeals to a general educated audience. The overline hailed Marx as "The Next Thinker," and the text of the essay was likewise chock-full of praise for Marx. "Many of the contradictions that he saw in Victorian capitalism . . . have begun reappearing in new guises . . . . [H]e wrote riveting passages about . . . issues that economists are now confronting anew, sometimes without realizing that they are walking in Marx's footsteps" (Cassidy 1997: 248).

Yet when he turned to Marx's value theory, Cassidy (1997: 252) was uncharacteristically curt and dismissive: "His mathematical model of the economy, which depended on the idea that labor is the source of all value, was riven with internal inconsistencies and is rarely studied these days." The alleged proofs of internal inconsistency are so pervasive and little-challenged that he did not need to elaborate, except to suggest that Marx lacked the necessary mathematical tools. Since the particular tools that Cassidy—a journalist, not an economist—mentions are irrelevant to the issue he is discussing (the "transformation problem"),[7] it is clear that "riven with internal inconsistencies" is not a judgment he arrived at on his own. In any case, it is hard for the reader to avoid concluding that, if even a great admirer of Marx has to acknowledge that his value theory is inconsistent, this surely must be so.

The following year, a major radical journal devoted an entire issue to a book-length essay on economic crisis by Robert Brenner (1998), an eminent Marxist historian. Its fortuitous appearance in the midst of the Asian economic crisis has helped make it the most widely discussed Marxist work, by far, of the last two decades. So has the editor's introduction, which suggested that Brenner should be awarded the Nobel Prize and which concluded, "Marx's enterprise has certainly found its successor" (*New Left Review* editors 1998: v).

Yet in his 265-page essay on economic crisis, Marx's successor devoted only one footnote to his law of the tendential fall in the rate of profit—and only in order to dispose of it and the theory of crisis based upon it. To dismiss the law summarily, he needed only to cite the Okishio (1961) theorem, which purportedly proves that the law is false: "Formal proofs of this result can be found in N. Okishio . . . as well as in J. Roemer . . . ." (Brenner 1998: 11–12, note 1). After rejecting some other theories (on the basis of somewhat more evidence and argumentation), the rest of the essay develops Brenner's own account of falling profitability and economic crisis. It is this account rather than Marx's that became the focal point of the ensuing discussion of Brenner's essay. Such is the power of the Okishio theorem.

In 2000, the leading U.S. journal of sociology carried a symposium in which the lead paper, written by a noted Harvard University professor (Sørensen 2000), put forth a new theory of exploitation as the basis for class analysis. Given that "Marx's explanation of inequality and oppression is a very attractive one" (Sørensen 2000: 1529), Sørensen felt the need to disqualify it before setting out his alternative. He did so by appealing to authority, especially to the fact that even the Marxist economists have abandoned Marx's value theory: "For most of this century, there has been agreement that the original concept of exploitation proposed by Marx is untenable. It is based on a labor theory of value abandoned long ago, even by Marxist economists" (Sørensen 2000: 1524). It is true that Sørensen then tried to defend the notion that the "transformation problem" is genuinely a problem, but his argument evinces a near-total lack of understanding of the issue, even on a charitable reading.[8] It thus seems clear that he declared Marx's theory untenable without having first seriously studied the value theory controversy. But if Sørensen was not qualified to reject Marx's theory, he also had no basis for recommending his own theory of exploitation to replace it.

Three papers were published in response to Sørensen, including one by a well-known Marxist sociologist (Wright 2000). All of them concurred with his conclusion that Marx's theory is untenable. None took issue with the way in which he arrived at this conclusion.

1.5 Why This Particular Book?

This book's focus on the internal inconsistency question will detract from its popularity (as will my position on the question). Most people interested in *Capital* wish to appropriate this or that particular aspect of it, not reclaim it as a totality. I have written this book rather than a different one, however, because I consider it a scholarly responsibility to set the record straight on the internal inconsistency question, a responsibility to defend norms of honesty and integrity in intellectual discourse.

I also consider this book a personal priority in the sense that, by helping to set the record straight, it makes a greater contribution than other things I wish to write about in the future. I think it is more important at the moment to help create a climate that allows Marx's ideas to be heard than to express my own ideas —including my own ideas about his work. I am convinced that popularizations of his work have made it harder, not easier, for his ideas to be heard, and that this is a major reason why they are still so misunderstood and little understood. Precisely because Marx's ideas are difficult and popularizations are easier, the latter become an easy substitute for the original texts. If we read the latter at all, we do so through the eyes of the popularizer.

Moreover, I believe that this is a propitious moment for this book to appear, for two reasons. First, if enough of its readers join in the effort to set the record straight on the question of internal inconsistency, this book can facilitate a reconsideration of Marx's value theory that extends well beyond its readership. Such reconsideration has become newly important, I believe, in light of the emergence of the movement against global capitalism. The movement is still searching for an understanding of that which it is against, and careful study of Marx's concept of capital as a process of "self-expanding value" would serve it well. An understanding of the tendency of value to expand limitlessly and inexorably, overcoming and integrating into itself all obstacles in its path, can help the movement recognize the insufficiency of merely institutional and political change, the need to transcend the system of value production itself (see Hudis 2000). Similarly, if capital is self-expanding value, then the current search for an alternative to capitalism needs also to become an inquiry into the extraordinarily difficult problem of precisely how an alternative to value production might get off the ground and sustain itself, given the tendency of the value-relation to overcome and absorb everything outside it.

Second, given that Marxian economics has disintegrated to the point of near-collapse, this is an appropriate moment to take stock of the internal contradictions within the field that helped bring about this situation. I emphasize the internal factors because the process of disintegration began before the resurgence of neo-liberalism and long before the collapse of the totalitarian state-capitalist regimes that called themselves "Communist." In my view, the disintegration of Marxian economics has a lot to do with the myth of internal inconsistency, and not only because some people who accepted the myth left the field.

A more important factor is the manner in which Marxist economists responded to the allegations of internal inconsistency. Instead of sitting down together, trying to reinterpret Marx in a way that makes his value theory make sense, and thereby reclaiming it as a basis of their research program, almost all Marxist economists took the opposite tack. An atmosphere of "every man his own Marxist" emerged.[9] As Marxist economists set about correcting Marx's supposed errors and overhauling their erstwhile research program, competing approaches and faddish solutions proliferated. So did various attempts to salvage Marxian economics (or make it respectable) by subsuming it under one or another variant of bourgeois economics.[10] Very little of this work has withstood the test of time—almost everyone who engaged in it has since turned to other matters—and in the end there was very little else to build upon.[11]

In retrospect, it seems clear that this whole way of responding to the allegations of internal inconsistency in Marx's theory served to weaken Marxian economics considerably. Lacking a focused research program and a common purpose, Marxian economics was unable to sustain itself once the ideological and political climate shifted to the right and Marxism became unpopular on the left. Much less was it able to offer something positive that might have acted as a countervailing influence. The ethos of "every man his own Marxist" also prevented the refutations of the internal inconsistency allegations from gaining acceptance and even from being treated as such. In the rare cases in which they were not ignored entirely, TSSI counterexamples that refuted the proofs of inconsistency were dealt with, not in their own terms, but as if they were economic models put forth by adherents of yet another competing approach.

I am certainly not suggesting that Marxist economists should have taken on faith that Marx was right about everything. The point is simply that it is reasonable and proper to try to resolve apparent inconsistencies, and to "think outside the box" in order to do so, before concluding that a theory is inadequate and heading off in every direction at once. This is how things are done in the physical sciences; the appearance of garden-variety anomalies does not provoke internal crisis (Kuhn 1970).[12] I hope that this book and other TSSI work can serve as a model for how Marxist economists might respond to such anomalies in a more sober and productive way than they responded in the past.

1.6 Whig History, Pluralism, and Dogmatism

I have also written this book as a contribution to the small but growing movement on behalf of pluralism within economics.[13] It contributes to this movement by offering a pluralistic alternative to the dominant Whig histories of the value theory controversy (e.g., Howard and King 1992).

1.6.1 Whiggism vs. Pluralism

Whiggishness and pluralism are antithetical. One can be against both Whig history and pluralistic practice (as Thomas Kuhn seems to have been, up to a point), but one cannot be in favor of both.

Whig historians "produce a story which is the ratification if not the glorification of the present" (Butterfield 1965: v). In other words, Whig history (1) is written from the perspective of those who currently hold power, and (2) assumes that the present is necessarily better than the past, that progress has taken place. The combination of these two factors makes Whig history profoundly anti-pluralistic. It can and often does serve as a justification for silencing dissidents on the ground that they are opponents of and obstacles to progress. It serves this justificatory function especially when the progress that supposedly has been made is progress toward clearly desirable ends such as knowledge and truth, the weeding out of error and internal inconsistency.

The controversy over Marx's value theory has been conducted on this Whiggish ground for more than three decades. The work of Paul Samuelson (1971), perhaps the pre-eminent economist of his generation, ushered in the modern phase of the controversy in the early 1970s, and everything written about it subsequently has been implicitly or explicitly a response to his work. Samuelson was a conscious and proud Whig historian. Defending the methodology of his critique of Marx, he wrote:

> [I]n the realm of cumulative knowledge, I believe there is a place for what might be called Whig History of Science. In it we pay past scholars the compliment of judging how their works contributed (algebraic) value-added to the collective house of knowledge. . . . I have thought it valuable to . . . appraise [Marx's] arguments on the transformation problem in the way a journal referee would treat any serious contributor. [Samuelson 1974b: 76]

Samuelson is suggesting, no doubt correctly, that journal referees would recommend that Marx's work on the "transformation problem" never see the light of day. He is also suggesting that they would be right to do so. The justification for this anti-pluralistic position is the Whiggish premise that economic knowledge has been "cumulative"—in other words, that it has progressed in an unambiguous way, culminating in Samuelson and his school. Thus, what counts as a contribution to knowledge is what counts from the perspective of this school and in light of the particular problems it addresses.

Yet it is well known that knowledge does not always move forward. Freeman (2004) points out, for instance, that the Copernican Revolution constituted a *return* to the heliocentric hypothesis of Aristarchus of Samos that had been abandoned nearly two millenia before, and he explores the implications of this fact for the controversy over Marx's value theory. Feyerabend (1988: 35) noted that reclamation of earlier ideas is a common phenomenon in science, and offered an explanation for why it occurs: "Theories are abandoned and superseded . . . long before they have had an opportunity to show their virtues." Facts such as these eliminate the main justification for anti-pluralistic practices.

1.6.2 The Most Effective Whiggish Strategy

What is more pertinent to the question of internal inconsistency is the very common case in which knowledge moves neither forward nor backward but sideways, as it were. Instead of a later theorist providing better or worse solutions than an earlier theorist to the same set of problems, the problems themselves have changed. In this case, it cannot be said that progress in solving the problems has been made, because "the" problems do not exist; there are two different sets of problems. But since Whig historians wish to extol the progressive character of the later theorist, they have to efface these differences. In doing so, they distort what the earlier theorist wrote, thereby creating inconsistencies where there were none—and this is construed as further evidence that what has subsequently occurred is progress! The more similar the two sets of problems are, the easier it is to cover over their differences.

In addition to being dishonest, this strategy is anti-pluralistic. By turning the earlier theorist into a flawed precursor of the later one, it effectively eliminates the distinctive character of her own thought.

This is exactly what has occurred throughout the controversy over Marx's value theory. *Some problems he addressed are very similar to those of neo-classicism, Sraffianism, and modern Marxian economics, with one key difference: Marx did not pose the problems in terms of the properties of static equilibrium states, and he therefore had no need to value inputs and outputs simultaneously.* But this difference has been repeated ignored. His theory is *transformed* into a theory of static equilibrium states, and thus into a simultaneist theory, causing a host of internal inconsistencies to appear. (This is the *real* transformation problem.)

I am not the first to call attention to this strategy. In a recent discussion of Thomas Kuhn's concept of "incommensurability," Sharrock and Read (2002: 144–145, emphases in original) characterize the strategy as follows: "The predecessor is made to look . . . rather *like oneself.* [This particular . . .] Whiggish strateg[y] . . . is the most effective if it can be pulled off, for it then becomes impossible to read predecessors as themselves. They read rather as if they've been trying to be you all along, *as if they've read you,* but ill-understood you."

Philip Mirowski (1988, chap. 10), the noted institutionalist historian of economic thought, showed how the same strategy was at work in Morishima's (1973) widely discussed critique of Marx. Mirowski (1988: 171) also noted that this strategy is a frequent device of neoclassical historians of economic thought, used to "demonstrat[e] that all that is valuable in economics has led up to the current orthodoxy." Frequently, their writings on Smith, Ricardo, and others

> consist of a marshaling of quotes, which are dragooned to justify the casting of some economic relationships in a specific functional form, which are then used to arrive at one of the two alternative conclusions[, . . . the second of which is that] the esteemed late economist in question had tripped himself up in self-contradiction, due to his unfortunate weaknesses in the area of mathematical expertise. [Mirowski 1988: 171][14]

This is also a perfect description of the strategy used to "prove" Marx's self-contradictions, including the appeal to lack of mathematical expertise as an explanation of why he blundered.[15] (Hegelianism and "Marx forgot" are other favorite explanations.)

Mirowski (1988: 172) goes on to ask, "What is wrong with this harmless bit of storytelling? After all, the classical economists are dead and in their graves." His answer—"Perceptions of progress do matter and are worth fighting over"— unfortunately leaves something to be desired. I do not think that such storytelling is harmless. It erodes respect for honesty and accuracy, debasing intellectual discourse. And some of us might wish to visit the graves of the dead—in other words, to reclaim their ideas—but, at least in Marx's case, false proofs of internal inconsistency have made this much more difficult. Recall Cassidy's (1997: 252) words: "was riven with internal inconsistencies and is rarely studied these days." That he connects these two things is no accident. Finally, by tending to justify exclusionary practices, the Whiggish story of linear progress is detrimental to intellectual development. Regression occurs when the only ideas that have the opportunity to be developed are wrong. Pluralistic practices act as a safeguard against this.

1.6.3 "Only One Path" Forward?

Marxist critics of the TSSI have frequently accused its advocates of dogmatism, orthodoxy, fundamentalism, and the like. These accusations are based mostly on the Whiggish story of linear progress. (Their other basis is the confusion, discussed above, between claims that something is logically valid and claims that it is true.) In a critique of what he calls "New Orthodox Marxism," for example, Laibman invokes the "proofs" of Marx's errors and he claims that the "20th-century Marxists" have corrected the errors. Thus, he contends, "there is only one path leading from the 19th century to the 21st, and that one lies through the 20th" (Laibman 2004: 16; the same volume carries responses by Kliman, Moseley, and Freeman). Those who wish to reclaim Marx's value theory in its original form are therefore dogmatically clinging to the past.

If the proofs of error to which Laibman appeals were valid, his anti-pluralistic position would have some merit. As Hodgson (2001: 35) has recently noted, there is a huge difference between "contradictory ideas in the academy and . . . inconsistent ideas within our own heads." Pluralism is no warrant for *internal* inconsistency.

Yet if the proofs to which Laibman appeals are invalid, as I hope to show—and especially if the charges of error and inconsistency are not even plausible, as I also hope to show—then his chain of reasoning collapses. If Marx has not been shown to be wrong, there is no need to correct him. I will argue that the so-called corrections are in fact simply alternative theories and models. This does not mean that Marx was necessarily *right* about everything, or even anything. What it does mean is that his original theory—when read in a manner that eliminates the appearance of inconsistency—is back in the running alongside alternative theories, including the "corrected" versions of his theory.

Hence, the shoe of dogmatism is now on the other foot. What is now dogmatic and orthodox is Laibman's insistence that there is "only one path" forward. Moreover, practices that hinder research rooted in Marx's value theory, including failure to acknowledge that refutations of the proofs of inconsistency have renewed the theory's viability, are acts of unacceptable censorship and suppression. All advocates of pluralism have a responsibility to speak out against such acts. Until conclusive proof of Marx's errors and inconsistencies is provided, this is how matters stand.

The myth of internal inconsistency has caused Marx's value theory and much of the rest of *Capital* to be relegated too hastily to the dustbin of Whig history. Whether his theory turns out in the end to be right or wrong, fruitful or fruitless, at the moment it is worthy of renewed consideration. Let history decide—non-Whig history.

1.7 Outline of Subsequent Chapters

The next two chapters are intended especially for readers who are new to the controversy over Marx's value theory. Chapter 2 provides a brief account of his theories of value, price, profit, and the tendential fall in the rate of profit, and then outlines the main differences between the standard interpretation, the TSSI, and some other interpretations that also arose in the 1980s. Chapter 3 is a short history of the controversy.

In chapters 4 through 6, I defend the book's theses in a general way, before turning to specific issues in the chapters that follow. Drawing on hermeneutic theory inside and outside of economics, and on our everyday interpretive practices, chapter 4 argues that the claims of internal inconsistency in Marx's theory should be rejected on the ground that they are implausible, because the interpretations of the theory that produce the inconsistencies are themselves implausible. The very point of an exegetical interpretation is to make the text make sense, but the interpretations in question fail to do so precisely because they create avoidable inconsistencies in the text. When one interpretation makes the text make sense by rendering the author's arguments internally consistent while another interpretation fails to do so, it is just not plausible that the latter is correct.

In chapters 5 and 6, I argue that the alleged proofs of inconsistency and error all depend crucially upon one key interpretive error, simultaneism—the notion that Marx held, or that his theory requires, that inputs into production and the outputs that subsequently emerge are valued simultaneously. Chapter 5 argues that simultaneism is simply incompatible with the key tenet of Marx's value theory, namely that value is determined by labor-time. Instead, simultaneism leads inevitably to *physicalism*—the notion that value, as well as price, profit, and the rate of profit, are determined by "physical quantities" (technology and real wages).

Surveying textual evidence of a more direct nature in chapter 6, I argue that it likewise shows Marx's theory to be temporalist rather than simultaneist. Later in that chapter, I also argue that the textual evidence shows Marx to have been a single-system rather than a dual-system theorist—that is, the values and prices of his theory are determined interdependently, not in two independent systems. This issue is important to the present work because Marx can be acquitted of internal inconsistency only if he was a single-system theorist as well as a temporalist.

Chapters 7 through 9 bring the foregoing analysis to bear upon two key interpretive controversies. In chapter 7, I take up Marx's law of the tendential fall in the rate of profit. This law, which he deemed "in every respect the most important law of modern political economy" (Marx 1973: 748), says that labor-saving technological changes tend to depress the rate of profit. Although the Okishio (1961) theorem is widely thought to have disproved the law, I argue that the theorem fails because it values inputs and outputs simultaneously and thereby substitutes an imaginary, physically determined, rate of profit for the temporally determined rate to which Marx's law refers. Furthermore, I show that labor-saving technological change *necessarily* tends to lower the temporal rate of profit relative to the physical rate, and thus that the rate of profit can indeed fall under conditions in which the Okishio theorem supposedly proved that it cannot.

Chapters 8 and 9 take up the so-called "transformation problem," the alleged error in Marx's account of the relationship between values and prices of production. It follows from Marx's account that his supposedly "metaphysical" theories of value and surplus-value hold true in the real world; in the aggregate, price and profit are determined by value and surplus-value, and thus the exploitation of workers is the exclusive source of profit. Yet Bortkiewicz (1952, 1984) supposedly proved a century ago (in 1906–1907) that inputs' and outputs' prices of production must be determined simultaneously, that Marx neglected this requirement, and that his theoretical conclusions no longer hold true once his error is corrected. I shall show, however, that Bortkiewicz's proof is invalid—inputs and outputs need not be valued simultaneously in order for prices of production to prevail—and that when Marx's account of the value-price relationship is interpreted in accordance with the TSSI, his conclusions do indeed follow from his premises.

One crucial claim of this book is that Marx cannot plausibly be interpreted as a simultaneist. This claim rests largely on the idea that simultaneous valuation is fundamentally incompatible with Marx's theory that value is determined by labor-time. Yet much of modern Marxian and Sraffian economics has seemingly rescued one or another of Marx's disputed theoretical conclusions within the simultaneist framework. In order to sustain my claim that simultaneist interpretations are implausible, it is important to show that these rescue efforts do not in fact succeed. I do so in the main text and the appendix to chapter 9 by considering some works that seemingly overcome the "transformation problem" without jettisoning simultaneous valuation, and showing that they overcome it only in a formal, not a substantive, sense. They force Marx's conclusions to go through by producing other absurd and impossible conclusions along the way, or they imply that the Okishio theorem is right while Marx was wrong—labor-saving technological change tends to raise, not lower, the rate of profit.

Continuing in the same vein in chapter 10, I examine the "Fundamental Marxian Theorem" (FMT) and related claims. The FMT is the crown jewel of simultaneist Marxian and Sraffian economics, for it supposedly demonstrates that failure to "solve the transformation problem" in a technical sense is no big deal, because Marx's principal conclusion—the exploitation of workers is the sole source of profit—remains intact. Consequently, proponents of the FMT claim, we can scrap his incoherent and metaphysical theory without doing damage to the essential core of his critique of capitalism.[16] Actually, the FMT demonstrates nothing of the sort, since it fails to vindicate Marx's exploitation theory of profit. I show that all simultaneist interpretations imply that profit can exist even though workers are not exploited, and that workers can be exploited even though there is no profit. These "internal inconsistencies" in Marx's value theory do not arise, however, when it is read as a temporal and single-system theory.

In chapter 11, I consider another body of work that also attempts to rescue Marx's conclusions without abandoning simultaneism. Many statistical studies have purportedly found that the correlation between industry-level prices and values is extremely strong, and that deviations between prices and values are small. On the basis of this evidence, the authors of these studies implicitly or explicitly dismiss the "transformation problem" as much ado about very little. I argue, however, that the evidence is invalid—in technical terminology, the strong price-value correlations are "spurious"—and I discuss my own recent studies which show that no statistically significant correlation remains after this problem is corrected. I also call attention to the fact that (as some authors of the above studies have acknowledged) the evidence would not tend to confirm Marx's *own* value theory even if it were valid.

Although the TSSI has existed for a quarter-century, Marx's theories of value, profit, and economic crisis are still regularly dismissed as internally inconsistent and error-ridden. Why is this so? Chapter 12, which concludes the book, explores some of the ideological, sociological, and psychological reasons. In the meantime, if any readers are tempted to discount this book's arguments on the ground that most experts—including experts *on Marx's side*—have not embraced the TSSI, I urge that they take note of Feyerabend's warnings quoted at the start of this chapter.

Notes

1. Feyerabend (2002: 16, 218).
2. It is of course possible to reclaim *particular aspects* of the work that are (largely) unrelated to its value theory without disproving the allegations of inconsistency. But that

is something different from reclaiming *Capital* itself, as a totality. Dunayevskaya (1991) puts forth the perspective of a return to Marx's Marxism as a totality.

3. For example, the Sraffian interpretation of Marx has frequently been charged (rightly, in my view) with a failure to appreciate the historically specific character of his value categories.

4. I will return to this issue in chapter 8, in connection with Postone's (1993) discussion of the transformation problem.

5. See, for example, Bellofiore (2002: 104, 2005: 9); Laibman (2004: 2–3, 16); Mongiovi (2002: 395, 414). Bellofiore (2002: 104, emphases added) writes: "Marx's project cannot be defended as it stands . . . some of the contradictions on which the critics have insisted are really there in *Capital*. . . . [Yet] Marx's progression from Volume I to Volume III [can] be *re*established on a *sound* theoretical basis." The "transformation problem" is apparently among the contradictions that are "really there," according to Bellofiore (2005: 9, emphasis in original): "Marx . . . does not transform the inputs, as he should do," and this is one of the reasons why Marxian value theory, "as it stands in Marx, *does not work*."

6. For a striking example of this phenomenon, see Saad-Filho (2001: 107, 90), who claims to "avoid[ ] the inconsistency charges" because, on his interpretation, Marx's solution to the "transformation problem" is only "incomplete," not incorrect. Yet once Saad-Filho "completes" Marx's solution—in other words, revises it in the standard (simultaneous dual-system) manner—his theories of value and the falling rate of profit are once again riven with all of the usual inconsistencies!

7. Cassidy (1997: 252) mentions "supply-and-demand curves, production functions, and game theory."

8. "Surplus has no implications for observable economic quantities like prices. Marx realized this in volume 3 and argued that the sum of surpluses in labor values and the sum of prices [sic] will be the same. However, 'as a general rule, profit and surplus value are really two different magnitudes'" (Sørensen 2000: 1529). Since the last sentence quotes Marx, Sørensen seems to be suggesting that Marx admitted that he was wrong. But the passage that Sørensen quotes pertains to "a particular sphere of production" (Marx 1991a: 267) and thus has no bearing upon whether the economy-wide sums are equal. On a charitable reading, Sørensen is appealing to a feature of some critics' "corrections" of Marx's theory: the sum of prices equals the sum of values, but the sum of profits differs from the sum of surplus-values. But his explanation is garbled on this reading as well: he pairs "the sum of surpluses" with "the sum of prices," the quotation from Marx is still irrelevant, and Sørensen fails to explain why Marx's theory needed to be corrected in the first place. On an *extremely* charitable reading, Sørensen is suggesting that surplus-value has no implications for profit—even though their totals are equal—because they differ at the industry level. To make sense, this novel and counterintuitive claim would require an explanation that he does not provide.

9. F. H. Hedge (1805–1890), a Unitarian clergyman, is widely quoted as having written (or said), "Every man is his own ancestor, and every man his own heir. He devises his own future, and he inherits his own past."

10. By "bourgeois economics," I mean all schools of economics that implicitly treat capitalism as natural and eternal by identifying peculiarly capitalistic categories (e.g. value, profit, wages) with categories applicable to all forms of society (e.g. wealth, increment to wealth, remuneration of workers).

11. Sraffianism may seem to be an exception to the rule, but its ties to Marxism have become increasingly tenuous.

12. It is also noteworthy that an insupportable lack of concern for internal consistency is prevalent throughout economics. Neoclassical economics is a congeries of mutually incompatible models (Desai 1988: 320–21) and Sraffian economics is beset by internal inconsistencies every bit as serious as those that supposedly beset Marx's value theory. (The conclusions of the Sraffian model fail when some inputs are not reproduced as outputs, which is always the case (Freeman 1997: 30–40). Its conclusions also fail when at least one "self-reproducing non-basic" commodity's "own-rate of reproduction" is less than that of the basic system (Sraffa 1960: 90–91, Kliman 1999a: 65–69), which seems likely as well.) Neoclassicists and Sraffians typically excuse these problems on the ground that theories are mere tools that necessarily differ from reality. But for them to excuse the internal inconsistencies of their own theories, while raising cain about the alleged internal inconsistencies of Marx's theory, is itself internally inconsistent. Will they excuse this internal inconsistency, too, on the ground that allegations of internal inconsistency are mere tools that necessarily differ from reality?

13. See the homepages of the International Confederation of Associations for Pluralism in Economics, www.icape.org (Jan. 7, 2006), the Association for Heterodox Economics, www.hetecon.com (Jan. 7, 2006), the International Working Group on Value Theory, www.iwgvt.org (Jan. 7, 2006), and the journal *Critique of Political Economy*, www.copejournal.org (July 14, 2006).

14. A minor difference in the way relationships are expressed mathematically— the "specific functional form"—can drastically affect the conclusions. For instance, the only mathematical difference between the TSSI and some other interpretations of Marx's theory is that the TSSI attaches time subscripts to variables (input and output prices are thus written as p_t and p_{t+1}, not p and p), but this leads to many diametrically opposite conclusions.

15. In Marx's case, the characterization of the issues and alleged errors as mathematical ones has additional advantages. His critics, especially Marxist and radical critics, are able to portray their critiques as purely scientific, not ideologically or politically motivated. Moreover, Marx is read by a great many people who lack the mathematics needed to understand the critiques. They end up taking the experts' conclusions on faith, or walking away from issues they perceive as technical and trifling, which likewise allows the experts' views to go unchallenged.

16. Such claims implicitly deny that Marx's law of the tendential fall in the rate of profit is part of the essential core of his critique, in marked contrast to his contention that the law is "the most important law of modern political economy."

Chapter 2

Marx's Value Theory and Contending Interpretations

This chapter, intended especially for readers unfamiliar with the details of Marx's value theory or the interpretive controversy surrounding it, provides the theoretical background to the rest of this work, while some historical background is provided in the next chapter. Almost all of the technical terms used in this book are defined in this chapter and set in boldface when they first appear.

In the first section, I present the basic elements of Marx's theory of how values, prices, and profits are determined. The second section briefly outlines the key controversies over the theory's interpretation. It is of course impossible to separate these two discussions neatly—one cannot present the theory without interpreting it—but I have tried to make the presentation as non-controversial as possible and I call attention to its controversial aspects.

Although it is also impossible to neatly separate what Sweezy (1970: 25) called the "quantitative" and "qualitative" dimensions of Marx's value theory,[1] my presentation of the theory emphasizes the former rather than the latter. I emphasize the quantitative dimension not because I consider it the more important one (the opposite is the case), but simply because the allegations of internal inconsistency focus on the theory's quantitative dimension.

2.1 Marx's Value Theory

2.1.1 Commodity Production

Marx's value theory is not a general explanation of why goods and services have prices, nor of why they have one price rather than another. The theory pertains

19

exclusively to **commodity production**, that is, to cases in which goods and services are "produced for the purpose of being exchanged" (Marx 1990a: 166) or, equivalently, produced as commodities. There have been a great variety of societies in which products are exchanged and thereby acquire the *form* of commodities. Yet if the products have been produced for a different purpose, that of satisfying the producers' and others' needs and wants, they have not been *produced* as commodities.

For instance, Malinowski (1921) reported that in the Trobriand Islands, production and distribution were governed by a complex system of customary rules which dictated, for instance, that a farmer's sisters and the tribal chief were the immediate recipients of his garden produce. Although gift-exchange and barter were common, both within and between communities, only a relatively few articles were exchangeable, and their rates of exchange were in all cases "rigidly prescribed by custom"; "competitive exchange of goods and services [determined by] the interplay of supply and demand" did not exist (Malinowski 1921: 14, 15). The Trobriand Islanders were not commodity producers, as defined above, and so Marx's value theory does not apply to them. (Nor does the theory apply to non-commodity production that takes place within capitalist societies—for instance, household production for the household's consumption.)

A key reason for distinguishing between commodity production and non-commodity production is that prices or rates of exchange are determined differently in the two cases. When things are not produced as commodities, the rates at which they exchange may depend exclusively upon the demand for them, or upon normative considerations, or—as in the case of the Trobriand Islanders—upon customary rules. It is only when products are produced for the purpose of being exchanged that their costs of production become significant determinants of their prices. Relatedly, the purpose of production exerts a profound influence upon the character of the production process; when products are produced as commodities, "their character as values has already to be taken into consideration during production" (Marx 1990a: 166). Producers who produce commodities must do more than produce useful things. They must produce things that command a sufficiently high value in exchange; they must produce efficiently in order not to lose money; and they must revolutionize their methods of production in order to keep up with the competition.

Some mistaken criticisms of Marx's value theory stem from a failure to understand these points. Although the theory cannot explain how prices are determined when products are not produced as commodities, it is not falsified by such cases. It is simply inapplicable to them.

Marx (1990a: 166) argues that when production is no longer just the production of useful things, but production of value as well, workers' labor acquires the same dual character. As an activity that produces a specific useful good or service, it is what Marx calls **concrete labor**. As an activity that produces value—abstract wealth, wealth as such, considered without regard to its specific physical form—it is what he calls **abstract labor** (Marx 1990a: 128, 131–37).[2]

2.1.2 Determination of Value by Labor-Time

Marx holds that a commodity's value is determined by the average amount of labor currently needed to produce it. Specifically, if twice as much labor is needed to produce commodity A as to produce commodity B, then A's value is twice as great as B's (Marx 1990a: 129–30). Marx often used the phrases **determination of value by labor-time** and **law of value** to refer to this theory (although he used the latter term in other senses as well).

The phrase "currently needed to produce" reflects the idea that the value of newly-produced items determines the value of already-existing ones. If wheat harvested last year had a value of $4/bushel, while wheat harvested today has a value of $3/bushel, then any wheat that remains from last year likewise has a value of $3/bushel today. The phrase "average amount of labor" is also significant. Marx (1990a: 129) holds that labor creates value only to the extent that it "is necessary on an average, or in other words is socially necessary"; any labor spent on the production of a commodity in excess of what he calls the **socially necessary labor-time** does not count as value-creating labor. This is his way of expressing the idea that less efficient producers cannot get higher prices for their products simply because their costs of production are above average, nor must more efficient producers charge less than others simply because their costs of production are below average.

Marx's theory that a commodity's value is determined by the amount of labor needed to produce it has often been construed as a *definition* of the commodity's value (see, e.g., Mongiovi 2002: 397–98), but this is incorrect for two reasons. First, Marx usually expressed commodities' values in monetary terms, which would not be possible if values were defined as amounts of labor. Values in that case would have to be expressed exclusively in terms of labor-time. Second, the theory can in principle be falsified, while definitions cannot.[3]

2.1.3 Value Transferred and New Value Added

In this theory, a commodity's value is the sum of two components (Marx 1990a, Chs. 7–8). One is the **value transferred** from used-up means of production—raw materials, machinery, etc.—to the product. (In the case of **fixed capital**, machinery and other inputs that last more than one production period, this transfer occurs piecemeal, as the fixed capital depreciates.)

Precisely how much value is transferred from the means of production has been the subject of considerable controversy, as we shall see. I and other proponents of the temporal single-system interpretation (TSSI) interpret Marx as having held that the amount of value transferred is the amount of value that is needed to acquire the means of production (rather than their own value). The word "needed" serves to indicate that the amount of value transferred depends upon (a) the current cost, rather than the **historical cost**, or original cost, of the means of production, and (b) the socially average expenditure on the means of production. Thus, if the efficiency with which a particular firm uses inputs is greater than (less than) the industry average, its actual expenditure will be less than (greater than) the sum of value transferred to its products.

The other component of a commodity's value is the **new value** added by what Marx calls **living labor**—the labor performed by workers during the production process. Their labor adds new value in proportion to the length of time they work, the intensity of their labor relative to the social average, and the "complexity" of their labor relative to "simple" (unskilled) labor.

2.1.4 Productivity and Value Creation

The workers' labor does not, however, add new value in proportion to its **productivity**, physical output per unit of labor. An hour of average, or socially necessary, labor "always yields the same amount of value, independently of any variations in productivity" (Marx 1990a: 137).[4]

This point is crucial to Marx's theory that labor-saving technological changes tend to depress the rate of profit. Although the technological changes boost productivity, they simultaneously tend to displace workers and thereby reduce the amount of new value added in production.

To better understand this perhaps counterintuitive idea, assume that productivity doubles *throughout an entire industry* and, for simplicity, that no value is transferred from the means of production to the product. In this case, when productivity doubles, an hour of labor produces twice as much output but the same amount of value, so each unit of output has only half as much value as it did before. If, on the other hand, the doubly productive hour of labor were to produce not only twice as much output but also twice as much value, output and value would both double. This seemingly obvious notion in fact implies that each unit of output has the same value that it had before, even though productivity has doubled!

What makes this latter notion seem obvious is a failure to distinguish between industry-wide and firm-specific increases in productivity. Marx's theory does imply that when an *individual* firm produces twice as much output with the same amount of labor, the amount of value it produces may (almost) double as well. This is because the per-unit value of its output does not depend upon how much labor this particular firm requires, but upon the *average*, socially necessary, amount of labor that is required throughout the industry. A doubling of productivity within a small firm will hardly affect this industry-wide average.

2.1.5 Constant Capital, Variable Capital, and Surplus-Value

Capitalist firms advance sums of capital, or **capital value**, to the production process. In other words, they invest in production. Marx (1990a: chap. 8) divides the capital value advanced into **constant capital** and **variable capital**, the sums of value used to acquire means of production and to hire workers, respectively. He calls the former constant capital because, as we saw, he holds that the using-up of means of production simply transfers value to the products. What goes into production is what comes out; value neither increases nor decreases.

Marx also uses the term constant capital in a rather different sense. He refers to the sum of value transferred as the constant capital component of a commodity's value. This is somewhat confusing since, as we saw, the value transferred can differ from the actual amount of value advanced for means of production that have subsequently been used up.

The portion of the advanced capital that is used to pay wages is called variable capital because the hiring of workers sets in motion a process that causes the firms' capital value to increase. The amount by which the capital value at the end of the process exceeds the original capital value advanced is what Marx (1990a: 251) calls **surplus-value**.[5]

2.1.6 The Origin of Surplus-Value

How can this increase in value occur? Marx argues that it cannot occur, in the aggregate, by buying cheap and selling dear. Some firms can certainly profit in this way, but he contends that such profit comes at the expense of, and is exactly offset by, other firms' losses. This is so even if all firms sell dear—because in this case they cannot all buy cheap. If everything sells for 10% more than its true value, everything is also bought for 10% more than its true value, and all firms lose as buyers exactly what they gain as sellers (Marx 1990a: 263).

Instead, he argues, what occurs is that the workers are made to perform **surplus labor**, and thereby to replace the variable capital used to pay their wages with a greater sum of value (Marx 1990a: chap. 7). Imagine that each hour of socially necessary labor adds $60 of new value, and that a particular worker (whose labor exactly meets the standard of social necessity) receives a weekly wage of $600. During the first ten hours of the workweek, her labor adds $10 \times \$60 = \$600$ of new value, and thus she fully replaces the variable capital advanced to pay her wages. But the worker is forced to work for an additional thirty hours, and thus to perform thirty hours of surplus labor, labor for which she has been paid no equivalent.[6] This adds an extra $30 \times \$60 = \$1800$ of new value, the surplus-value.

How can she be forced to do this? Marx's answer ultimately depends on his theories of how wages and the length of the workweek are determined, discussion of which is beyond the scope of this chapter. Yet a brief comment on the legality and morality of surplus-value production is in order. Marx argues that, although the source of the surplus-value is the exploitation of the worker, this exploitative relationship is completely consonant with bourgeois law and bourgeois morality. The firm does not purchase her labor or her product at less than their full value—because it does not purchase labor or a product from her at all. It, not she, is the lawful owner of the product, and what it purchases from her is not her actual labor, her activity, but **labor-power**, her *ability* to work. For the sake of argument, Marx assumes that the firm pays her the full value of her labor-power, the money she needs in order to produce this ability to work once again. In other words, $600 is what she needs in order to return to work next week without her ability to work having been diminished through hunger, lack of shelter, etc.

Having bought her labor-power at its value, the firm is legally—and within this society, morally—entitled to get a full week's work out of her, during which time she just happens to produce a new value of $2400 instead of $600. From within the standpoint of present-day society, there is nothing to criticize. The exploitation of the worker can only be criticized from the standpoint of the possible non-exploitative, classless society of the future.

To quantify the degree of exploitation, Marx (1990a: chap. 9) takes the ratio of surplus-value, s, to variable capital, v. The result, s/v, is what he calls the **rate of surplus-value** or **rate of exploitation**.

2.1.7 Two Distinctions between Value and Price

Marx distinguishes between price and value in two different ways. The two distinctions have nothing to do with one another, so it is important not to confuse or conflate them. One reason why his value theory is alleged to be internally inconsistent is precisely that prominent critics have indeed confused and conflated the two distinctions.[7]

One distinction is between two ways of *measuring* value. Marx (1990a: 188) holds that value has two measures, money and labor-time. He generally measures commodities' values in terms of money, but he sometimes measures them in terms of labor-time, and occasionally he compares the two (see, e.g., Marx 1991a: 266). When measuring a commodity's value in money terms, he often calls it simply the "value," while at other times he calls it the "monetary expression of value" or, equivalently, the *price*. "Price, taken by itself, is only the monetary expression of value" (Marx 1971: 35, emphasis omitted; cf. Marx

1990b: 1068). In this sense, then, "price" refers to value measured in terms of money rather than in terms of labor-time.

The other distinction between "value" and "price" is *quantitative*. In this context, if we are speaking of a firm's or industry's output, "value" refers to the sum of **value produced** within a firm or industry—the value transferred plus the new value added—while "price" refers to the sum of **value received** by the firm or industry. Similarly, if we are speaking of a single commodity, "value" refers to the commodity's actual value, determined by the labor-time needed to produce it, while "price" refers to the sum of money that the commodity's owner can receive in exchange for it.[8]

Note that we can meaningfully discuss these quantitative differences only if we are measuring price and value in the *same* units. It makes no sense, for example, to say that the $5400 a firm receives for its output is greater or less than the 100 hours of labor needed to produce that output. This shows that the two value-price distinctions are indeed wholly independent of one another.

2.1.8 The Monetary Expression of Labor-Time (MELT)

A numerical example may help to further clarify the difference between the two distinctions. To measure value and price in the same units, a conversion factor is needed. Marx frequently employed such a factor (see, e.g., Marx 1990a, chap. 7, section 2), but did not give it a name. In recent years, owing largely to the work of Alejandro Ramos (e.g., Ramos 2004), the term **monetary expression of labor-time** (MELT) has become popular. If each hour of socially necessary labor adds $60 of new value, as in the example above, the MELT is $60/hr.[9] Multiplying labor-time figures by the MELT, we get dollar figures; dividing dollar figures by the MELT, we get labor-time figures.

Now assume again that (1) the worker works a 40-hour week, (2) her weekly wage is $600, and (3) the MELT is $60/hr throughout the week. Also assume that (4) $3600 is the current necessary cost of the means of production that are used up during the week, and (5) the firm receives $5400 at the end of the week when it sells the output the worker has produced. Given these five bits of information, we can derive the remaining figures of Table 2.1. The symbols stand for the following:

c_{VT} sum of value transferred
v variable capital, value of the wage
n new value added
w value of output (value produced)
p price of output (value received)
s surplus-value, surplus labor
π profit

Table 2.1. Two Distinctions between Value and Price

	c_{VT}	v	n	$w = c_{VT} + n$	p	$s = n - v$	$\pi = p - (c_{VT} + v)$
Dollars	3600	600	2400	6000	5400	1800	1200
Labor-hrs	60	10	40	100	90	30	20

The fact that there are not two, but 2 × 2, value and price figures illustrates clearly that two different distinctions are in play. The value and the price of the firm's output (value produced and value received) can both be measured in terms of money and in terms of labor-time. It is only when they are measured in the same units—either dollars or labor-hours—that we can conclude that the price of the firm's output is 10% below its value.

2.1.9 "Value" and "Price" Rates of Profit

Marx (1991a, chap. 2) measures the **rate of profit** as s/C, where s is the total surplus-value produced throughout the period (e.g., a year), and C is the total capital advanced at the start. This ratio expresses the relative extent to which the capital expands in and through the production process. Yet his theory recognizes that price and value can differ quantitatively, and therefore that the amount of profit a firm or industry receives can differ from the amount of surplus-value it produces (see Table 2.1). Hence, there is also implicit in his work a second rate of profit, π/C, where π is the total profit received throughout the period.[10] These two ratios are now commonly called the **value rate of profit** and **price rate of profit**, respectively.

If we think of s and C as economy-wide totals, then s/C is the economy-wide average rate of profit. Marx (1991a, chap. 9) also calls it the **general rate of profit**. He maintains that there is no difference between the value and price rates of profit at the level of the economy as a whole:

> [Profit and the rate of profit are] different[,] for the individual capital[,] from profit, and therefore from the rate of profit, in so far as the latter consists of the surplus value really produced. . . . But it was also shown that considering the sum total of the capitals . . . the total capital of the capitalist class, the average rate of profit is nothing other than total surplus value related to and calculated on this total capital. [Marx 1991b: 104, emphasis omitted]

2.1.10 The Tendency of Profit Rates to Equalize

Value rates of profit can differ widely across firms and industries, even if their rates of surplus-value are identical, because some production processes are more, and others are less, labor-intensive. Assume that the capital advances in the restaurant and chemical industries are $100 and $200 respectively. Although the chemical industry is larger, the restaurant industry is much more labor-intensive, employing perhaps five workers for every worker employed in chemical production. If the two industries' rates of surplus-value are the same, and a surplus-value of $8 is produced in the chemical industry, then the restaurant industry's surplus-value is 5 × $8 = $40. Hence the value rate of profit is $40/$100 = 40% in the restaurant industry and $8/$200 = 4% in the chemical industry.

Yet capital migrates in search of the highest possible rate of profit, and this process *tends* to eliminate differentials among the price rates of profit. The capital invested in the chemical industry will therefore tend to contract while the capital invested in the restaurant industry will tend to expand. As output in the chemical industry declines, its price and the associated profit rise above the actual sums of value and surplus-value the industry produces, and conversely for the restaurant industry. This results in a narrowing of the difference between their rates of profit.

2.1.11 Average Profit and Price of Production

In the hypothetical case in which rates of profit were exactly equal—that is, in which all industries realized the general rate of profit—they would each receive what Marx calls **average profit** and each industry's output would sell for what he calls its **price of production** (Marx 1991a, chap. 9). He stressed that this situation never occurs in reality. Instead, he argued, actual **market prices** fluctuate around prices of production, and thus actual profits fluctuate around average profit, given a sufficiently competitive (non-monopolistic) environment.

What is the relationship between price of production and average profit, on the one hand, and value and surplus-value, on the other? To answer this question, it will be helpful to introduce the concept of **cost price**. This is Marx's (1991a, chap. 1) term for the sum of value transferred plus variable capital—in other words, what it costs a capitalist to produce a commodity. According to his theory, the value produced in an industry equals cost price plus surplus-value,[11] while the price of production equals cost price plus average profit.

Let us imagine that cost price, k, is $30 in the restaurant industry and $40 in the chemical industry, and that these are the only two industries in the economy.

Table 2.2. Prices of Production and Average Profits

Industry	C	k	s	s/C	π/C	π	$w = k + s$	$p = k + \pi$
Restaurant	100	30	40	40%	16%	16	70	46
Chemical	200	40	8	4%	16%	32	48	72
Total	300	70	48	16%	16%	48	118	118

Using this information and the figures given above for surplus-value and capital advanced, we can derive the remaining information in Table 2.2. In accordance with Marx's theory, each industry's price of production rate of profit, π/C, is equal to and determined by the general rate of profit for the total economy, 16%, and thus each industry's average profit, π, is equal to 16% of the capital it advanced.

Note that total profit and total surplus-value both equal 48, and that total price of production and total value both equal 118. Also, of course, the economy-wide price and value rates of profit both equal 16%. The first two equalities are consequences of the latter. Marx attached great importance to these three **aggregate equalities**, holding that they confirmed his value theory. In the aggregate, the production of value and surplus-value does determine price, profit, and the rate of profit (see, e.g., Marx 1991a: 984–85). Yet as we shall see, especially in chapter 9, critics have persistently denied, for almost 100 years, that the aggregate equalities hold true.

2.1.12 The Tendential Fall in the Rate of Profit

Marx held that as capitalist production develops, capitalists tend to adopt more productive, labor-saving technologies; that is, they turn increasingly to methods of production that replace workers with machines. On the basis of this tendency, as well as his theory that value is determined by labor-time and his conclusion that the general price and value rates of profit are equal, he deduced the **law of the tendential fall in the rate of profit** (LTFRP) (Marx 1991a, part 3). The law is that productivity increases under capitalism produce a tendency for the general rate of profit to fall. "The progressive tendency for the rate of profit to fall is thus simply *the expression, peculiar to the capitalist mode of production*, of the progressive development of the social productivity of labour" (Marx 1991a: 319, emphasis in original).

Why do productivity increases resulting from labor-saving technological change tend to lower, not raise, the rate of profit? Note, first, that when labor-saving technological changes are introduced, more of each dollar of advanced capital is invested in means of production, while less is used to hire workers. But according to the theory that value is determined by labor-time, it is workers' living labor that adds all new value. Moreover, as we have seen, an average hour of labor "always yields the same amount of value, *independently of any variations in productivity*" (Marx 1990a: 137, emphasis added), which is Marx's way of expressing the tendency of rising productivity to reduce prices. Technological innovation thus causes a fall in the amount of new value created per dollar of advanced capital. Given a constant rate of exploitation (rate of surplus-value), the amount of surplus-value created per dollar of advanced capital—in other words, the rate of profit—necessarily falls as well.

This is easily shown algebraically. The general rate of profit can be expressed as the product of two factors, the rate of surplus-value (s/v) and the percentage of the total capital advanced (C) that is laid out as variable capital (v) in order to hire workers, (v/C):

$$\frac{s}{C} \equiv \left(\frac{s}{v}\right)\left(\frac{v}{C}\right)$$

If the rate of surplus-value is constant, then every fall in the percentage of capital advanced that is used to hire workers leads to a proportionate fall in the rate of profit. For instance, if the rate of surplus-value is 2 (or 200%), and 20% of the capital advanced is used to hire workers, then the rate of profit is 2 × 20% = 40%. But if, owing to technological change, the percentage of capital advanced used to hire workers falls to 15% and then to 10%, the rate of profit falls to 30% and then to 20%.

2.1.13 The Rising Rate of Surplus-Value and Its Limited Effect

Marx's initial presentation of the LTFRP at the start of part 3 of *Capital*, volume III does assume a constant rate of surplus-value. He recognized, however, that there is a tendency for the rate of surplus-value to rise as a result of rising productivity (see esp. Marx 1991a, chap. 14). Although workers create no more value when their productivity increases, they do create more *surplus*-value. The increase in productivity lowers the value of the goods and services that workers consume, and thus, if the workers' physical standard of living remains unchanged, the *value* of their wages (i.e., their wages in money or labor-time terms) falls. Consequently, their necessary labor-time (the portion of the workday during which they create a sum of value equivalent to their wages) is reduced and their surplus labor-time, the time during which they create surplus-value, is extended. Increases in the workers' physical standard of living can offset this tendency, but unless their standard of living fully keeps pace with productivity—increases at the same (or a greater) rate—the value of wages will fall and thus the rate of surplus-value will rise.

It might seem, therefore, that a sufficient rise in the rate of surplus-value can always offset, or more than offset, the tendency for the rate of profit to fall stemming from the replacement of workers by machines. Marx anticipated and countered this claim, first in volume I of *Capital* (Marx 1990a: 419–20) and then twice in volume III (Marx 1991a: 355–56, 523). He pointed out that a rising rate of surplus-value has a strictly limited effect on the *total amount* of surplus-value created, and therefore on the rate of profit, even if the rate of surplus-value were to rise to infinity! This is because there is a strict limit to the total amount of surplus labor extracted; it cannot be greater than the total amount of living labor performed.

Imagine that at first, for each $1 million of advanced capital, there are five workers, and that each worker supplies five hours of surplus labor per day. The total daily surplus labor is $5 \times 5 = 25$ hours. Now if, as a result of mechanization, the workforce is reduced to one worker per million dollars of advanced capital, the total daily surplus labor must fall, since in no case can it exceed twenty-four hours per worker. The rate of profit must therefore fall as well. "[T]herefore, the compensation for the reduced number of workers[,] provided by a rise in the level of exploitation of labour[,] has certain limits that cannot be overstepped" (Marx 1991a: 356).

2.1.14 The Meaning of "Tendential Fall"

None of this, however, should be taken to imply that Marx predicted that the rate of profit will actually display a falling *trend* in the long run. Despite a common belief to the contrary, he seems nowhere to have put forth such a claim. On the contrary, he held that "[c]ounteracting influences [are] at work, checking *and cancelling* the effect of the general law," and that the LTFRP "has constantly to be overcome by way of crises" (Marx 1991a: 339, 367, emphasis added). Thus what Marx meant by the "tendency" of the rate of profit to fall was not an empirical trend, but what would occur in the absence of the various "counteracting influences," such as the tendency of the rate of surplus-value to rise.

He singled out one of these counteracting influences, the recurrent devaluation of means of production, for special consideration. Like the tendential fall in the rate of profit itself, and the tendency of the rate of surplus-value to rise, the devaluation of means of production is a consequence of increasing productivity. Capitalists incur losses (including losses on financial investments) as a result of this devaluation; a portion of the capital value advanced in the past is wiped out. In this way (as well as by means of their tendency to cause the price of output to fall), increases in productivity tend eventually to produce economic crises. Yet since the advanced capital value is the denominator of the rate of profit, the annihilation of existing capital value acts to raise the rate of profit and thus helps to bring the economy out of the crisis (see Marx 1991a, chap. 15, esp. pp. 356–58, 362–63).

In short, although the falling tendency of the rate of profit is "constantly . . . overcome," the tendency is not nullified. It makes its presence felt, since it is only "overcome by way of crises." Recurrent economic crises, not a declining rate of profit over the long term, are what Marx's theory actually predicts. Researchers who wish to test his theory empirically should therefore focus their attention, not on the observed trend of the profit rate, but on ascertaining whether, and to what degree, the recurrent crises of capitalism are traceable to recurrent declines in capital values, and a tendency for prices to fall, as a result of increasing productivity.

The most likely source of the belief that Marx predicted a long-term downward trend to the rate of profit is the fact that the classical economists to whom he was responding did indeed make this prediction. It is thus assumed that he and they were discussing the exact same issue. However, Marx (1989b: 128, starred note, emphasis in original) explicitly repudiated this notion: "When Adam Smith explains the fall in the rate of profit [as stemming] from a superabundance of capital . . . he is speaking of a *permanent* effect and this is wrong. As against this, the transitory superabundance of capital, overproduction and crises are something different. Permanent crises do not exist."

That Marx regarded capitalism's economic crises as *transitory*, though unavoidable and recurrent, is also important to stress. The common belief that he predicted the collapse of capitalism, as a result of the LTFRP alone or in conjunction with other causes, is yet another belief for which evidence is lacking. Mandel (1991: 79), a prominent advocate of the view that Marx predicted a collapse of the system, acknowledged that no textual support for this claim can be found in his presentation of the LTFRP or elsewhere in volume III of *Capital*. However, according to Mandel (1991: 79), "a number of passages . . . from Volume 1" support the theory of collapse. Yet he cited only one such passage, the end of the penultimate chapter, and this passage says nothing about the system's *collapse*. Marx (1990a: 929–30) projects that the system's tendencies will result in *social revolution* ("The expropriators are expropriated"), and not because of any collapse, but because of the centralization of capital and growing revolt of the working class.

Quite apart from such misinterpretations of the LTFRP, critics have continually claimed that the law is internally inconsistent; when correctly applied, Marx's value theory leads to the conclusion that labor-saving technological change causes the rate of profit to rise. The reasoning behind this claim, and its validity, will be examined in chapter 7.

2.2 Contending Interpretations

2.2.1 Dual-system Interpretations

Dual-system interpretations of Marx's theory have their origin in Bort-kiewicz's (1984) "correction" of Marx's account of the value-price relationship. On these interpretations, values and prices are determined independently of one another. There is a **value system**, in which the values of the products depend upon the values of the inputs; in other words, the sum of value transferred to the product is the *value* of the means of production that get used up. And there is a separate **price system**, in which the prices of the products depend upon the *prices* of the used-up means of production.

Putting the same point differently, dual-system interpretations hold that a commodity has two distinct cost prices, not one. Proponents of these interpretations recognize that Marx himself theorized in terms of a single cost price, but claim that this was an error. Some argue that he acknowledged the error and indicated that it should be corrected.

The relevant distinction between values and prices here is the *quantitative* one. No one denies that there are two distinct systems of money magnitudes and labor-time magnitudes, in the sense of Table 2.1. It would be absurd to mix-and-match them. To say, for instance, that the labor-time value of used-up inputs is part of the product's money price simply makes no sense. What is controversial about the dual-system interpretation is rather its contention that values and prices constitute separate systems when they are measured in the same units. For instance, according to the dual-system interpretation, the *money value* of used-up inputs is part of the *money value* of the output, while the *money price* of used-up inputs is part of the *money price* of the output.

In recent years, some interpreters have said that their interpretations are non-dualistic because they, unlike other dual-system interpreters (e.g. Morishima 1973: 73), recognize that values as well as prices can be measured in money terms. They are certainly entitled to use words as they wish, but then a second term is needed to denote interpretations according to which money values and money prices are determined independently. Changes in terminology do not efface the substantive distinction between dual- and single-system interpretations.

The statement that values and prices are determined independently in dual-system interpretations is subject to one minor qualification. One can always alter the monetary unit—redefine one "old dollar" as 0.1234, or 5.6789, etc. "new dollars"—and thereby cause some price aggregate (such as total price) to equal some value aggregate (such as total value). This procedure has no effect on *relative* prices—the rates at which commodities are exchangeable with one another—or other important relative magnitudes such as the rate of profit and the ratio of profit to wages.

Dual-system interpretations have traditionally held that there are also two separate "value" and "price" variable capitals. This notion follows from their reading of Marx's (1990a: 276) statement that the value of labor-power is determined by the *values* of the goods and services the worker needs. Dual-system interpreters inferred from this that there is a separate price of labor-power in the price system, determined by the *prices* of the goods and services the worker needs.[12] And since the value of labor-power is also the variable capital of the value system, if workers happen to be paid the value of their labor-power, dual-system interpreters inferred that there is a distinct variable capital in the price system.

A different dual-system interpretation appeared in the 1980s (Duménil 1980, 1983; Foley 1982). Sometimes called the New Solution or New Approach, it is now usually referred to as the **New Interpretation** (NI). The NI holds that workers' actual money wages are the variable capital of *both* the price system and the value system. The usual reasons given for this interpretation (e.g. Foley 1986: 42–43) are that workers and firms haggle over what money wage will be paid, not over workers' consumption levels, and that the statement of Marx's cited in the previous paragraph is not a postulate of his theory.

On both the traditional dual-system interpretation and the NI, cost prices and capital advances differ across the value and price systems. There are consequently two distinct and unequal *general* rates of profit as well, and the remaining aggregate equalities cannot both hold true, contrary to what Marx concluded. Dualists justify these discrepancies by arguing that his conclusions are incorrect, a consequence of his alleged error to which I referred above.

2.2.2 Single-system Interpretations

Like the NI, the **temporal single-system interpretation** and the first of what I shall call the **simultaneous single-system interpretations** (SSSIs) also appeared first in the early 1980s.[13] On these interpretations, values and prices are determined interdependently, in two ways.

First, prices of production and average profit depend upon the general (value) rate of profit, s/C, so there is no distinct price system.[14] Second, prices influence value magnitudes, so there is no distinct value system either. The constant-capital value advanced and the value transferred depend upon the prices, not the values, of means of production. Moreover, the single-system interpretations concur with the NI's conclusion (though not necessarily with its reasoning) regarding the variable-capital value advanced; it depends upon workers' actual wages, not the values of the things they consume.

All three aggregate equalities hold true under the single-system interpretations. Nonetheless, some dualists (e.g. Naples 1993) have argued that single-system interpretations contradict Marx's theory that a product's value is determined by the amount of labor needed to produce it. Dual-system interpreters hold that the amount of labor needed to produce the product is (1) the amount of labor needed to produce the means of production that are used up in order to produce the product, plus (2) the amount of new labor that workers need to perform.

Single-system interpretations do contradict this reading of the theory, but an alternative reading is possible. Shoe manufacturers do not produce leather, nor do tanneries raise cattle. In order to produce its product, a firm needs to *acquire* means of production. Hence, the amount of labor needed to produce the product is (1') the amount of labor needed to *acquire* the means of production that are used up in order to produce the product, plus (2). To acquire the needed means of production, moreover, the firm needs to buy them at their actual *price*—not at their value, which might be much less. Thus the amount of labor needed to acquire them is their price measured in labor-time, that is, their money price divided by the MELT.

Other aspects of this particular interpretive controversy and the relevant textual evidence will be taken up in chapter 6.

2.2.3 Simultaneous vs. Temporal Valuation

Simultaneous valuation is the *a priori* stipulation that the per-unit value (or price) of each input must equal the per-unit value (or price) of the same good or service when produced as an output of the same period. **Simultaneists** maintain, for instance, that a bushel of seed corn planted at the start of the season must have the same value as a bushel of corn harvested at the end. Goods and services that workers consume are generally also regarded as inputs in this context.

With the exception of the TSSI, all interpretations discussed above are simultaneist; they hold that input and output values—and, subject to a couple of qualifications, input and output prices—are determined simultaneously in Marx's value theory. Although they all recognize that actual input prices and output prices can differ, some simultaneist interpretations deny that actual input prices are relevant to the determination of the capital advanced, the value transferred, and variable capital. The relevant input prices, they maintain, are those that equal the output prices. Most simultaneists, however, acknowledge that actual input prices are determinants of the capital advanced, etc. They insist upon simultaneous determination of input and output prices "only" insofar as prices of production are concerned.[15]

Temporal valuation is simply non-simultaneous valuation. Proponents of the TSSI deny that there is any sense in which Marx held, or in which his theory implies, that inputs entering production now and outputs emerging later must have the same prices or values. This of course does not preclude the abstract possibility that inputs and outputs *may happen to have* the same prices or values.

It is quite unclear how the notion arose that Marx's theory is simultaneist. All simultaneist interpretations have their origins in Bortkiewicz's "correction" of Marx's theory along simultaneist lines, but Bortkiewicz (1952: 23–24) himself interpreted the original theory as non-simultaneist. My conjecture is that Marxian theorists began at some point to read Marx as a simultaneist in an ex-post effort to justify the authenticity of the Bortkiewicz-style models they were already employing.

There are two main ways in which these models' authenticity has been justified. The first pertains to Marx's (1990a: 317–19) notion that commodities' values do not depend upon the original, historical cost of the inputs used to produce them, but upon the inputs' current cost. According to some simultaneists, this means that commodities' values depend upon the post-production **replacement cost** of the inputs. If that is so, then inputs and outputs must indeed be valued simultaneously, but **temporalists** deny that it is so. They interpret Marx as having held that commodities' values depend upon what the inputs cost when they enter into the production process, which might be quite different from both their historical cost and their replacement cost.

Other interpreters argue that Marx was implicitly a simultaneist because he sometimes assumed that commodities sell at their prices of production and— these interpreters maintain—the prices of inputs and outputs must be equal in order for prices of production to exist. However, temporalists deny, on textual and mathematical grounds, that prices of production exist only when input and output prices are equal.

Chapters 5 and 6 will take up these two issues in greater detail.

2.2.4 Simultaneism and Physicalism

Simultaneous valuation is inextricably bound up with what I shall call **physicalism**, a shorthand expression for what Steedman (1977: 67, 72) called "physically based analysis" and "the physical quantities approach." Physicalism holds that "physical quantities" or, more precisely, **technology** and workers' **real wages** are the sole proximate determinants of values, surplus-value, prices of production, average profit, and rates of profit. (Roughly speaking, technology refers to the relationship between physical inputs and physical output, and real wages are wages in physical terms. Technological progress occurs when a given quantity of inputs yields more output than before, and when a given amount of output can be produced with a smaller quantity of inputs. A worker's real wage rises if she is able to consume more goods and services than before, either because her money wage rises or because the goods and services become cheaper.)

Although Steedman is a **Sraffian**—a follower of Sraffa (1960)—
Sraffianism is but one variant of physicalism, since all simultaneist interpretations and theories are physicalist. As I shall show in chapter 5 (and in chapters
7–10), simultaneous valuation itself is what leads, necessarily and inescapably,
to physicalism and its theoretical conclusions. Chapter 5 will also show that
physicalism—and thus simultaneism—are incompatible with Marx's theory that
value is determined by labor-time.

This point is critically important. The internal inconsistency controversy is
almost entirely reducible to it. Because simultaneism and the law of value are
fundamentally incompatible, it is inevitable that Marx's value theory becomes
inconsistent when it is construed as a simultaneist theory. In almost every case,
Marx's alleged inconsistencies are nothing more than particular examples of this
elemental incompatibility. Thus, if it is shown that Marx himself was in fact a
simultaneist, or that he committed errors that must be corrected by means of
simultaneous valuation, then his value theory must indeed be deemed internally
inconsistent. If neither of these things can be shown, however, then the contradictions between his results and those of physicalism cannot be used to convict
him of internal inconsistency.

2.2.5 The "Value-Form" Paradigm

Another strand of Marx-inspired value theory has been called the "social
paradigm" or "abstract labor approach" and is increasingly known as "**the
'value-form' paradigm**" (Arthur 2001: 16, emphasis added). I shall not have
much to say about it in this book, for two reasons. First, the "value-form"
paradigm has little to do, in a direct sense, with the internal inconsistency
controversy. It seems to have emerged as an effort to *circumvent* the controversy, and the paradigm as such neither affirms nor denies the allegations of
internal inconsistency. Second, the "value-form" paradigm is generally not
intended as an interpretation of Marx's theory in the same sense as those
surveyed above. Krause (1982: 8), for example, holds that it is "not important"
whether his position is "in line with Marx," and Reuten forthrightly acknowledges that there can be "hardly any doubt" that Marx's position differs from his
own. He rejects Marx's position not because he deems it false or logically
incoherent, but because he cannot see how it can be made "operational" (Reuten
1993: 98–99, 103).

A short discussion of the paradigm is nonetheless in order. Although its
proponents do not have a unified position, they tend to suggest that an act of
labor becomes abstract (or fully abstract) only when its product is subsequently
exchanged. "[T]he real, historical process which abstracts from the heterogene-
ity of concrete labors is the process of exchange. Only through exchange . . . can
it be determined *a posteriori* whether the concrete labors of a particular

production process are to count as a portion of society's total labor" (Mohun 1984–85: 401). It follows from this that "value is . . . established in the market (hence a market concept) rather than having existence prior to it" (Reuten 1993: 105). Although other "value-form" theorists put the matter less baldly (and clearly), they seem to be saying much the same thing.

If such notions are taken as an accurate representation of Marx's views— which, I repeat, is not what "value-form" theorists generally intend—then his theory that value is determined by labor-time becomes meaningless. Mohun's statement, for instance, indicates that whether the concrete labor used to produce a commodity counts as abstract labor is "determined *a posteriori*." It all depends upon whether or not the commodity is subsequently sold.[16] Marx (1990a: 128, 131–37) holds that abstract labor, not concrete labor, is what creates value. If we try to combine the two ideas, the result is that value is created if and when the commodity is sold. There is no meaningful sense in which labor-time can be said to be determining value here. Instead, both labor-time and value are being determined by whether the commodity sells or not.

The source of the problem is that, when the "value-form" paradigm and Marx's value theory are combined, the temporal sequence of determination is altered. In order to make sense of his theory, it is crucial to get the sequence of determination right. Labor must be abstract already in the production process if it is to create the product's value as well as the product itself.[17] It follows that the product's value is created in production and comes into being at the moment when the product is produced, rather than being "established" only subsequently, when the product goes to market, as Reuten proposes.

It is not for the sake of textual fidelity, but in order to make sense of Marx's value theory, that I offer the following comment on a recent interpretation that (unlike Reuten's statement) seems to suggest that Marx *himself* held that value is established in the market. According to Arthur (2001: 31, emphasis added), "Marx said that 'labour is not itself value'; although 'labour creates value' it 'becomes value' only in 'objective form' *when the labour embodied in one commodity is equated with the labour embodied in another commodity* (Marx [1990a]: 142)."[18] Now compare Arthur's statement and what it says about the temporal process of determination to Marx's original text:

> Human labour-power in its fluid state, or human labour, creates value, but is not itself value. It becomes value in its coagulated state, in objective form. The value of the linen as a congealed mass of human labour can be *expressed* only as an 'objectivity' [*Gegenständlichkeit*], a thing which is materially different from the linen itself and yet common to the linen and all other commodities. [Marx 1990a: 142, emphasis added]

In Arthur's version of the passage, the "objective form" of labor is money (the second of the two commodities). The labor embodied in the first commodity (the linen) only "becomes value" when it is equated with the labor embodied in the money. In the original version, however, the "objective form" of the labor that produced the linen is clearly the linen itself. It is when the "fluid state" ends and the "coagulated state" begins—in other words, when the labor process concludes with the emergence of the completed linen—that the labor acquires its "objective form." This is the moment when labor "becomes value"—*prior* to any exchange of the linen for money.

Marx says, moreover, that the value of the linen must be expressed in terms of money (the "materially different" thing). Since something—an idea, a feeling, value, etc.—can be expressed only if it *already exists* apart from that expression, this statement likewise goes against Arthur's interpretation. As Marx (1990a: 188) noted in a passage that explicitly distinguishes between "objectified human labour" and money, "It is not money that renders the commodities commensurable. Quite the contrary. Because all commodities, as values, are objectified human labour, and therefore in themselves commensurable, their values can be communally measured in one and the same specific commodity, . . . money."

Notes

1. Sweezy attributes the distinction to Franz Petry (1916).

2. Although I shall generally omit the qualifying adjective when referring to the notion that labor produces value, I always mean abstract, not concrete, labor.

3. I have argued, for instance, that if value is determined by labor-time, a faster rate of productivity growth causes the rate of increase in the aggregate price level to fall, *ceteris paribus*, and this in turn tends to reduce the aggregate rate of profit, leading to various forms of economic crisis (Kliman 2003). There are several testable hypotheses here. As Quine (1980: viii, 40–42) stressed, theoretical propositions are testable only in clusters, not one-by-one. (This and subsequent references to Quine pertain to particular aspects of his work only, and should not be construed as endorsements of his overall anti-dialectical philosophy. Non-critical references to other authors in particular contexts are likewise not endorsements of their work in general.)

4. Marx recognizes that the *nominal* amount of value produced by an hour of labor —the value produced as expressed in money—can vary. Such variations, however, are not caused by changes in productivity, at least not directly.

5. Marx often refers to the surplus-value as *profit,* though he uses the latter term to mean several other things as well. In some contexts, for example, profit refers to extra value received, while surplus-value refers to extra value produced. Marx also argues throughout much of *Capital,* volume III (parts 4–6) that the sole source of all non-labor incomes (interest, rent, profits of commercial firms, etc.) is the surplus-value produced. The industrial firms which produced the surplus-value can therefore retain only part of the surplus-value as profit, since they have to "share" it with other kinds of capitalists.

6. Marx calls the first ten hours of labor, the period for which an equivalent is paid, the **necessary labor**. It is important not to confuse necessary labor with socially necessary labor-time, which refers to something very different.

7. Steedman (1977: 29–30), for example, jumbles together the difference between the labor-time and money *measures* of the rate of profit with the (alleged) difference in *magnitude* between the value and price rates of profit.

8. Thus a commodity's price, in this sense, is one of its **exchange-values**—its exchange-value in terms of money. For a discussion of the development and significance of Marx's distinction between (intrinsic) value and exchange-value, see Kliman (2000a).

9. There are other, equivalent, ways of defining the MELT. It is the reciprocal of the amount of labor a unit of money commands. It is also the economy-wide ratio of the total money price of output to the total labor-time value of output. See Kliman and Freeman (2006).

10. Here, and throughout section 1 of this chapter, "profit" refers to the monetary expression of surplus-value. Only a portion of this profit is retained, as "industrial profit," by the firms in which the surplus-value is created. The remainder is paid out as interest, rent, and dividends, used to purchase commercial services such as buying, selling, and accounting, and so forth. Most of volume III of *Capital* is an extended argument that all property incomes (industrial profit, interest, rent, dividends, etc.) have a single source—the surplus-value created in production—and thus that the total of these property incomes is determined by and limited to the total surplus-value. Phenomena such as rising rents and interest rates, capital gains, etc., therefore merely alter the way in which the already-created surplus-value is divided; they do not negate the theory that value is determined by labor-time (see, e.g., Marx 1991a: 984–85).

11. This is mathematically equivalent to the statement, above, that the value of the product equals the value transferred plus the new value added, since the new value added equals the variable capital plus surplus-value.

12. Marx's distinction between the value and price of labor-power is unrelated to his distinction between the value of labor-power and the price of *labor*. The latter two magnitudes differ to the extent that workers consume more or less than they need to renew their ability to work (Marx 1990a: 769–72).

13. The earliest published TSSI works are Perez (1980), Ernst (1982), Carchedi (1984), and Kliman and McGlone (1988). In a personal communication, Eduardo Maldonado-Filho has indicated that prior drafts of his temporal single-system refutation of the "transformation problem" (Maldonado-Filho 1997) were written in 1981 and 1986. Wolff, Roberts, and Callari (1982) put forth the first SSSI. Ramos (1991), Lee (1993), and Moseley (1993a) subsequently came out with other SSSIs.

14. In the case of the SSSIs, however, it is more accurate to say that s/C depends upon prices of production and average profit.

15. I put "only" in quotes because, when testing the cogency and consistency of Marx's value theory, they seem always to assume that commodities sell at their prices of production.

16. McGlone and Kliman (2004) argue that this was not Marx's position, and that he instead regarded labor as already abstract in the process of production.

17. Dunayevskaya's (2000: 103–06) 1958 discussion of Marx's concept of abstract labor was perhaps the first to interpret him as having held that labor is made abstract by, and is abstract within, the capitalistic labor process. She emphasizes the close relationship between his concepts of abstract labor and alienated labor.

18. I said that this statement "seems to" indicate that Marx held that value is established in the market because the "equat[ing]" here might possibly be a mental act rather than an exchange. Arthur's interpretation of Marx's meaning is incorrect in either case.

Chapter 3

A Brief History of the Controversy

3.1 Introduction

This chapter briefly surveys the history of the controversy over Marx's value theory, focusing on debates over the theory's internal consistency. Its main purpose is to provide some historical background that will be helpful for an understanding of the chapters that follow; it is not a complete account of the controversy. Subsequent chapters provide additional historical background and explore many of the issues sketched out here in greater depth. Although this chapter is intended especially for readers who are new to the controversy, other readers may find it of interest as well, since some of what I discuss is not well known and my anti-Whiggish perspective on the controversy makes this survey rather different from earlier ones.

Although the controversy is a century old, it is possible to survey it fairly briefly because the fundamentals of the simultaneist-physicalist critique of Marx have been in place from the start. Subsequent critiques have generally been little more than extensions and elaborations, and often plain repetitions, of points made by Dmitriev (1974) in 1897 and Bortkiewicz (1952, 1984) in 1906–1907. Indeed, Steedman (1977: 17, n19) "wondered whether 'Marx after Dmitriev' or 'Marx after Bortkiewicz' might not be a proper title" for his now-famous *Marx after Sraffa*. He opted for the latter title on the ground that Sraffa's model was a generalization of theirs.

3.2 Dmitriev's Laborless Theory of Value

Dmitriev's work, written in Russian, had little direct influence on the controversy until the 1970s, because it was almost unknown in the West until its translation into French in 1968 and English in 1974. According to Desai (1988: 312),

"Sraffa is said to have possessed the only copy of the original Russian publication in the western world." Yet Dmitriev was indirectly an important influence on the controversy from the beginning, since Bortkiewicz studied and drew upon his work.

Dmitriev was the first modern physicalist. Anticipating Sraffa's (1951: xxxi) interpretation of Ricardo by more than a half-century, Dmitriev argued that the rate of profit is physically determined in Ricardo's theory, and he set out to defend the notion that it is physically determined in reality as well. Profit, he argued, depends upon technology—the relationship between physical inputs (including the goods that workers consume) and physical outputs—not surplus labor specifically: "the origin of industrial profit does not stand in any 'special' relationship to the human labour used in production" (Dmitriev 1974: 64). The same argument is crucial to the Okishio (1961) theorem, which allegedly disproves Marx's law of the tendential fall in the rate of profit (LTFRP).

Unlike many later physicalists, Dmitriev unflinchingly pursued the logic of this argument to its conclusion; there could be profit even if no living labor were performed at all:

> [We can] imagine a case in which all products are produced exclusively by the work of machines, so that no unit of *living labour* . . . participates in production. . . . [A]n industrial profit may occur . . . [,] a profit which will not differ essentially in any way from the profit obtained by present-day capitalists. [Dmitriev 1974: 63, emphasis in original]

> [Although] *wage labour is not used* in production, . . . *'surplus value' will nevertheless arise, and* . . . consequently, *there will be profit on capital*. [Dmitriev 1974: 214, emphases in original]

Dmitriev did not mention Marx by name, but his use of specifically Marxian terminology makes clear who his target was. That the editor of Dmitriev's book could state that "his system of thought is compatible with Marxian economics" (Nuti 1974: 7) only indicates how far Marxian economics had departed, already by 1974, from Marx's own work.

To prove his claim, Dmitriev (1974: 63–64) constructed a complex example in which a certain type of machine produces new machines of the same type and, directly or indirectly, all other types of machines and consumer goods. He then tried to demonstrate that the rate of profit will be positive, even though no human labor is performed in production, if more units of this machine are produced than are used up in production.

For our purposes, it will be sufficient to study Dmitriev's proof procedure by means of a simpler example. There is a single kind of machine, each unit of which lasts one production period and then wears out. We assume, as Dmitriev did, that no human labor is performed, and that more machines are produced than are used up in production. Imagine, for instance, that four machines are used up in order to produce five machines. In this case, Dmitriev holds, the rate of profit is given by the following equation:

$$5p = 4p + r(4p)$$

where p is the per-unit price of the machine and r is the rate of profit (profit divided by cost). In other words, the total price of the output ($5p$) equals the total cost of the input ($4p$) plus the profit or mark-up on the cost ($r(4p)$). Dividing through by p—as Dmitriev himself did—we obtain $5 = 4 + 4r$. And after a bit more algebra, we find that $r = 1/4$ or 25%. Note that this rate of profit is physically determined: it equals 25% because the output of machines exceeds the input by 25%.

Given that Dmitriev's book opens with paeans of praise to mathematics, and that his work has regularly been extolled as a model of rigor, this argument is surprisingly slipshod. Dmitriev assumes a case in which no labor is performed, and thus a case in which there is arguably no value. Yet he took for granted that the machine has a positive price. In other words, he assumed precisely what he needed to prove. If the machine is free, then $p = 0$, and it is impermissible to divide through by p as he did. Instead of finding that the rate of profit is positive, we find that the original equation becomes $0 = 0$. The rate of profit is therefore undefined.

There is good reason to believe that the machine will indeed be free. Dmitriev's fully automated economy is able to generate an ever-increasing output of the machine, unconstrained by any natural resource limitations, and *at no additional cost*. It is thus quite plausible, at the very least, that the machine's price would quickly fall to zero. Curiously, Dmitriev himself reaches an analogous result when he goes on to consider a system of goods produced solely by animals. Hence, he concludes, there is "no foundation for any of the references to various 'natural' processes (such as the breeding of animals and yields which do not necessitate human tending of the plants etc.) as independent sources of 'profit on capital'" (Dmitriev 1974: 69).

One can only wonder why he failed to notice that this conclusion applies equally to his system of goods produced solely by machines, which is strictly analogous, and why the secondary literature has also missed the connection. Time and again, Dmitriev's demonstration that the rate of profit would be positive in a fully automated economy has been accepted uncritically (see, e.g., Dobb 1972: 213, 217; Nuti 1974: 18–19; Desai 1988: 311–12; and Howard and King 1992: 256).

Yet even if we assume that the machines have a positive price, Dmitriev's demonstration is marred by another fatal error. He does not prove, but simply assumes, that valuation is simultaneous—in other words, that the machine's input price equals its output price. It seems to me that Marx's theory implies that they are not equal. Marx holds that the value of output equals the value transferred from the inputs plus the new value added by living labor. But since Dmitriev assumes that the economy is fully automated, there is no living labor and thus no new value added in this case. The five output machines are therefore worth only as much as the four input machines were worth. Thus the price of a machine falls by one-fifth and the rate of profit is consequently zero. This last result is what Dmitriev claims to disprove, of course, but he fails to do so because he assumes, rather than proves, that the input and output prices are equal.

As we shall see throughout this book, subsequent physicalist "proofs" of Marx's errors and inconsistencies are rather similar to Dmitriev's. They, too, rely crucially on the equality of input and output prices, and they, too, fail because this equality is arbitrarily assumed, not proved.

3.3 The Falling Rate of Profit Controversy

Owing to its revolutionary political implications and its dependence on a supposedly "metaphysical" value theory, Marx's LTFRP has been subjected to unrelenting criticism ever since volume III of *Capital* was published in 1894.[1] Many critics have argued that countertendencies—especially a rising rate of surplus-value and the cheapening of means of production—can offset or more than offset the tendency of the rate of profit to fall (see, e.g., Robinson 1941: 243–45, Sweezy 1970: 102–104). Marx was aware of this possibility, of course, and his LTFRP in fact predicts recurrent economic crises that restore profitability—largely by means of the cheapening of the means of production—rather than a falling trend in the rate of profit (see section 2.1.14).

In any case, arguments that the rate of profit *may not* fall do not discredit Marx's theory as effectively as the argument that it *cannot* fall for the reasons he stated. The Okishio (1961) theorem allegedly proves this latter claim. Once it became widely known in the 1970s, this theorem caught on quickly, largely eclipsing the debate over whether the countertendencies offset the tendency of the rate of profit to fall (see Cullenberg 1994).

Like Dmitriev's model, the Okishio theorem employs simultaneous valuation in order to arrive at physicalist conclusions. The crux of the theorem is that, because labor-saving technological change boosts productivity, it causes the rate of profit to rise, not fall as Marx claimed. For instance, if the four input machines in the above example beget six output machines instead of five, the rate of profit rises from $\frac{5-4}{4} = 25\%$ to $\frac{6-4}{4} = 50\%$. Once again, however, this result holds true only if input prices happen to equal output prices. Okishio does not prove that they will be equal.

Although they were not widely known prior to the 1970s, similar critiques of the LTFRP—based upon simultaneous valuation models or directly upon physicalist reasoning—had been around from the beginning. In 1899, both the Russian-Ukrainian "legal Marxist" Mikhail Tugan-Baranowsky (1901) and the Italian philosopher Benedetto Croce (1914) criticized Marx's law from a physicalist perspective. Similar critiques came from Bortkiewicz (1952) in 1907, von Charasoff (1910) in 1910, Moszkowska (1929) in 1929, Shibata (1934) in 1934, and Samuelson (1957) in a brief passage in a 1957 paper. Okishio's theorem is a generalization of Shibata's work. Roemer (1981, chap. 5) and others later generalized the theorem even further to allow for the employment of fixed capital.

In reaction to this theorem, many Marxist and Sraffian authors produced models in which the rate of profit falls even though labor-saving technological change occurs. In almost all cases, these alternative models failed to disprove the Okishio theorem. Because they employed simultaneous valuation, and their conclusions were therefore physicalist, they were unable to vindicate Marx's claim that the rate of profit can fall *because* productivity increases (see section 7.2.3 below). They obtained a result that differed from Okishio's only because they altered one or another of the theorem's assumptions, such as the assumption that the real wage rate remains constant, or the assumption that capitalists adopt new technologies only if they believe that their rates of profit will rise as a result. Counterexamples to the Okishio theorem put forth by proponents of the temporal single-system interpretation (TSSI) are an exception to this rule. They do show that the rate of profit can fall *because* productivity rises (see section 7.4 below).

3.4 Origins of the "Transformation Problem"

Like the LTFRP, Marx's account of the transformation of values into prices of production in chapter 9 of *Capital,* volume III, was first critiqued shortly after the publication of that volume in 1894. The critique put forward in 1896 by Böhm-Bawerk (1984), a leader of the Austrian school of economics, remains highly influential in some circles. According to Böhm-Bawerk, Marx had asserted in volume I that commodities tend to sell at their values, and he had promised to show that real-world phenomena which appear to contradict this assertion do not in fact contradict it, but chapter 9 of volume III failed to overcome the contradiction. Moreover, Böhm-Bawerk argued, Marx's account is tautological and meaningless, because his aggregate value-price equalities are irrelevant. (See sections 8.3 and 8.4, below, for further discussion of this issue.)

Simultaneist authors' critiques of Marx's transformation account are rather different. They are not based on the claim that Marx asserted that commodities tend to sell at their values, and they do not allege that his solution is tautological or meaningless. Simultaneist authors instead argue that his solution is internally inconsistent; Marx's conclusions fail to follow from his own theoretical premises in chapter 9. During the last sixty years at least, the specialist literature has focused on the latter critique almost exclusively. This may be partly because the critics realize that it is harder to rebut charges of internal inconsistency than charges of meaninglessness. And it is undoubtedly due in part to the theoretical-political orientation of Marx's principal critics during this period. Böhm-Bawerk's arguments have a pronounced Austrian flavor, while these critics have mostly been Marxists or Sraffians.

The simultaneist critique was traditionally thought to have begun with Bortkiewicz's (1952, 1984) 1906–1907 essays. Actually, Mühlpfort (1895) and Komorzynski (1897) put forth similar critiques a decade earlier. Yet Bortkiewicz was the first—and, to this day, the only—author who actually tried to *prove* that Marx's account of the transformation is internally inconsistent. Subsequent simultaneist critiques almost invariably appeal to this alleged proof (although they often misunderstand it). The crux of Bortkiewicz's argument is that Marx's account produces a difference between input and output prices, and that this difference leads to "internal contradictions"—specifically, to a spurious disruption of the reproduction process. After supposedly proving this claim, Bortkiewicz "corrected" Marx's account by means of a model that eliminated the difference between input and output prices and, in doing so, severed values and prices into two discordant systems. The magnitudes of constant and variable capital in the value system differ from the magnitudes of constant and variable capital in the price system.

This model fails to preserve two of Marx's three aggregate equalities, and it preserves the remaining one—the equality of total profit and total surplus-value—only by assuming particular circumstances in which it holds true. Thus, if Bortkiewicz's solution is indeed the correct one, Marx's value theory is untenable in its original form. And since Bortkiewicz obtained the equality of total profit and total surplus-value in a rather arbitrary manner, Marx's theory that all profit arises from exploitation is seriously called into question as well. Moreover, as Bortkiewicz noted, several other implications of his solution also contradict Marx's theory. For instance, it implies that the LTFRP is incorrect. Nonetheless, Bortkiewicz's "correction" and his alleged proof of Marx's self-contradiction were heartily endorsed, and brought to the attention of the English-speaking world, by Sweezy, the most prominent Marxist economist of his generation. In his famous 1942 work, *The Theory of Capitalist Development*, Sweezy (1970: 123) went so far as to call Bortkiewicz's model the "final vindication of the labor theory of value, the solid foundation of [Marx's] theoretical structure."

3.5 Marxian Economics as General Equilibrium Theory

Bortkiewicz was acutely aware that his simultaneist conception of price determination diverged markedly from Marx's. This is an important piece of knowledge that has been lost over the decades. As Bortkiewicz-style models came to be standard tools of Marxian economics, it became natural to think of their properties as properties of Marx's value theory and to seek textual justification for their Marxian heritage. Moreover, input-output techniques became a popular tool of economists, ready and waiting for Marxian economists to apply them to problems of value determination. To do so, they had to value their inputs and outputs simultaneously. It was in this environment that there arose the nearly ubiquitous interpretation that Marx's *own* value theory was simultaneist (if not indeed physicalist as well).

Bortkiewicz saw the situation much more clearly, I believe. He vigorously attacked what he called Marx's "successivist" conception of determination, in which economic factors are "regarded as a kind of causal chain, in which each link is determined, in its composition and its magnitude, only by the preceding links." Against this, he praised the "school led by Léon Walras" for propagating a more "realist[ic]" view of economic relations, in which "the various economic factors or elements condition each other *mutually*" (Bortkiewicz 1952: 24, emphasis in original). Although Bortkiewicz spoke of successivist and mutual determination, not temporal and simultaneous determination, which are now the more common terms, they mean much the same thing.

The "school led by Léon Walras" is now the dominant one. A somewhat more developed version of his general equilibrium model is the foundation of modern neoclassical economics. His and most subsequent general equilibrium models have been simultaneist, though superficially temporal versions have been formulated in recent decades. Moreover, various adaptations of Walras' model—those of Bortkiewicz, Dmitriev, Leontief (a student of Bortkiewicz's), von Neumann, and Sraffa—have become the foundation of Sraffianism and most of modern Marxian economics.

Bortkiewicz's debt to Walras was strong and abiding. At the age of nineteen, in a letter to Walras that initiated an extensive correspondence between them, Bortkiewicz wrote, "Your writings, sir, have awakened in me a lively interest in the application of mathematics to political economy, and has [sic] pointed out to me the road to travel in my researches into the methodology of economic science" (quoted in Freeman and Carchedi 1996a: xx, n11; cf. xiii).

3.6 The Master's Tools

Particularly after Sweezy called attention to Bortkiewicz's work in 1942, other authors proposed various generalizations of his "correction" of Marx. His three-department model was generalized into one with an indefinite number of sectors (Seton 1957), and the "transformation problem" was presented in explicitly physicalist terms—using technical coefficients rather than values as its data (Samuelson 1957). Alternative "corrections" of Marx's transformation account were also put forth (see section 9.2 below). Whereas Bortkiewicz's model preserved the equality of total profit and total surplus-value, but not Marx's other two equalities, the alternative solutions privileged a different aggregate equality. Because all of these generalizations and alternatives were simultaneist and dual-system, as Bortkiewicz's model was, they too failed to preserve the full set of aggregate equalities and they contradicted Marx's theoretical conclusions in several other respects.

Until the 1970s, such issues did not engage the interest, much less the passions, of more than a handful of "transformation problem" buffs. By the early 1970s, however, civil rights and antiwar struggles had given rise to the New Left, and many Ph.D. students and junior professors of economics had become radicalized. An attempt to create an alternative, a specifically "radical economics," was underway. Some of the young radical economists were beginning to study *Capital* seriously and to conduct research based upon it. The global economic crisis that erupted shortly thereafter further weakened confidence in the existing order of things.

As Desai (1988: 316) and Howard and King (1992: 268) have noted, it was owing to this atmosphere that Samuelson's (1971) critique of Marx's solution touched off a new and heated debate. Almost everything written on value theory since that time has been a direct or indirect reaction to this paper.

A Nobel laureate, and perhaps the leading economist of his generation, Samuelson was given a National Science Foundation grant and thirty-three pages in the most widely-read journal of economics in order to state his case. Such funding and promotion of a discussion of Marxian theory was unique within economics, and remains so. Since Samuelson was a neoclassicist theoretically and a liberal (in the American sense) politically, it is not surprising that he vigorously championed Bortkiewicz's critique and "correction" of Marx. What was, or at least should have been, surprising was that Samuelson's purpose was *not* to steer his readers away from Marx's theory that profit arises from exploitation. (Nor was his primary purpose to expose the fact that the dual-system models obtained their aggregate equalities in a spurious fashion, though his discussion of that fact was the main thing that angered his critics.)

Ultimately, Samuelson's purpose was instead "to demonstrate that anyone who believes in the relevance [of Marx's theory of profit . . .] will do better to jettison as unnecessary and obfuscating to his *own* theory the letter of Volume I's analysis of inter-industry values" (Samuelson 1971: 414–15, emphasis in original). To formulate their own theory rigorously, Marx's followers need to adopt "*the tools of bourgeois economics (i.e., of simple general equilibrium pricing)*" (Samuelson 1971: 405, emphasis added).

Why did Samuelson care whether a theory he rejected was formulated rigorously? Why did he not critique it directly? And why was he advising the young radical economists to *strengthen* their critique of mainstream profit theory by employing the tools of general equilibrium pricing (i.e., simultaneous valuation)?

I suspect that Samuelson may have understood something that Audre Lorde (1984: 112), the African-American lesbian poet, wrote about some years later in a different context: "the master's tools will never dismantle the master's house. They may allow us temporarily to beat him at his own game, but they will never enable us to bring about genuine change." Samuelson may have understood, in other words, that simultaneous valuation is incompatible with Marx's critique of political economy. Given Samuelson's exceptional abilities as a mathematical economist, this is not unlikely. He may thus have suspected that the tools of equilibrium theory would help reshape the views and research of young radical economists who adopted them.[2] The disintegration of the Marxian school during the last thirty years suggests that its adoption of these tools has indeed had a profound effect.

Another striking feature of Samuelson's paper is that his reference to "the tools of bourgeois economics (*i.e.,* of simple general equilibrium pricing)" was not a reference to neoclassical tools alone. As he later explained, "My vantage-point in the discussion was *not* neoclassical. It was Sraffian!" (Samuelson 1973: 64, emphasis in original). That a leading neoclassicist should suddenly become a Sraffian, however temporarily, is remarkable enough. What makes it even more surprising is the fact that Sraffa's followers had engaged in a major theoretical battle against Samuelson and his followers only a few years earlier (see Harcourt 1969), and Samuelson had been obliged to concede a crucial point in print (Levhari and Samuelson 1966). Yet he was now donning a Sraffian hat.

Indeed, Samuelson often seemed to be consciously publicizing and promoting Sraffa's work, which was not widely known at the time, in his 1971 critique of Marx. He cited Sraffa, always favorably, in eleven separate places. In the third paragraph of the paper, Samuelson (1971: 400) referred to "this age of Leontief and Sraffa," thereby putting a relatively unknown leftist critic of mainstream economics on the same pedestal as Wassily Leontief, who would be awarded the Nobel Prize in economics two years later. This reference gave rise to another paper, published shortly thereafter in the same journal, entitled "This Age of Leontief . . . and Who?" (Levine 1974).

Why did Samuelson decide to adopt a Sraffian vantage-point? Why did he praise Sraffa's work to the point of presenting him as equal in status to Leontief? Perhaps Samuelson simply wanted to suggest that if even the model of a leftist like Sraffa implies that Marx's theory is flawed, this surely must be so. Yet perhaps he suspected that he would not get very far with the young radical economists if he recommended that they adopt specifically neoclassical tools, but that they might find the Sraffian version of general equilibrium theory more palatable, a halfway house between Marx and orthodoxy, so to speak. If this was Samuelson's strategy, it seems to have succeeded.

3.7 The Transformation of Physical
Quantities into Values and Prices

Samuelson's paper is also important because it was the first work to make a
wide readership aware of the *physicalist* character of the simultaneist revisions
of Marx's transformation account. Since these models preserved one or another
aggregate value-price equality, they were frequently regarded as demonstrations
that prices and profits did, in the end, depend upon the production of value and
surplus-value. As Samuelson (1971: 417–18, 426–28) emphasized, however,
prices and values in these models are both derived from physical data.

Six years later Steedman hammered home the same point. He argued forcefully and repeatedly that value is at best an irrelevant concept: "physical quantities . . . suffice to determine the rate of profit (and the associated prices of
production) . . . . [I]t follows that value magnitudes are, at best, redundant in the
determination of the rate of profit (and prices of production)" (Steedman 1977:
202). "Marx's value reasoning—hardly a peripheral aspect of his work—
must therefore be abandoned, in the interest of developing a coherent materialist
theory of capitalism" (Steedman 1977: 207).

Recognition that the dual-system model was physicalist led to an equally if
not more damaging demonstration by Morishima (1973, chap. 14) that Steedman
(1977, chap. 11) played to the hilt. Morishima combined a joint production
model—a physical input-output system in which, roughly speaking, industries
produce multiple products—with simultaneous valuation, and found that values
and surplus-value may be negative even though prices and profits are positive.
This is why, in the passage quoted above, Steedman stated that value magnitudes are "at best, redundant." At worst, simultaneist value magnitudes are
downright meaningless.

Morishima and Steedman proposed a way of circumventing this problem,
but it required that values not be defined in Marx's "additive" manner, as the
value transferred plus the new value added. Few Marxist economists were willing to accept this solution. Quite a few of them argued that Morishima's results
were due to the improper manner in which he had aggregated individual values
into social values.

The peculiar aspect of this controversy is that almost everyone was troubled
only by the *coexistence* of negative values and surplus-values with positive
prices and profits. Few seemed to be troubled by the notion of negative values as
such. In simultaneist interpretations of Marx's theory, negative values arise even
in the absence of joint production, but this fact did not lead to any significant
questioning of the notion that Marx was a simultaneist. Nor did another paradox
of simultaneist value theory that also arises even in the absence of joint production: profit can be negative although workers are exploited, and positive even if
workers are not exploited.[3]

Instead, such problems led Marxian economists to restrict their analyses to cases in which the paradoxes do not arise—cases in which each industry continually produces more of its product than it and other industries use up. The ostensible justifications for this restriction are that economies must be able to reproduce themselves, and that we should follow Marx by trying to understand the reproduction of the capitalist system. Yet reproduction can and does occur when this restriction does not hold true, as we shall see in chapter 10. Thus it seems that the underlying purpose of the restriction was simply to expunge the perverse cases. The desire to make simultaneous valuation "work" has come to dictate how capitalist reproduction is conceived and analyzed.

The arguments put forth in response to the physicalist critiques were at first very weak. Even though values are redundant once physical quantities are specified, it was argued, values exert their influence by determining the physical data (Wright 1981). The value rate of profit sets limits to movements in the price rate of profit (Shaikh 1982). These and similar claims were little more than wishful thinking.

Shaikh (1977) also tried to reconcile physicalism-simultaneism with Marx's value theory. He argued that Marx's account of the value-price transformation was not incorrect, but merely incomplete, the first stage of an iterative process that leads to the "'correct'" (Shaikh 1977: 128ff.)—that is, simultaneist—solution. This work was quite popular in its time, even though Shaikh's was not the first "iterative solution,"[4] and even though its end result, which is all that really matters, was Bortkiewicz's, not Marx's. Recognizing that this was a problem, Shaikh later initiated a research program that attempts to circumvent the theoretical and interpretive problems in value theory by defending "the labor theory of value" on empirical grounds. Its findings will be examined in chapter 11.

Wielding impressive and seemingly rigorous mathematical tools, the Sraffians made mincemeat out of the attempts to defend Marx's value theory. Unless the proponents of value analysis repudiated the simultaneist algebra that generated the physicalist conclusions, they could not prevail. They did not repudiate it and they did not prevail. Steedman's (1977) *Marx after Sraffa* effectively settled the debate.

By the start of the 1980s, the Sraffians' victory was an established fact. This was partly because of the apparent invincibility of their analytical tools, and partly because the radicalization of the late 1960s and early 1970s had petered out. The Fundamental Marxian Theorem, made widely known by Morishima (1973), also helped to secure the victory of Sraffianism. This theorem was (wrongly) thought to have proved—using physicalist analysis rather than Marx's value theory—that the exploitation of workers is the source of all profit. It thus seemed possible to embrace both physicalism and the core of Marx's critique of capitalism. One had to exclude the LTFRP from the core of his critique in order to do so, but few Marxist economists regarded this as a serious problem.

Many Marxist and radical economists thus became Sraffians or proposed explicitly physicalist versions of Marxian value theory. Others surrendered the terrain of quantitative price and value determination to the Sraffians, but sought to preserve the insights of Marx's "qualitative" value theory. These efforts developed into what is now known as the value-form paradigm. Some other Marxist economists acknowledged that value and surplus-value are redundant, but tried to argue that they are still somehow the key underlying determinants of prices and profit. Finally, a few die-hards continued (and still continue, as we shall see in the appendix to chapter 9) to deny that simultaneous valuation makes value redundant.

Thus the disintegration of the Marxian school was well underway by the early 1980s, and the process of disintegration accelerated with the rise of Reaganism and Thatcherism. The transformation of academic institutions in the English-speaking countries into largely vocationally oriented institutions, which has reduced the space for oppositional thought, also contributed to the disintegration. Finally, since many if not most Marxian economists were pro-Stalinist to varying degrees, disillusionment set in after the collapse of the state-capitalist regimes in Eastern Europe and the USSR and the rise of neoliberalism, and this led to further disintegration.

3.8 Reinterpreting Marx

At the same time, however, various theorists began to question whether the standard Bortkiewiczian interpretation of Marx was correct. As a result of this rethinking, the New Interpretation (NI), the first simultaneous single-system interpretation (SSSI), and the TSSI emerged, independently and more or less concurrently, in the early 1980s.

The NI was put forth independently by Duménil (1980, 1983) and Foley (1982). Focusing on the value-price relationship, they challenged Bortkiewicz's dualistic conception of variable capital (or the value of labor-power), arguing that workers' actual money wages are the variable capital of both the price and value systems. They also proposed a new aggregate value-price equality that they construed as an improved version of Marx's equality of total price and total value: the sum of variable capital plus profit equals the sum of variable capital plus surplus-value. It follows immediately that total profit and total surplus-value are also equal. Thus the NI arguably preserves something akin to two of Marx's three aggregate equalities.

Yet Duménil and Foley refrained from challenging Bortkiewicz's dualistic conception of constant capital. Consequently, their interpretation fails to preserve Marx's original equality of total price and total value, or the equality of the aggregate price and value rates of profit. And because their interpretation is simultaneist, it implies that the LTFRP is false, and that the other allegations that Marx's value theory is internally inconsistent are correct.

The first SSSI was that of Wolff, Roberts, and Callari (1982). A decade later, Ramos (1991), Lee (1993), and Moseley (1993a) put forth other SSSIs, though Ramos' more recent and better-known work upholds the TSSI. Proponents of the SSSIs do not themselves use this label, since they tend to stress their internal differences and justify their interpretations in different ways. Yet since the key analytical features of their interpretations—simultaneous valuation and a single-system conception of constant and variable capital—are substantially identical, the term SSSI is appropriate.

Like the NI, the SSSIs focus on the value-price relationship. They interpret Marx's concepts of constant and variable capital in a manner that eliminates Bortkiewicz's distinct value system entirely. Consequently, all three of Marx's aggregate equalities are preserved by the SSSIs. Yet because these interpretations are simultaneist, the rate of profit remains physically determined, as Marx's critics maintain, despite the fact that the price and value rates of profit are defined in a manner that makes them equal. Thus, the SSSIs also imply that the LTFRP is false and that Marx's value theory is internally inconsistent in other respects.

The first published TSSI works on the "transformation problem" were Perez (1980) and Carchedi (1984).[5] Ernst (1982) was the first temporalist refutation of the Okishio theorem. In a mathematical sense, the TSSI is just like the SSSIs, except that it holds that Marx had a temporal, rather than simultaneous, conception of price and value determination. Because it is a single-system interpretation like the SSSIs, it too preserves all three aggregate equalities. But because it is temporalist as well, it implies that Marx's price and value magnitudes are *not* physically determined. Consequently, the TSSI vindicates the logical coherence of the LTFRP and eliminates all of the other apparent inconsistencies in Marx's value theory.

Adherents of the standard, simultaneous dual-system interpretation have persistently charged that all of these new interpretations are mere definitional tricks. If the alleged internal contradictions in Marx's value theory are not eliminated from within their own interpretive framework, they are not eliminated at all. Even Mohun (2003: 93, emphasis in original), a proponent of the NI, recently felt the need to warn his readers that the TSSI manages to preserve Marx's equality of total price and total value only because it interprets his concept of value "*differently from how it is conventionally understood.*" Such critiques ignore the hermeneutic principle, which I will discuss in detail in the next chapter, that a successful interpretation is one that makes the text make sense.

Notes

1. For an insightful discussion of the LTFRP's revolutionary implications and its relationship to Marx's humanism, see Dunayevskaya (2000: 140–45). The LTFRP has revolutionary political implications because it suggests that economic crises stem from an internal contradiction of value production—increases in physical productivity cause reductions in commodity values and a tendency for the rate of profit to fall—that cannot be resolved within capitalism. In contrast, theories that trace crises to low productivity, sluggish demand, competition, high wages, etc. suggest that the capitalism's crisis tendencies can in principle be substantially lessened or eliminated.

2. For further discussion of how economists' tools influence their views, see chapter 5, below.

3. This paradox will be discussed in chapter 10. It has frequently been claimed that the Fundamental Marxian Theorem proves that this paradox cannot arise, but that claim is incorrect.

4. Howard and King (1992: 230) suggest that Charasoff (1910) was, in effect, the first to propose an iterative solution. Shibata, Okishio, Morishima, and Bródy also proposed iterative solutions prior to Shaikh.

5. Manuel Perez was a pseudonym used by Michel Husson.

Chapter 4

Making Marx Make Sense: On Interpretive Method

4.1 Introduction

It is highly unusual for a work on Marx's critique of political economy to discuss interpretive method in any detail. I do so here because I believe that this discussion is sorely needed. Interpreters of Marx's value theory often flagrantly violate standard norms of interpretation, and such violations are unfortunately considered acceptable within economics. This is undoubtedly the foremost reason why the myth that Marx's value theory is internally inconsistent is allowed to persist. If Marxian and Sraffian economists had embraced the hermeneutic principle that the task of exegetical interpretation is to make the text make sense (if it is possible to do so), the question of internal inconsistency would have been settled long ago, in Marx's favor.

In order to help clarify why I find current interpretive practices so troubling, this chapter begins with a brief case study: Screpanti's (2003) recent "proof" that Marx's theory of exploitation is logically inconsistent. The remainder of the chapter then explains and defends the principle that successful interpretations are ones that make the text make sense. This principle is, of course, the foundation of my argument that the allegations of internal inconsistency are mythical. Because there exists an interpretation that makes Marx's value theory make sense, by removing the apparent inconsistencies, interpretations that produce the inconsistencies should be rejected as inadequate. Thus the allegations of inconsistency, which rest upon these flawed interpretations, should be rejected as well.

I stress, once again, that I am discussing whether Marx's arguments should be judged internally consistent, *not* whether the theoretical conclusions resulting from these arguments should be accepted as true. The principle to which I am

appealing does not imply that a deductive argument should be read in a way that
makes the conclusion true. What it implies is only that the argument should (if
possible) be read in a way that makes it make sense—a way that makes the conclusion follow logically from the premises. If some premise of the argument is
false, then the conclusion might be false as well, even though the argument itself
makes sense (i.e., it is logically valid).

4.2 How Not to Interpret

A fairly prominent Sraffian Marxist (Screpanti 2003: 160, 157) recently claimed
to "prove[ ]" that Marx's value-theoretic account of exploitation is "logically
inconsistent." Marx stated one conclusion while his premises imply a contrary
conclusion. The relevant premises are Marx's definitions of commodities' values and prices of production, plus two measures of the rate of exploitation. One
rate of exploitation is applicable when commodities sell at their values; the other
is applicable when they sell at prices of production. On the basis of his aggregate value-price equalities, Marx concluded that the two rates of exploitation are
equal. As Screpanti (2003: 157) notes, this conclusion enabled him to "go on
treating profits as evidence of surplus labour, i.e. exploitation" when analyzing
the real world, in which commodities do not sell at their values.

Screpanti then claims to prove that the two rates of exploitation are actually
unequal. Yet his proof is invalid for a very simple reason: it does not employ
Marx's own premises. Screpanti uses his own interpretations (mathematical for-
malizations) of Marx's definitions instead of the original ones (Screpanti 2003:
156–57, Equations (1), (3), (4), and (6)). But this means that he fails to demonstrate any *internal* inconsistency in Marx's theory. The two rates of exploitation
that he finds to be unequal are his interpretations of Marx's rates, not the original ones. What Screpanti actually proves, then, is only that his interpretation is
unable to deduce Marx's conclusion. Whose fault is this, Marx's or his own?

To prove his claim of logical inconsistency, Screpanti would have had to
prove that his interpretation of Marx's premises is correct. Failing that, he would
have made a strong case for the claim if he had provided solid evidence and arguments in support of his interpretation and against alternatives. He did none of
this. He simply wrote down three of his four premises (Equations (3), (4) and
(6)) without any accompanying justification. In support of the remaining premise, Equation (1), Screpanti quoted two sentences from *Capital*: "How, then, is
the magnitude of this value to be measured? By means of the quantity of the
'value-forming substance', the labour, contained in the article." Immediately
thereafter, he wrote: "This second axiom establishes that $\lambda = \lambda A + l$" (Screpanti
2003: 156).

This equation is surely not a plausible reformulation of the passage he
quoted. For one thing, the passage does not even say that values (λ) are the sum

of two components.[1] Thus, Screpanti offered *no* credible evidence in support of his interpretation.

Nor did he offer any evidence or arguments against alternative interpretations. The section of his paper that supposedly proves Marx's inconsistency does not even mention other interpretations (the temporal single-system interpretation (TSSI) is briefly discussed in the appendix, but in a different context). This omission is quite serious, since, according to both the TSSI and the simultaneous single-system interpretations (SSSIs), it does indeed follow from Marx's premises that the two rates of exploitation are equal. Had Screpanti acknowledged this fact, the illegitimacy of his proof procedure would have been obvious to his readers.[2]

Despite all of this, at least one editor of a respected heterodox journal of economics, and presumably some referees as well, deemed Screpanti's "proof" worthy of publication. This case is far from unique. As we shall see throughout this book, those who have "proved" that Marx is internally inconsistent, and those who publish their work, seem rarely if ever to have considered the possibility that Marx's arguments may admit of a different interpretation. And when their interpretations are unable to make Marx's texts make sense, this is invariably taken to be proof of his inconsistency rather than evidence of their own misinterpretation.

4.3 The Meaning and Interpretation of Analytical Arguments

The task of textual interpretation is to establish the meaning of the text. Yet there are different types of meaning and, accordingly, different types of interpretation.

Hirsch (1967: 8) distinguishes between the text's "significance" (to the reader) and its "meaning"—"what the [author's] signs represent." Rorty (1991: 85–86) specifies four meanings of "the meaning" of a text, ranging from "What the author would, under ideal conditions, reply to questions about his inscriptions which are phrased in terms which he can understand right off the bat" to "The role of the text in somebody's view of . . . its relation to the nature of man, the purpose of my life, the politics of our day, and so forth." Hogan (1996: 5) lists nine different possible meanings of a text's "meaning," everything from "the conscious, truth-conditional meaning of the author" to "the publisher's political aim," and he suggests that there are many, many more. Rescher (2001: 60–61) distinguishes between "creative" interpretations (which develop what the interpreter finds significant), "exploitative" interpretations (which use the text to serve a purpose, such as the formulation of one's own theory), and "exegetical" interpretations (which try to understand the author's position, for instance by clarifying her "claims and contentions").

Thus, when we assess whether an "interpretation" succeeds in establishing "the meaning" of a text, it is important to specify precisely what we are talking about. By doing so, we overcome many difficulties that would otherwise arise. It is very difficult, if not indeed impossible, to judge the relative success of alternative interpretations when one thinks of "the meaning" of a text as a sort of undifferentiated whole (Hogan 1996: 107). "Which is the best interpretation of Marx's value theory?," for example, is a frustratingly broad and vague question that admits of no clear answer. But if we specify what we are referring to more precisely, the assessment of alternative interpretations becomes more tractable. Moreover, we may be able to avoid the kind of interpretive dispute that arises unnecessarily when the parties are talking at cross purposes (see Hogan 1996: 122). Two people who disagree vociferously about "Which is the best interpretation of Marx's value theory?" might agree on the answer to such questions as "Which interpretation of Marx's texts best 'exploits' (in Rescher's sense) his value theory in furtherance of the physicalist research program?," and "Which interpretation best establishes what Marx would, under ideal conditions, reply to questions about the terms of his analytical arguments which are phrased in terms which he could understand right off the bat?"

This book deals exclusively with this last question. The reason why it does so is simple: the claim that Marx's arguments are internally inconsistent is a claim that it is impossible to deduce his conclusions from his premises *when the premises and conclusions are construed as he intended them to be construed.*[3] It is therefore simply untenable to declare that Marx is internally inconsistent while simultaneously declaring that what he really meant is not the issue.

Accordingly, I assess the interpretations considered herein exclusively in terms of their success as "exegetical interpretations," their ability to establish the "meaning" (in Hirsch's sense) of some of Marx's inscriptions. Although some of these interpretations are also "creative" and/or "exploitative," it is appropriate to consider them as exegetical interpretations because their proponents have defended them, at least partly, on exegetical grounds.

Some years ago, Foley (2000a: 36) noted correctly that "empirical investigation of the development of world capitalism need not wait on the resolution of every knotty interpretive and theoretical issue in the labor theory of value." In light of the distinctions sketched out above, it should also be clear that resolution of the specifically interpretive controversy over Marx's value theory need not wait on any consensus regarding theoretical and empirical matters. "Is this interpretation a good basis for theoretical or empirical analysis?" and "Does it succeed as an exegetical interpretation of Marx?" are quite different questions, and they might have quite different answers. The fact that one believes that the answer to the first question is "yes" is not a good reason to refrain from acknowledging that the answer to the latter question is "no," and vice-versa.

4.4 Knowing What an Author Meant

It has sometimes been argued that we cannot know what an author meant, especially when, as in Marx's case, we cannot ask him or her. This argument presupposes that the author can know what he or she meant in a way that we cannot—directly, through introspection. Empirical evidence suggests, however, that this is not so. Hogan (25–26, cf. p. 61, pp. 133–34)) notes that "many psychological studies have indicated [. . . that] our introspective judgment is highly fallible. Even on ordinary matters, my analyses of myself are as much matters of uncertain theoretical inference as are my analyses of other people," rather than reports of knowledge obtained directly through introspection. The difference between the problems we face in knowing what someone else meant and what we ourselves meant is therefore at most a difference of degree, not a difference of kind.

The notion that we cannot know what an author meant is also often based on confusion between knowledge and certainty. We can never be certain that a particular interpretation is correct or incorrect. Yet, as many authors emphasize, all empirical investigation is like interpretation in this respect (see, e.g., Hirsch 1967: 17–18, chap. 5; Hogan 1996: 13, 28, 42; Rescher 2001: 68; Stigler 1965). Whether the empirical data are texts, thumbprints, economic statistics, or readings of the movements of subatomic particles, we can never say with certainty that a particular explanatory hypothesis—which is what an exegetical interpretation is—must be correct or incorrect.

But this is no obstacle to knowledge of a less ambitious, fallible kind. The goal of all empirical investigation is to decide, on the basis of the currently available data, which hypotheses are more *plausible* and which are less so. In other words, when we conclude that a theory or interpretation is correct or incorrect, we mean that the way in which it explains the available evidence is plausible or implausible. (All of the authors cited in the preceding paragraph make this point in one way or another.) As twentieth-century philosophers of science have taught us, all theories can be made to fit the facts. But they cannot all do so plausibly, and thus their relative plausibility is the basis for discriminating among them. The same thing holds true in the case of interpretation.

Hence, the fact that we cannot know with certainty what an author meant provides no warrant for the conclusion that "anything goes" in interpretation. To my knowledge, *no* school of interpretation holds that one interpretation is as good as another. For instance, although Fish (1980) makes much of the fact that no interpretation is decisive, he seems to mean by this mostly that it is always possible, in principle, that new evidence (regarding the author's attitudes, intentions, concerns, etc.) might make an accepted interpretation untenable, and he affirms no fewer than five times in a single essay that "We are right to rule out at least some readings."

Similarly, in a paper discussing an exchange between Hyppolite and Derrida on Einstein's physics, Plotnitsky (1997, para. 17), a well-known practitioner of deconstruction, argues that his own interpretation of what they meant is "more plausible" than the interpretation put forth by scientists who had poked fun at Derrida. He also urges that their statements be given "the most sensible rather than the most senseless interpretation"; in other words, an interpretation should make the text make sense (Plotnitsky 1997, para. 18). In a subsequent reply to a critic, Plotnitsky (1998, para. 9, emphasis added) even stated that "it can be ascertained with a *reasonable degree of certainty* that Hyppolite suggests the possibility of some connections between Derrida's ideas and relativity."

In a critique of *Marx and Non-equilibrium Economics,* a 1996 collection that challenged the allegations of internal inconsistency in Marx's value theory, Foley (1997: 494) wrote that "Marx's writings on economics are voluminous, and exist in various states of revision. So it is hard to rule out the possibility of inconsistencies in his . . . theory of value." He is correct in one sense. Since certainty is unattainable in empirical matters, the possibility of some inconsistency can never be ruled out definitively. Yet as the foregoing discussion indicates, this is a red herring. Marx's critics throughout the last century have not merely reminded us of the innocuous truism that inconsistency in his value theory is an abstract possibility. They have alleged that inconsistency has been proved in several particular cases. Thus the real issues are whether these proofs are valid and—if they are not—whether it is *plausible,* in light of currently available evidence, that Marx is guilty of these particular inconsistencies. Rather than address these issues, Foley suggests on abstract, *a priori* grounds that Marx should be presumed guilty of inconsistency until proven innocent.

4.5 The Criterion of Coherence

A principal founder of textual hermeneutics, Friedrich Schleiermacher, wrote that "as the whole is of course understood from the individual, so too the individual can only be understood from the whole" (quoted in Connolly and Keutner 1988: 10). His point was to distinguish genuine understanding from misunderstanding. We genuinely understand a text (for example) only if the individual parts are reconciled, brought together as aspects of the whole.

Students of textual interpretation since that time have embraced Schleiermacher's criterion, which Hirsch (1967: 236) called the "criterion of coherence." For instance, part of Kosík's (1976: 95) distinction between "a substantiated interpretation" and "textual distortions or modifications" is that the former will "leave no opaque, unexplained or 'accidental' passages in the text." In other words, it must not be selective, but must explain the text as a whole. If some passages cannot be explained or are incompatible with the interpretation, then it must be regarded as unsubstantiated. Similarly, Rescher (2001: 62) writes: "in exegetically interpreting philosophical texts we seek . . . to remove, overcome, or explain away obscurities, ambiguities, conflicts, and other such obstacles to understanding." Even a practitioner of deconstruction such as Plotnitsky (1997, note 6) embraces this and other "classical protocols" of interpretation, though he cautions that they "cannot guarantee determinate results."

Few critics of Marx's value theory disagree openly with this criterion. They simply find it inapplicable to cases in which they have found his theory to be inconsistent. In such cases, they maintain, it is just not possible to reconcile the conflicting parts of the text. But this argument begs the question. It takes for granted that the interpreter's inability to understand the texts as a coherent whole is the author's fault, not the interpreter's, although this is precisely what is at issue here. The claim that Marx is at fault must be demonstrated, not presumed. But since his critics fail to embrace a clear *criterion* by which successful interpretation can be distinguished from misinterpretation,[4] they have no way to demonstrate that the fault is his, not theirs.

Because they lack such a criterion, they inevitably fall prey to a quite common problem that Hirsch (1967: 166) called "circular entrapment." They defend their interpretations of particular passages by appealing to "what Marx wrote" in those passages and elsewhere. Yet their appeal to "what Marx wrote" is actually an appeal to *their own interpretations* of what he wrote—not his words *per se*, but his words as construed by them. In other words, they defend their interpretations by appealing to their interpretations.

This also leads inevitably to unintentional dogmatism. When Marx's critics insist that their interpretations are correct because they are "what Marx wrote," they are actually insisting upon *their own interpretations* of what he wrote. In other words, their interpretations are correct because they say so. To avoid dogmatism, one needs to escape from this vicious circularity. One needs to specify the conditions under which one would be willing to concede that one's interpretation is incorrect. To uphold a belief, come what may, is precisely what dogmatism is. Yet in the absence of a clear criterion of interpretive adequacy, it is impossible to specify the conditions that would falsify one's interpretation. Over the years, I have asked many critics of Marx and/or the TSSI to specify such conditions, but none has done so. The "best" answer I have received is that they would abandon their interpretations if new evidence came along that contradicted them. This answer clearly begs the question. Under what conditions would they be willing to concede that the new evidence *does* contradict their interpretations? To this question there has been no answer.

The criterion of coherence allows us to break out of such question begging, circularity, and dogmatism, because it allows us to specify the conditions under which an interpretation should be rejected. Warnke (1993: 21) draws out this implication clearly: "the adequacy of a given textual interpretation depends on the extent to which it can show the text's coherence as a unified whole." Thus an interpretation that resolves apparent inconsistencies within a text is superior to ones that either fail to do so or do so only to a lesser extent.

Sound interpretation thus makes sense of a text by *making the text make sense*. This means, first, that an interpreter must try to make the text *make sense*. Rosenberg (1984: 73) writes that the test of philosophical interpretation is "whether the philosopher's arguments indeed make sense when his vocabulary is understood in the suggested way." It also means that one needs to *make* the text make sense. Thus, when certain passages seem to contradict others, "Interpretation here calls for the removal of [the] apparent conflicts" (Rescher 2001: 64). They are often removed by introducing distinctions, qualifications, and the like. The texts of Marx's critics provide little if any evidence that they have employed such procedures before declaring his work internally inconsistent.

A particular text may of course be genuinely inconsistent. Yet it follows from the criterion of coherence that an allegation of inconsistency should not be taken at face value. On the contrary, it should be regarded as *prima facie* evidence of misinterpretation. As Warnke (1993: 21) notes, "if certain parts of the text seem to contradict others, the initial presumption of the critic has to be that they do so because one or the other set has been misunderstood [by the critic]."

Warnke (1993: 33) acknowledges, of course, that it may not be possible to make the text cohere. If attempts to do so repeatedly fail, it becomes increasingly plausible that the text is indeed inconsistent. The initial presumption that the text has been misunderstood must give way to the conclusion that the author, rather than her interpreters, is at fault. As we saw in the case of Screpanti, however, Marx's critics have claimed that his value theory has been proven internally inconsistent merely because it becomes so under their own interpretations, even though—as the TSSI demonstrates—it is possible to make Marx's texts cohere. In cases such as this, the criterion of coherence clearly implies that interpretations that fail to make the text cohere are inadequate.

4.6 Stigler's "Principle of Scientific Exegesis"

The great merit of George Stigler's (1965) "Textual Exegesis as a Scientific Problem" is that it showed how to apply the criterion of coherence to the interpretation of an analytical work. His "principle of scientific exegesis" (PSE) says that such an interpretation should be rejected if it cannot deduce the author's main analytical conclusions from her definitions and premises.

The PSE has profound implications for the interpretive controversy in value theory. It implies that the interpretations on which Marx's theory becomes internally inconsistent must be rejected. The evidence that Marx was inconsistent is therefore unsound. And since the evidence is unsound, Marx should be judged not guilty.

A Chicago School economist who later won the Nobel Prize, Stigler articulated his principle in the midst of a debate over the meaning of Ricardo's theory of the demand for corn. Haim Barkai (1965) had argued that Ricardo's theory implies that a rise in the price of corn would cause the amount demanded to fall. Stigler argued, to the contrary, that Ricardo had in effect asserted that the demand for corn is perfectly inelastic. A rise in its price would not lead to a reduction in the quantity demanded.

My concern here is not to decide who was right, but to discuss the test of interpretive adequacy that Stigler proposed. He objected to Barkai's selective use of quotations in order to make his case. "Why," Stigler (1965: 448) asked, "should we allow the hand-picked quotation to carry an interpretation when we would reject the hand-picked fact as an empirical test of a hypothesis? In fact the two problems are basically the same."

This point is important because it pinpoints precisely what is wrong with quoting out of context, and why battles of quotations fail in the end to clarify matters. These are "unscientific" ways of deciding among interpretations. Issues of interpretation are empirical issues, textual evidence is empirical evidence, and so the "scientific," scholarly procedure is to evaluate competing hypotheses about a text's meaning in essentially the same way that one evaluates competing hypotheses about the external world.[5] One needs to test whether they fit with the empirical evidence—taken as a whole.

Yet the really brilliant aspect of Stigler's paper is his apparently novel understanding of what constitutes empirical evidence in the case of an analytical text. He recognized that textual evidence is not limited to passages in which an author sets out her definitions and premises; another part of the evidence consists of her theoretical conclusions. Stigler thus proposed that a textual interpretation be judged according to whether it can hold both types of evidence together as a unified whole. The test of an interpretation, in other words, is whether it can deduce the author's theoretical conclusions from her definitions and premises:

> textual interpretation must uncover the main concepts in the man's work, and the major functional relationships among them. . . .
> . . . We increase our confidence in the interpretation of an author by increasing the number of his main theoretical conclusions which we can deduce from (our interpretation of) his analytical system.
> The test of an interpretation is its consistency with the main analytical conclusions of the system of thought under consideration. If the main conclusions of a man's thought do not survive under one interpretation, and do under another, the latter interpretation must be preferred. (The analogy to maximum likelihood is evident.)
> . . . This rule of consistency with the main conclusions may be called the principle of scientific exegesis. [Stigler 1965: 448]

A few aspects of this passage are worth emphasizing here. First, Stigler did not say that "consistency with the main conclusions" is one desirable feature of an interpretation. He proposed it as *the test* of interpretive adequacy. Thus, an interpretation that one believes to have other desirable features, but which fails the test of consistency with the main conclusions, must be rejected. Conversely, an interpretation that one regards as undesirable for other reasons, but which is consistent with the author's conclusions, must be accepted. One may not, for instance, favor the former on the ground that the latter "distorts our understanding" of the text. Clearly, if an interpretation fails *the test* of interpretive adequacy, its understanding of the text must be regarded as a misunderstanding.

Second, just as the criterion of coherence implies that an interpretation which finds the text to be internally coherent is better than one that does not, so too does the PSE. "If the main conclusions of a man's thought do not survive under one interpretation, and do under another, the latter interpretation must be preferred."

Finally, Stigler's "analogy to maximum likelihood" is a reference to the inferential character of interpretation. The concluding words of his paper were: "Let us recognize the fact that the interpretation of a man's position—especially if the man has a complex and subtle mind—is a problem in inference, not to be solved by the choice of quotations" (Stigler 1965: 450). Maximum likelihood estimation is a statistical technique in which one works backwards, beginning with the results—the sample data—and uses them to infer the mathematical relationship between the variables that exists in the larger population. The relationship one selects is the one that is most likely to have produced the observed data.

Analogously, Stigler was saying, one should use a theory's conclusions as evidence of what its premises and definitions actually are. One should infer from the conclusions how to interpret otherwise ambiguous textual evidence pertaining to definitions and premises. Thus he worked backwards when attempting to understand Ricardo's theory of the demand for corn. Beginning with the conclusion that the rate of profit tends to fall with the progress of capital accumulation, plus some other premises of Ricardo's theory, Stigler tried to show that it implies a perfectly inelastic demand for corn. That must be so, he argued, since Ricardo's conclusion that the rate of profit falls would otherwise not follow from his premises.

The PSE is an application of the criterion of coherence in two senses. First, it proposes that interpretations be tested according to whether they can establish coherence between two different aspects of a text—definitions and premises on the one hand, conclusions on the other. Second, it requires a holistic rather than a linear method of reading a theoretical text. It denies that the meaning of an author's premises and definitions can be determined by focusing solely on passages that discuss them directly. It thereby also implicitly denies that one can judge whether a work is internally coherent by determining whether its conclusions follow from an interpretation of its premises and definitions that was worked out prior to and without regard to the conclusions.

The meaning of the premises is instead established when an interpretation is able to take passages that contain conclusions, and passages that set out premises, and make them cohere with one another. And while we must no doubt proceed from premises to conclusions in order to ascertain whether an argument is internally consistent, the PSE stipulates that we must also proceed from conclusions to premises in order to ascertain what an author's premises really are.[6] This is a classic example of what has been called the "hermeneutic circle."

4.7 Barkai and Hollander on the PSE

Barkai (1967) responded to Stigler about a year later. That he continued to affirm his own interpretation of Ricardo's theory is not surprising. What may be surprising is that Barkai nevertheless endorsed the PSE. After quoting Stigler in the opening sentence of his reply—"The test of an interpretation is its consistency with the main analytical conclusions of the system of thought under consideration"—Barkai (1967: 75) remarked that "[t]his is undoubtedly a useful criterion, and I propose to apply it here."

Thus Barkai accepted the terms of the debate as Stigler had just (re-) formulated them. He agreed that it was not possible to decide which interpretation of Ricardo's theory of the demand for corn was correct simply by examining isolated passages that address the issue directly, or even by examining the totality of such passages. To be considered correct, Barkai conceded, an interpretation of Ricardo's theory must be able to deduce his conclusion that the rate of profit falls with the progress of accumulation:

> I do not dispute the strategic position of this 'law' [of the falling profit rate] in Ricardo's conceptual structure. Consequently, *I would have to concede that my interpretation of Ricardo's position on demand is untenable if it were true that a 'conventional' demand relation and the law of the falling profit rate are incompatible, or that the latter is 'weakened' when the former applies.* [Barkai 1967: 76, emphasis added]

Barkai thus set out to substantiate his interpretation of Ricardo in the way Stigler proposed. He endeavored to "show . . . that 'the law of the falling profit rate' can be deduced rigorously from the premises of the Ricardian model, even if one assumes a negatively sloped (and not a zero) elastic demand curve" (Barkai 1967: 76).

For those of us who are not Ricardo specialists, what is noteworthy about this exchange is that Stigler and Barkai agreed about method despite their disagreement about substance. Both authors acknowledged that the test of an interpretation is whether it can derive an author's conclusions from (its understanding of) her premises, and both willingly applied this test to the case at hand. In recent years, another prominent historian of Ricardo's thought, Samuel Hollander, has also returned to and endorsed Stigler's view that the test of an interpretation of an analytical work is whether it is consistent with the text's main conclusions.

Hollander does take issue with Stigler's 1965 paper, but his criticisms pertain solely to other aspects of Stigler's position on interpretation. According to Hollander (1990: 730–32), Stigler suggested that we should not test interpretations against the text's main conclusions *as the author herself formulated them*. Our goal should not be to understand what the author intended, but "to maximize the value of a theory to the science." We should thus formulate a text's "central theoretical position . . . in a strong form capable of contradiction by the facts," even if what the author herself wrote must first be "amended" in order to produce the falsifiable hypothesis we desire.[7] Stigler (1990) replied to Hollander's paper, but did not contest this interpretation of his position, so Hollander may well have understood him correctly.

Whether that is so or not, I believe that Hollander (1990: 731, 733) was absolutely right to insist that "[w]e must isolate the central theoretical position from the texts without amendment" and to affirm that "the primary requisite of exegesis . . . is to get the model right on the author's own terms." The point is to make the text make sense, but we do not really make it make sense if we falsify or discard textual evidence in order to produce the *semblance* of coherence.

In any case, the dispute between Stigler and Hollander was limited to whose version of the "main conclusions" to use, the author's original ones or the interpreter's possibly "amended" ones. Hollander agreed with Stigler that an interpretation needs to be consistent with the main conclusions in order to be considered correct. "The 'scientific rule of exegesis' is . . . acceptable provided it is limited to a test of interpretation understood simply as consistency with the main analytical conclusions" (Hollander 1990: 131).

4.8 In Defense of the Criterion of Coherence and the PSE

Although Hollander and some other historians of economic thought (e.g., Graça Moura 2000, note 25) reject Stigler's own formulation of the PSE, I am not aware of anyone who argues against the basic point that "[t]he test of an interpretation is its consistency with the main analytical conclusions of the system of thought under consideration."[8] Yet almost all Marxist and Sraffian economists reject this test implicitly, since they fail to employ it and decline to discuss its validity. It will therefore be helpful to offer some arguments in its favor.

The PSE may at first seem to be a "trick." Interpretation of definitions and premises in the light of the conclusions may at first appear to be analogous to the case in which statisticians adulterate the data in order to reach their favored results. There are three key differences, however. First, it is not the case that the "data" (the authors' statements) are altered when they are reinterpreted in a way that makes them cohere with the conclusions. The reinterpretation changes the meaning ascribed to the statements, not the statements themselves. Those who insist that their own interpretations are self-evident will of course *feel* that the reinterpretation changes the statement, because they see no difference between the statement and their interpretation of it, but this is simply not what has taken place.

Second, statisticians' data are generated independently of, and exist prior to, the procedures that produce the statistical results. This is why adulterating the data is a fraudulent practice. It destroys pre-existing information. In contrast, interpretations of definitions and premises have no privileged status as against interpretations of theoretical conclusions. A single interpretive process produces both. Moreover, it produces them simultaneously. Every interpreter produces her "data"—her interpretation of definitions and premises—and her interpretation of the text's conclusions at the same time, in a back-and-forth manner, in order to try to make the two cohere. The notion that "the author's" definitions and premises are pre-existing facts (relative to the conclusions) evidently arises because interpreters forget that, and how, they themselves generated these "facts."[9]

Finally, by doctoring one's data, one can always produce the desired statistical results, but it is quite difficult to make different parts of a text cohere with one another. All responsible interpreters try to do so, but they often fail. Thus, an interpretation that succeeds in making the text cohere should be accepted precisely because coherence is so difficult to achieve. One might be able to explain away this or that particular incongruity in a text by arbitrarily imposing a "forced" interpretation upon it, but such a procedure cannot succeed in making the various parts of a text fit together into a coherent whole.

To see more clearly why interpretations that succeed in deducing the author's conclusions are not "forced" but, on the contrary, more plausible than those which do not, consider Rescher's comment on the interpretation of texts that have a "how-to aspect." "[When a] text . . . has a how-to aspect, whether this be small-scale (recipes for baking bread, instructions for cleaning a rifle) or large-scale (prescriptions for successful merchandizing, guidelines to scanning Latin poetry) . . . there is no anything-goes plasticity; some ways of interpreting that text and implementing the lessons of such an interpretation are *materially better* than others" (Rescher 2001: 67, emphasis added).

Now notice that a deductive argument has a how-to aspect in much the same way that a recipe for baking bread does. By manipulating the ingredients according to the steps of the recipe, one should end up with bread. If one baker ends up with bread, while another (working under similar conditions) fails to do so, we conclude that it is highly probable that the first baker's interpretation of the recipe is right while the second baker's is wrong. She either did not use the specified ingredients or did not correctly follow the steps.

Similarly, by manipulating the author's premises according to the rules of inference, one should end up with the author's conclusion. If some scholars end up with that conclusion while others fail to do so, we should conclude that it is highly probable that the first group's interpretation of the text is right while the second group's is wrong. The second group either did not interpret the premises correctly or did not properly apply the rules of inference. The first group's interpretation is *materially better* than the second group's.

The PSE and the criterion of coherence can also be defended by showing that analogous tenets are regularly employed in various scholarly disciplines and in daily life. The widespread employment of these principles, especially their employment in daily life, is evidence that they are principles of responsible interpretation that have withstood the test of time, if indeed they are not inevitable.

The criterion of coherence has often been defended by noting that we employ essentially the same criterion "*wherever* there is anything unfamiliar . . . in the expression of thoughts through speech" (Schleiermacher, quoted in Connolly and Keutner 1988: 9, emphasis in original). We try to understand the speaker's utterances as a coherent whole, and in two senses. First, we interpret the individual words, phrases, etc. in the context of her statement as a whole. Second, we choose to interpret her statement in such a way that it makes sense—if that is at all possible. Quine, following Wilson (1959: 532), called this the "principle of charity," and noted that "the commonsense behind the maxim is that one's interlocutor's silliness, beyond a certain point, is less likely than bad translation" (Quine 1960: 59).

Essentially the same criterion has been applied in anthropology. On the basis of first-hand reports of what certain non-Western peoples "believe," some anthropologists and philosophers concluded that these peoples are "irrational," at least by Western standards. Another anthropologist (Sperber 1982) challenged this conclusion. He first drew a distinction between factual beliefs and "representational beliefs with a semi-propositional content." He then argued that "there is no reason, either theoretical or empirical, to assume that the apparently irrational beliefs reported by anthropologists and historians are factual beliefs. . . . [T]he very fact that, when assumed to be factual, these beliefs appear irrational is reason enough to assume, on the contrary, that they are representational beliefs with a semi-propositional content" (Sperber 1982: 175).[10] In other words, the very fact that one interpretation of the beliefs makes sense of them by *making them make sense,* while another does not, is sufficient reason to infer that the former interpretation is right while the latter is wrong.

Darwin invoked something analogous to the criterion of coherence when defending his theory of natural selection against critics, as Rescher (2001: 140) recently pointed out. The critics balked at his theory on the ground that no direct evidence supports it; evolutionary change is not observed. Darwin (1872: 421) acknowledged this fact but argued that "[i]t can hardly be supposed that a false theory would explain, in so satisfactory a manner as does the theory of natural selection, the several large classes of facts above specified. It has recently been objected that this is an unsafe method of arguing; but it is a method used in judging of the common events in life, and has often been used by the greatest natural philosophers." Since, on his interpretation of the indirect evidence, "several large classes of facts" become a coherent whole, effects of a single process, Darwin concluded that his interpretation is correct.

As we saw, Stigler himself defended the PSE by arguing that analogous principles are generally accepted and employed in the sciences, particularly in statistical work. Analogous principles have also been employed by historians of ideas outside of economics. For instance, Thomas Kuhn came to the conclusion that Aristotle's physics—especially his writings on motion, which were commonly deemed preposterous—had long been misinterpreted. What convinced Kuhn of this was his "discovery of a way of reading Aristotelian physics, one that *made the texts make sense*" (Kuhn 2000: 17, emphasis added). This of course does not mean that Kuhn came to believe that Aristotle's theories are true.

Similarly, Freudenthal (1986), a historian of science, considered four claims contained in Newton's *Principia Mathematica* that seem not to make sense. He argued that the basis of Newton's claims was a certain unstated set of assumptions about the properties of particles. Endorsing Freudenthal's argument, Chalmers (1990: 107), a philosopher of science, writes: "[T]he main case for the fact that Newton did assume [that particles have these properties] is that, once assumed, otherwise problematic arguments and assertions in the *Principia* make sense."

4.9 Critics' Responses

Few critics of Marx's value theory and/or the TSSI have thought it necessary to respond to TSSI theorists' plea that the criterion of coherence and the PSE be brought to bear upon the interpretive controversy in value theory. The only papers that have engaged the issue are Moseley (2000a) and Mohun (2003).

Moseley (2000a, introduction, emphasis in original) upheld his SSSI against the TSSI by rejecting the principle of scientific exegesis:

> Andrew [Kliman] suggests that the main criterion for choosing between different interpretations of Marx's concept of constant capital is which interpretation can better derive more of Marx's main conclusions (most importantly, the falling rate of profit). I disagree. I argue that the main criterion for choosing between different interpretations of the determination of constant capital in the case of a change in the value of the means of production is *what Marx himself actually wrote* about this subject. . . . [E]very time Marx wrote specifically

about this subject, he assumed that constant capital is valued in [sic] current replacement costs, in the sense indicated above. In this situation, it does not make sense to accept Andrew's interpretation of the valuation of constant capital simply because this interpretation makes it easier to derive a falling rate of profit. It may be easier to derive the falling rate of profit, but this interpretation contradicts everything Marx ever wrote specifically on this subject. Maybe if the texts were more ambiguous, Andrew's criterion might be more appropriate. But in this case, the texts are unusually clear and consistent throughout Marx's manuscripts.

It is interesting that Moseley rejects the idea of testing his interpretation of Marx by seeing if it can be used to deduce a falling rate of profit. As we have seen, neither Stigler nor Barkai had any qualms about testing their interpretations of Ricardo in precisely this manner. Part of the reason why Moseley rejects such a test is that he falsely counterposes "what Marx himself actually wrote" to the derivation of a falling rate of profit, as if the issue were the "eas[e]" with which different interpretations can make the rate of profit fall. In fact, what is at issue is the ability of different interpretations to make two aspects of the text— premises and conclusions—cohere. The question is: which interpretation of the premises that "Marx himself actually wrote [down]" coheres with the conclusions of the law of the tendential fall in the rate of profit (LTFRP) that "Marx himself actually wrote [down]" as well?

Yet the more fundamental reason why Moseley rejects the PSE is that he simply refuses (without explaining why) to accept that interpretations should be judged by their ability to make the texts cohere *as a whole*. Notice that, rather than taking the whole of Marx's texts into account, he excludes everything from consideration except what Marx wrote "specifically about this subject." More- over, he defines "this subject" in a very narrow way. Not only is the LTFRP not part of "this subject," neither is Marx's overall theory of how constant-capital value is determined. For Moseley, "this subject" is only what Marx wrote specifically about the determination of constant-capital value *in the particular case in which the value of the means of production changes*. This definition of the subject enables him to dismiss as irrelevant a great many passages in which Marx states that the constant capital component of commodities' values is determined temporally (see section 6.4, below). Moseley contends that these passages are irrelevant because they do not *explicitly* address the case in which values change![11]

Why does this make such passages irrelevant? Moseley is arguing, in effect, that a general statement never applies to a particular case unless it explicitly *includes* that particular case. This is simply not so; general statements automatically apply to all particular cases that they do not explicitly *exclude*. For instance, if I say "vitamins are good for you" without explicitly listing all of the particular cases to which I intend it to apply (". . . in months ending in 'r,' and in years in which Brazil wins the World Cup, and when it is sunny, and if you stop liking reggae . . ."), is my statement inapplicable to these cases? Similarly, Marx wrote at the start of *Capital* that abstract labor is the substance of value, without explicitly stipulating that this statement applies to the case in which commodities' values change. Does this make the statement irrelevant to that case? Clearly not.

Moseley (2000a: section 2.3, emphasis added) contends, however, that "[i]mplicitly, all these passages [in which Marx discusses the determination of constant-capital value in temporal terms] are under the assumption that the value of the means of production *does not* change." But he provides no evidence to substantiate this assertion, and no evidence seems to exist. Thus he apparently regards it as a logical deduction: since the passages do not state explicitly that they apply to the case in which values are changing, they implicitly assume that values are not changing. This is like saying that, since my statement "vitamins are good for you" does not explicitly stipulate that it applies to months ending in "r," its scope is implicitly restricted to the remaining months!

Moseley also argues that the evidence is too clearly in his favor to make the PSE applicable. The primary criterion of interpretive adequacy is the interpretation's correspondence to the texts; the PSE "might be" appropriate if the texts were ambiguous, but not here. The problem with this argument, of course, is that the evidence favors Moseley's interpretation only if one accepts his exclusion of a great deal of evidence, interprets the remaining evidence as he does, and accepts his framing of the issue. (He frames it as "the determination of constant capital," while I think that this phrase conflates distinct processes, and that he misinterprets the texts because of this.) Under such circumstances, what good does it do to appeal to "what Marx wrote"? We are locked in an interpretive disagreement of the kind that no one has found a way to unlock, except by appealing to the criterion of coherence.

Having rejected this criterion, however, Moseley inevitably succumbs to the circular reasoning and unintentional dogmatism that I alluded to above. He has no choice but to justify his interpretation of what Marx wrote by appealing to (his interpretation of) what Marx wrote, and no choice but to insist that his interpretation is correct because it is (his interpretation of) what Marx wrote.[12]

Mohun's recent reply to Kliman (2001) is far more encouraging. He is the first critic of the TSSI to acknowledge that, in order to properly evaluate the adequacy of different interpretations of Marx's value theory, a clear "criterion of decidability" is needed (Mohun 2003: 97). Although he does not explicitly endorse the PSE, which he calls the "criterion of replication" (Mohun 2003: 97), Mohun employs it in order to test the relative adequacy of the TSSI and the New Interpretation (NI) as interpretations of Marx's theory that exploitation is the source of all profit. He concludes that the TSSI and the NI perform equally poorly, while I believe that this conclusion is incorrect (see Kliman and Freeman 2006 and sections 10.6 through 10.8, below). Yet I am confident that this particular controversy can be resolved relatively quickly and easily, because we are both appealing to an explicit criterion of interpretive adequacy, and especially because we are both appealing to the same criterion. If other critics of the TSSI follow Mohun's lead and employ the PSE as well, there is good reason to believe that the interpretive controversy over Marx's value theory can finally be settled, once and for all.

Notes

1. Although proponents of the TSSI and the SSSIs agree that values are the sum of two components, they reject other features of Screpanti's reformulation that he also fails to substantiate.

2. For additional discussion of Screpanti's paper, see Kliman (2006b).

3. Otherwise, all arguments could properly be judged internally inconsistent. Readers could always interpret them in a way that makes them inconsistent, justifying their interpretations on the ground that "this is what the terms of the argument mean to me" or "this is a useful way of understanding the terms of the argument" (interpretations that make Marx's arguments internally inconsistent have indeed been very useful to his critics), etc., and there would be no way to rule out such practices.

4. A recent paper by Mohun (2003), which I discuss below, is evidently the first non-TSSI work to employ such a criterion.

5. "There *are* standards of scholarship, and any proposition about the real world must be right or wrong. Even when that real world is a writer's mind-state or intentions when composing a work, it is perfectly possible, at least in principle, to test the validity of inferences and hypotheses. . . . [S]uch tests may be difficult to devise and somewhat less than perfect to implement. But that is nothing new in science" (Dunbar 1995: 178, emphasis in original).

6. A recent handbook on philosophical technique recommends exactly the same procedure: "In working out precisely what the premises are in a given argument, ask yourself first what the claim is that the argument is trying to demonstrate. Then ask yourself what other claims the argument relies upon (implicitly or explicitly) in order to advance that demonstration" (Baggini and Fosl 2003: 3).

7. In this and the preceding sentence, all words and phrases inside quotation marks are Stigler's (1965: 448).

8. Some historians of economic thought do point out that there is not always agreement as to what the "main analytical conclusions" are. In such cases, the PSE cannot be used to settle interpretive disputes, of course, but the interpretive controversy over Marx's value theory is not such a case. I am not aware of anyone who denies, for instance, that Marx's LTFRP, aggregate value-price equalities, and theory that exploitation is the source of all profit are among his main analytical conclusions.

9. Resistance to the idea that one should not only work forward, from definitions and premises to conclusions, but backward as well, might also be partly psychological in origin. Polya (1988: 230–32) observes that, although mathematicians have regularly employed the method of working backward since the time of the ancient Greeks, people often find it difficult to employ this method, and he conjectures that the difficulty may be psychological.

10. Although Sperber does not mention Quine, his argument may stem directly or indirectly from Quine's (1960: 69) contention that "the more absurd or exotic the beliefs imputed to a people, the more suspicious we are entitled to be of the translations; the myth of the prelogical peoples marks only the extreme."

11. As we shall see in section 6.4, a few of these passages *do* explicitly address what happens when values change.

12. In Kliman (2000b), I discuss Moseley's paper, especially the substantive issues at stake, in greater detail.

Chapter 5

Simultaneism, Physicalism, and the Law of Value

5.1 Introduction

Prior to the development of the temporal single-system interpretation (TSSI), it was not recognized that the various allegations of internal inconsistency leveled against Marx's value theory have a common source. Many authors tried to defend his theory in piecemeal fashion, focusing on some issues but not others. For instance, the New Interpretation (NI) and the simultaneous single-system interpretations (SSSIs) do not address the claim that Marx's law of the tendential fall in the rate of profit (LTFRP) is false. Other authors challenged one or another particular assumption that Marx's critics made in this case or that. For example, Shaikh (1978) tried to defend Marx's theory of the rate of profit by challenging its critics' conception of competition, while Naples (1989) tried to refute the notion of a "transformation problem" by questioning the assumption that the rate of profit is uniform.

It seemed as though there were many different problems, each of which needed to be solved in its own particular way. And it seemed to the would-be defenders of Marx's theory that its critics had committed many little interpretive errors rather than one big one.

Yet the allegations of internal inconsistency do have a common source, one big interpretive error: simultaneous valuation. The models that supposedly prove that Marx was inconsistent all employ the simultaneist method. This method necessarily leads to physicalist conclusions rather than to Marx's conclusions. Repudiation of simultaneous valuation is almost sufficient, and in conjunction with the single-system interpretation, *is* sufficient, to refute the whole set of alleged proofs of inconsistency. Conversely, if simultaneism is not repudiated, Marx's value theory cannot really be vindicated.

The purpose of the present chapter is to show the incompatibility between Marx's theory, on the one hand, and simultaneism and physicalism on the other. (Claims that the textual evidence shows Marx himself to have been a simultaneist will be taken up in the next chapter.) "Physicalism" and "simultaneism" are defined in the next section, after which I show that the latter is incompatible with Marx's theory that value is determined by labor-time, since it necessarily leads to physicalist conclusions which contradict that theory. This conclusion then receives further support from a demonstration that the incompatibility between physicalism and the determination of value by labor-time cannot be overcome. Theorists who try to combine them necessarily end up in logical contradictions.

5.2 Definitions

I use the term *physicalism* as shorthand for Steedman's (1977: 72, 216–17) "physical quantities approach," a term he coined to designate his approach to questions of value, price, and profit. Steedman is a prominent Sraffian, but Sraffianism and physicalism are not synonymous. The latter term refers to *any* approach that draws conclusions about the workings of capitalist economies from models in which the sole proximate determinants of values, relative prices, profits, and the rate of profit are "physical quantities" or, more precisely, technology and real wages. Note that this definition refers to models and the conclusions deduced from them, not to the views of the theorists who employ such models. Also note the term "proximate determinants": proponents of physicalism recognize that technology and real wages are themselves determined by other factors, including factors emphasized by Marx. Their point is that one needs no information other than the physical data in order to determine values, relative prices, and the rate of profit.

Physicalist conclusions depend crucially upon a particular method of valuation, *simultaneous valuation* or *simultaneism*, and simultaneous valuation leads, necessarily and inevitably, to physicalist conclusions. Simultaneist theorists solve their mathematical models by imposing the constraint that per-unit prices (or values) of inputs into the production process must equal the per-unit prices (or values) of the outputs subsequently produced. Since input and output prices are constrained to be equal, they are solved for together (i.e., simultaneously). Note that this definition, like the one above, refers to theorists' models rather than their views.

Such models are also simultaneist in the sense that they determine prices and the rate of profit simultaneously, but this is simply a consequence of the simultaneous determination of input and output prices. Thus, although proponents of simultaneism (e.g. Sraffa 1960: 6) frequently claim that prices and the rate of profit must be determined simultaneously, they need not and cannot be so determined if input and output prices are permitted to differ.

The terms physicalism and simultaneism cast a wide net. In addition to Sraffians and pre-Sraffians such as Dmitriev and Bortkiewicz, encompassed within this net are works of Marxist critics of Sraffianism such as Medio (1972) and Shaikh, of neoclassicists such as Samuelson, and of theorists such as Okishio and Morishima whose debt is more to Leontief and von Neumann than to Sraffa. Also encompassed within this net are the NI and SSSIs, despite the fact that many of their proponents would wish to emphasize the role of monetary variables rather than physical quantities.

My classification may seem to be absurdly reductive. By focusing exclusively on a technical apparatus that these authors have in common—a mere "tool," in the jargon of economists—am I not sweeping aside the important respects in which their views differ? My answer is that their views are not all that important in the end, which is why my definitions of physicalism and simultaneism refer to theorists' models rather than their views. Economists' tools dominate over their views. Simultaneist models have their own logic, a logic that leads inexorably to physicalist conclusions.

Different economists may *wish* to say quite different things but, on pain of self-contradiction, they will end up saying essentially the same thing if their models are essentially the same. They will, of course, emphasize their differences from one another, but so do the makers of Bayer and Excedrin, even though all aspirin really *is* alike. In the appendix to chapter 9, I shall show that authors who claim to deduce Marx's anti-physicalist conclusions, despite their employment of the simultaneist method, are simply mistaken. They tell one story; their models tell another. And throughout this book, I shall show that theorists who have tried to use the simultaneist method to defend the consistency of Marx's value theory have at best vindicated it in a formal, not substantive, sense.

5.3 Simultaneous Valuation vs. the Law of Value

Almost without exception, the alleged internal inconsistencies and errors in the quantitative dimension of Marx's value theory are produced by simultaneous valuation.[1] Once Marx's theory is formulated in simultaneist terms, his LTFRP does not hold true. His claim that exploitation of workers is necessary in order for profit to exist is falsified (Dmitriev 1974: 62–64, 214), as is his claim that Ricardo was wrong to deny that production conditions in luxury industries have an influence upon the economy-wide rate of profit. The production of value becomes redundant—at best—to the determination of the rate of profit and prices of production. Values can be negative, and surplus-value can be negative although profit is positive. And once Marx is construed as a simultaneist and as a dual-system theorist, his account of the transformation of values into prices of production becomes internally inconsistent.

The immanent connection between simultaneism and the charges of inconsistency can be seen in another way, too. Non-simultaneous valuation combined with a single-system interpretation is sufficient to eliminate the appearance of inconsistency in every case.

How can a seemingly innocuous tool of analysis wreak such havoc? The answer is simple. *Simultaneous valuation is absolutely incompatible with the principle upon which Marx's value theory is founded, the principle that value is determined by labor-time.* To see this, consider a favorite expository device of simultaneist theorists, especially Sraffians—the "corn model." Corn (called "grain" in the U.S.) is produced using only corn of the same kind, planted as seed, plus the labor of farmworkers. Simultaneist theorists impose the constraint that a bushel of seed corn planted at the start of the year is worth exactly as much as a bushel of corn harvested at the end. If the value of a bushel of seed corn is $5, then the value of a bushel of corn output must also be $5, no matter how much or how little the farmworkers have had to labor in order to produce it. They may have had to toil a thousand hours, or only ten hours—or not at all! It makes no difference; the per-unit value of the corn output cannot rise above nor fall below the per-unit value of the seed corn. There is therefore no meaningful sense in which the corn's value depends upon the amount of labor needed to produce it.

Since the very concept of value is frequently dismissed as "metaphysical," opponents of metaphysics might benefit from a rephrasing of the point: simultaneous valuation in effect prevents changes in productivity from affecting the price, or value, of corn. Contrast this to the real world. When productivity rises —when the same amount of labor yields more output—commodities' prices tend to fall. This is essentially what Marx meant by saying that value is determined by labor-time. But we don't need a Marx to tell us this; every farmer knows that he can get a higher price for a bushel of his corn after a bad harvest than after a good one. Simultaneism, on the contrary, implies that a bushel of corn output cannot be worth more than a bushel of seed corn after a bad harvest, nor less than a bushel of seed corn after a good one.

Of course, no one actually believes that real-world prices or values remain constant over time. Nevertheless, when they "correct" Marx or try to prove him guilty of internal inconsistency, simultaneist theorists do stipulate that the prices of inputs cannot differ from the prices of the outputs that emerge later. If Marx's theoretical conclusions contradict the conclusions that they obtain by valuing everything simultaneously, they regard this as the fault of his theory rather than of their own interpretations, in violation of accepted interpretive practice.

Although I have explained why simultaneous valuation produces theoretical conclusions that contradict Marx's value theory, I have not yet explained why the conclusions it produces are necessarily physicalist. This, too, can be explained very simply. The aggregate value (or price) of a particular type of item is its per-unit value (or price) times the physical quantity of the item. There are thus two things that cause the aggregate value to change, changes in the physical quantity of the item *and* changes in its per-unit value. *But simultaneous valuation eliminates the change in the per-unit value that occurs during the production period. Hence, there is only one remaining cause of changes in the item's aggregate value—changes in its physical quantity.*

Assume, for example, that ten bushels of corn are invested (to plant as seed and pay farmworkers) at the start of the year, while twelve bushels are harvested at year's end. If the value (or price) of corn is $6/bushel at the start of the year but only $5/bushel at the end, then the capital value invested is $6 × 10 = $60 and the total value of output is $5 × 12 = $60. Although the physical quantity of corn increases by 20%, there is no increase in the corn's aggregate value, because the drop in its per-unit value has offset the physical increase. Yet proponents of simultaneism, valuing the corn invested and the corn harvested at the same price—for example, $5/bushel—declare that the capital value invested is only $5 × 10 = $50. They therefore find that aggregate value increases from $50 to $60. This is an increase of 20%, precisely the percentage by which physical output exceeds physical input. The economy has grown in value terms only because, and to the extent that, it has grown in physical terms.

5.4 Simultaneous Valuation and the Redundancy of Value

Beginning with Samuelson (1971: 417–18, 426–28), much has been made during the last few decades of the alleged redundancy of the concept of value. Even when rates of profit can be *expressed* in terms of values, Marx's critics maintain, they are actually *determined* by technology and real wages. The issue has usually been discussed in connection with the "transformation problem"—which pertains to deviations of prices from values across industries—but in fact the redundancy of value has nothing to do with such deviations. As was noted above, it is purely a consequence of simultaneous valuation. Simultaneist models make value redundant even when prices are equal to values.

For instance, it is easy to show redundancy in the corn-model case. Since there is only one industry in this case, value cannot be transferred across industries, so the price of corn equals its value. Now imagine again that the capitalist farmers invest ten bushels of corn at the start of the year, to use as seed and to pay wages, while twelve bushels are harvested at year's end. If we value the investment and the output simultaneously—that is, stipulate that they have the same value per bushel—then the twelve bushels of output must be worth exactly 20% more than the ten bushels initially invested. Profit must thus be equal to 20% of the sum of value invested. But profit as a percentage of investment is precisely what is meant by the rate of profit. So the rate of profit must equal 20%.

Note that value is redundant, first, because the rate of profit is exactly 20% whether the value (= price) of corn is high or whether it is low. (What a wonderful world! The farmers need not worry about the price of their corn falling, nor waste money on marketing and advertising in order to get a higher price.) Second, the rate of profit is identical to the rate of increase in corn, the 20% difference between the corn produced and the corn invested. This will always be the case. If the harvest had yielded eleven bushels, the rate of profit would have been 10%; had it yielded thirteen bushels, the rate of profit would have been 30%. So the rate of profit is determined exclusively by physical quantities—input, output, and the farmworkers' corn wages.

These conclusions depend crucially on simultaneous valuation. If the price of corn is not constant, but is determined by labor-time—if, in other words, its price falls as productivity rises, all else being equal—the results are quite different. Assume that the price of corn is $156/bushel at the start of the year, so that $1560 is invested. Also assume that the price of the corn output is $156 if eleven bushels are harvested, falling to $143 if output is twelve bushels or $132 if output is thirteen bushels. In all three cases, sales revenue is $1716, profit is $1716 − $1560 = $156, and the rate of profit is a constant 10%. The rate of profit no longer depends solely upon physical quantities. It also depends upon the decline in the price (= value) of corn that results from the increase in productivity.

Multisector simultaneist models yield the same, or essentially the same, results as the corn model. I noted above that simultaneist critics claim to have disproved Marx's contention that, contrary to what Ricardo argued, the level of the general (i.e. economy-wide) rate of profit is affected by production conditions in luxury industries. Their attempted refutations assume that the rate of profit is equalized. Imagine, then, that the economy consists of our corn industry plus an industry that uses corn and labor to produce corn liqueur, a luxury good, and that the rate of profit is equalized. Since the rate of profit is 20% in the corn industry, it must be 20% in the liqueur industry as well, no matter how much or how little surplus labor is pumped out of the distillery workers.

If values and prices are temporally determined, however, this proof does not go through. The price of each industry's output is cost price plus profit. The cost price is a datum, a known magnitude determined prior to production. What is the amount of profit? The equal-rate-of-profit assumption implies only that both industries obtain the *same* amount of profit per dollar of investment; it does not tell us what that amount *is*. One may therefore argue, as Marx did, that the total amount of profit (and thus profit per dollar invested) is determined by the total surplus-value produced in the economy *as a whole*. It follows that the level of the general rate of profit depends in part on the amount of surplus labor pumped out of the distillery workers.

Even when rates of profit are unequal, value is redundant at best under simultaneism, and for reasons that have nothing to do with price-value deviations. Consider a two-sector economy without fixed capital in which goods sell at their values. Sector 1 produces twelve units of good 1, a means of production, using seven units of good 1, and pays wages that allow its workers to purchase two units of good 2, a consumer good. Sector 2 produces ten units of good 2, using five units of good 1, and pays wages that allow its workers to purchase four units of good 2. When input values are constrained to equal output values, the general rate of profit turns out to be

$$\frac{(0.4)L_1 + (0.4)L_2}{3L_1 + (0.6)L_2}$$

where the L_1 and L_2 are the amounts of new value added by living labor in the two sectors.[2]

Thus if ten units of new value are added in each sector, the general rate of profit is 22.2%. (The rates are 33.3% and 11.1% in Sectors 1 and 2, respectively.) Now assume that productivity doubles in both sectors. This causes the new value added in each sector to fall to five. The general rate of profit remains unchanged (as does each sector's rate)! If, however, the productivity increase occurs in Sector 1 alone, the general rate *rises* to 28.6%. Both results contradict Marx's key claim that, all else being equal (as it has been here), the rate of profit should fall when less labor is pumped out of the workforce.

Neither result holds true when the values are determined temporally. The general rate of profit is the ratio of surplus-value (new value added minus variable capital) to total capital, and the capital advances are data, already determined prior to the production process. Thus the general rate of profit necessarily rises and falls together with the amount of new value added.

5.5 Simultaneous Valuation and Negative Values

The negative-value problem has typically been discussed in connection with multisector models of joint production (roughly, multiple outputs resulting from a single production process), but it arises even in the simplest cases. For instance, assume that corn, produced by means of seed corn and living labor, is the economy's only product. Also assume that, in the economy as a whole, the farmworkers plant ten bushels of seed corn at the start of the year, perform L person-years of labor during the year, but, owing to a drought, harvest only nine bushels of corn output at year's end. It is natural to suppose that the price of corn will rise, and indeed this is what Marx's value theory, as understood by the TSSI, suggests. The total value of the nine bushels of output is the sum of the value transferred from the ten bushels of seed corn that are used up *plus* the new value added by the farmworkers' labor. Thus the nine bushels of output are worth *more* than the ten bushels of seed corn, which implies that the per-bushel price of corn increases.

Yet simultaneist models prevent this increase from occuring, and by doing so they create the negative-value problem. If v is the simultaneously determined value of a bushel of corn and L is the value added by living labor, then

$$9v = 10v + L$$

and subtracting $10v$ from both sides, we obtain

$$-v = L.$$

Thus v must be negative if L is positive. Conversely, if v is positive then L is negative—the workers' labor subtracts value instead of adding it![3]

5.6 Accumulation for the Sake of Non-Accumulation

Some theorists have failed to recognize the fact that the determination of value by labor-time is incompatible with simultaneous valuation.[4] Others have failed even to recognize that the determination of value by labor-time is incompatible with physicalism. For instance, in his influential work on economic crisis published as a special issue of the *New Left Review*, Brenner (1998: 11–12) succeeds in demolishing the physicalist ("Malthusian") theory of the falling rate of profit. Yet he wrongly presents this as a critique of Marx's theory, even though he recognizes that Marx's theory refers to the fall in the *value* rate of profit. In other words, Brenner fails to recognize any difference between the value and physical rates. "Marx was, of course, fiercely anti-Malthusian. The Malthusian character of his theory of the fall of the rate of profit is therefore highly incongruous, though logically unavoidable, given that it has the decline in profitability result from a decline [sic] in productivity"—that is, a decline in *physical* output per unit of *physical* input (Brenner 1998: 11, n1).

Brenner's own account contains three crucial pieces of evidence that, taken together, allow us to conclude that his interpretation of Marx's theory is almost certainly incorrect. First, the theory's allegedly Malthusian character is "highly incongruous." Second, the theory is internally inconsistent under Brenner's interpretation. Finally, as Brenner himself acknowledges in the same footnote, Marx claimed that the decline in profitability results from a *rise* in productivity.[5] In other words, what Brenner calls "his theory of the fall of the rate of profit" is exactly the opposite of what Marx actually claimed! Unfortunately, Brenner did not construe any of this as evidence that his interpretation is a misinterpretation. He instead held Marx responsible for all of the inconsistencies and incongruities. Part of the problem seems to be that Brenner, a historian, relied on the authority of physicalist Marxist economists. They, too, typically identify their theory with Marx's theory and overlook the fact that physicalism is incompatible with the idea that value is determined by labor-time. But it is indeed a fact, as I shall now demonstrate.

Those who have tried to merge physicalism and the determination of value by labor-time, by means of simultaneous valuation, have often asserted three important propositions which, taken together, are incompatible. Within the space of a few pages, for instance, Laibman (1997) asserts all of them. The three propositions are:

1. Commodities' values fall as labor productivity rises (Laibman 1997: 28–29). This proposition follows from the determination of value by labor-time.
2. In a one-commodity world, the value rate of profit and the physical "rate of profit" (physical surplus divided by physical input) are identical (Laibman 1997: 23).
3. The rate of profit is capital's "potential rate of self-expansion" (Laibman 1997: 23).[6]

"Potential" in this context means maximum: when all profit is reinvested, the growth rate of capital, also known as the rate of accumulation, equals the profit rate. This follows from the fact that the growth rate of capital is the ratio of net investment to capital. *By definition*, this ratio is equal to the ratio of net investment to profit times the ratio of profit to capital,

$$\text{growth rate of capital} \equiv \frac{\text{net investment}}{\text{capital}} \equiv \left(\frac{\text{net investment}}{\text{profit}} \right)\left(\frac{\text{profit}}{\text{capital}} \right)$$

and the rate of profit is defined as the ratio of profit to capital (see Laibman 1997: 63–64). Thus the growth rate of capital equals the rate of profit when net investment equals profit.

Now assume that the conditions of the problem are satisfied. There exists a single commodity (serving as both a means of production and a consumer good), labor productivity rises, and all profit is reinvested. Thus capital is growing at its maximum potential rate. Let *ROP* stand for the rate of profit and *MGRC* stand for the maximum growth rate of capital. To distinguish between value (= price) variables and their physical counterparts, the subscript φ (the Greek letter *phi*) will be attached to the latter.

Since labor productivity is rising, Proposition 1 implies that the commodity's value is falling, which in turn implies that capital value grows more slowly than physical capital (see Laibman 1997: 28–29):

$$MGRC < MGRC\varphi \qquad\qquad (5.1)$$

Moreover, Proposition 2 implies that

$$ROP \equiv ROP\varphi \qquad\qquad (5.2)$$

while Proposition 3 implies that

$$MGRC \equiv ROP$$
$$\qquad\qquad (5.3)$$
$$MGRC\varphi \equiv ROP\varphi$$

Taken together, identities (5.2) and (5.3) imply that $MGRC \equiv MGRC\varphi$. But this contradicts (5.1). Hence the set of propositions is self-contradictory. The three propositions cannot all be true.

Any two of the propositions are compatible, but then the third must be jettisoned. As we just saw, if both (5.2) and (5.3) are true, then (5.1) is false. This means that, if the value rate of profit is physically determined, as in (5.2), then means of production do not become cheaper when productivity increases. Hence, value is not determined by labor-time. If both (5.1) and (5.3) are true, then $ROP < ROP\varphi$, so (5.2) is false. Thus, if value is determined by labor-time, as in (5.1), then the value and physical rates of profit necessarily differ. Rising productivity cheapens constant capital *and* it makes the value rate of profit fall below the physical rate. The first is impossible without the second.[7] Finally, if both (5.1) and (5.2) are true—that is, if value is determined by labor-time and the physical quantities approach holds true—then (5.3) is false. Yet (5.3) is true by definition. *It is therefore impossible consistently to embrace both the idea that value is determined by labor-time and the physical quantities approach.* All attempts to do so are self-contradictory.

Notice also that no sense can be made of the claim that the physical rate of profit governs the rate of accumulation in value terms. If value is determined by labor-time and productivity is rising, then the maximum growth rate of capital value must be lower than the physical rate of profit; taken together, relations (5.1) and (5.3) imply that $MGRC < ROP\varphi$. Since this result was derived without reference to (5.2), it holds true even if one chooses to define the value rate of profit in a way that makes it identical to the physical rate.

If one chooses to identify the value and physical rates of profit, then it is *also* the case that $MGRC < ROP$; the maximum growth rate of capital value must be lower than the value rate of profit (although this cannot be true, since it contradicts (5.3), which is necessarily true). The link between profitability and accumulation is thereby severed. The value rate of profit no longer governs the rate of accumulation of capital value in any fundamental sense, especially because the gap between these two rates can be quite large.

5.7 A Simple Example

The following corn-model example should help clarify the foregoing points. Assume that corn input (seed), corn output, workers' corn wages, and corn profit all increase by 20% per year. Also assume that the amount of labor performed by the farmworkers remains constant over time. It follows that labor productivity and the corn wage rate both increase by 20% each year. Given appropriate initial conditions, such as those of Table 5.1, the physical rate of accumulation is always the maximum rate—the output of one year is fully reinvested, as new seed corn and wages, in the next. Accordingly, the rate of accumulation equals the rate of profit, as must be the case.

Table 5.1. Physical System

Year	Total Capital (Seed + Wages)	Seed	Wages	Output	Profit*	Rate of Profit
1	125	75	50	150	25	20%
2	150	90	60	180	30	20%
3	180	108	72	216	36	20%

*Physical "Profit" is Output minus (Seed + Wages)

Given our assumption that the amount of labor performed by farmworkers remains constant, it follows that the same amount of new value is added each year if value is determined by labor-time. Assume that the amount of new value added is seventy-five. If we now equate input and output values, we find that the corn's per-unit value falls by 1/6th each year, from 1 to 5/6 to 25/36, etc.[8] Using these figures to value the seed, wages, and output, we obtain the physicalist "value" system of Table 5.2.

In accordance with Proposition 1, the corn's value falls as productivity rises, and, in accordance with Proposition 2, the value rate of profit equals the physical rate. Yet Proposition 3—which, I repeat, is true by definition—is violated. Although the value rate of profit is always 20% and the entire output is always reinvested, the total capital advanced fails to increase. In other words, the rate of accumulation of capital value is always zero!

Table 5.2. Physicalist "Value" System

Year	New Value Added	Per-unit Value	Total Capital $(c + v)$	c	v	s	Value of Output $(c+v+s)$	Rate of Profit $(s/[c+v])$
1	75	1	125	75	50	25	150	20%
2	75	5/6	125	75	50	25	150	20%
3	75	25/36	125	75	50	25	150	20%

Note: c, v, and s stand for constant capital, variable capital, and surplus-value.

To see what has gone wrong, notice that the value of output at the end of Year 1 is 150, and all output is reinvested as seed and wages, so it would seem that the total capital invested at the start of Year 2 should also be 150. It is only 125, however; 25 units of capital value have been conjured away. As we shall see in chapter 7, this "trick" is the secret behind the attempts to disprove Marx's LTFRP on logical grounds. Clearly the rate of profit cannot fall with the progress of capital accumulation when accumulation is artificially prevented from taking place!

Simultaneist authors typically defend the computations in Table 5.2 by arguing that the inputs have simply been valued at their *replacement cost*, the amount of value that would be needed to replace them at year's end. The capital value actually advanced at the start of Year 2 is indeed 150, they say—none of it has been conjured away—but the inputs' replacement cost is 125, and the rate of profit computed on the basis of such costs is 20%. The problem with this argument is that the "replacement-cost rate of profit" is not a rate of profit in any real sense. It is not what firms seek to maximize, and it fails to accurately measure either their actual rates of return or their potential rates of accumulation—in other words, their ability to grow (see sections 7.3.2 and 7.3.3 below).

Note that the replacement-cost defense maintains that the value rate of profit is a healthy 20%, even though the capitalist farmers actually invested a value of 150 at the start of Year 2 and the value of their output is 150 at the end. The farmers, on the other hand, are a wee bit disappointed. They think that they made no profit at all. Some readers may wish to explain to the farmers that they have been taken in by a metaphysical value theory: "You have actually done quite well. You've ended up with 20% more corn than you invested initially, and your potential rate of accumulation is therefore 20% as well—you can expand your operations by up to 20%."

Such readers are advised to think twice. If the farmers borrowed the 150 start-up capital from their bankers, then they end up with nothing, indeed less than nothing. They must sell off their entire corn output, and use their sales revenue of 150 to repay the principal on the bank loans. They have nothing left over to expand their operations. *Even in physical terms,* they are unable to accumulate. Moreover, they have not yet paid, and cannot pay, the interest that they owe the bankers.[9] The same situation occurs year after year, and soon the farmers are drowning in debt.

The example makes clear that, if physical quantities and value increase at different rates, as they do if value is determined by labor-time, then physicalism is incompatible with the (necessarily true) proposition that the value rate of profit is the potential growth rate of capital value. Simultaneous valuation seems to eliminate this problem because it seems to eliminate the difference between the growth rates of physical quantities and value—corn and value increase by the same percentage *within* each period, and thus the value rate of profit equals the physical rate. But then, as we have seen, the actual difference between the growth rates of corn and value re-emerges *between* periods. Value mysteriously disappears, or appears from out of nowhere.

Analysis of economic dynamics is therefore simply not possible when value is held to be determined by labor-time but simultaneously as well. As Mirowski (1989: 184), the influential institutionalist historian of economic thought, has noted, "the real-cost [i.e. simultaneist] method, devoid of explicit invariants, can only calculate a sequence of static equilibria in which the labor-value unit is not comparable from one calculation to the next." (Table 5.2 exhibits such a sequence.) Duménil and Lévy (2000: 142), authors widely recognized for their contributions to dynamic analysis, similarly acknowledge that their simultaneist interpretation of the "labor theory of value does not provide the framework to account for disequilibrium and dynamics in capitalism." It is therefore unable to serve as the foundation of a "theory of crisis or of historical tendencies" (Duménil and Lévy 2000: 142).

Notes

1. The sole exception is Böhm-Bawerk's charge, which will be discussed in chapter 8, that the value theories of volumes I and III of *Capital* contradict one another. This charge has had almost no influence on the value theory controversy for more than thirty years.

2. The equations determining simultaneist per-unit values, v_1 and v_2, are $12v_1 = 7v_1 + L_1$ and $10v_2 = 5v_1 + L_2$. (The left-hand sides are the total value produced in each sector, and each right-hand side is the sum of value transferred from means of production plus new value added.) Solving, we find that $v_1 = (0.2)L_1$ and $v_2 = (0.1)(L_1 + L_2)$. The expression for the general rate given in the text is obtained by substituting these solutions into the formula for the general rate of profit, $\dfrac{12v_1 + 10v_2 - (7+5)v_1 - (2+4)v_2}{(7+5)v_1 + (2+4)v_2}$.

3. Actually, both results are "true." Measured in terms of labor-time, value added is the living labor, which is positive, so the corn's value is negative. Measured in money terms, the price (= value) of corn is positive, so value added is negative.

4. A few theorists continue to deny that they are incompatible. See the discussion of Loranger's (2004) and Moseley's (1993a, 2000a, 2000b) solutions to the "transformation problem" in the appendix to chapter 9, below.

5. Brenner tries to explain away this fact by claiming that Marx's theory implies that, although the productivity of (living) labor rises, the productivity of other inputs falls enough to cause "overall" productivity to fall. Yet Brenner offers no textual support for this claim and, to my knowledge, none exists. Instead, he deduces it (improperly) from the Okishio theorem. Given a constant rate of exploitation, *Okishio's physicalist* rate of profit cannot fall unless the productivity of non-labor inputs falls, but this is irrelevant to Brenner's claim, which has to do with *Marx's* rate of profit.

6. Laibman (1997: 23) writes that "[t]he rate of profit, then, is the central measure of the effectiveness of capitalist production from the point of view of capital: its potential rate of self-expansion." "The" rate of profit refers both to the value rate and the physical rate, since he asserts that the two are the same. Hence, "potential rate of self-expansion" clearly refers to the self-expansion of both capital value and the physical capital stock.

7. This conclusion does not contradict the notion that the cheapening of means of production tends to counteract the fall in the rate of profit. Current productivity growth tends to lower the *current* rate of profit, while the cheapening of means of production tends to enhance *future* profitability. Continued productivity growth, however, will counteract this latter tendency.

8. If v_t is the simultaneist per-unit value in year t, we have $(v_t \times \text{Output}_t) = (v_t \times \text{Seed}_t) + 75$, from which it follows that $v_t = \dfrac{75}{\text{Output}_t - \text{Seed}_t}$.

9. Nothing is really different if the farmers are able to finance their own operations. Their books may not show that they owe interest to themselves, but if they continually extend zero-interest loans to themselves, they continually forego the interest that they could acquire by investing their money capital externally.

Chapter 6

Was Marx a Simultaneist?

6.1 Introduction

Chapter 5 showed that simultaneous valuation necessarily leads to physicalist results and that simultaneism is therefore incompatible with Marx's own theoretical results, derived from his theory that value is determined by labor-time. Thus Marx could not have been a *consistent* simultaneist. If his value theory is consistent, then its theoretical premises cannot be simultaneist. If, conversely, Marx did employ simultaneist premises, then his theory must be inconsistent. But this latter possibility is, in effect, what his critics have charged all along. Thus the demonstration in chapter 5 is insufficient—by itself—to refute the charges of inconsistency. It is also necessary to refute the claims that Marx employed simultaneist premises. That is the task of this chapter.

In the next section, I discuss what needs to be, and does *not* need to be, shown in order to refute the charges of inconsistency. The third section then examines the claim made by some simultaneist interpreters, especially Sraffians, that Marx's concept of prices of production presupposes that a static equilibrium rate of profit prevails. If this were true, then his theory would indeed be simultaneist, since input and output prices must be equal in a static equilibrium. In the fourth section I consider the claim that, in Marx's theory, the sum of value transferred from used-up inputs to outputs is the post-production replacement cost of the inputs. If this were true, it too would make Marx a simultaneist, since he would have valued both inputs and outputs at the prices or values that prevail when the output emerges. Finally, I conclude with a brief discussion of the textual evidence that pertains to whether Marx was a single- or dual-system theorist.

6.2 What Remains to be Shown?

Before turning to the texts, it is important to be clear about what remains to be shown and what does not. I shall not be able to prove conclusively that this or that passage is absolutely incompatible with simultaneism. All texts of all sorts permit multiple interpretations—which does not imply that all interpretations are equally acceptable. Nor shall I be able to show that simultaneist interpretations perform more poorly than the temporal single-system interpretation (TSSI) on a case-by-case basis, taking each contested passage in isolation. When construed in this fashion, I find many passages to be simply ambiguous. (Some passages even seem to support the dual-system interpretation—when taken out of context. One only needs to read "the quantity of labor needed to produce" and similar phrases technocratically, as a modern input-output analyst would read them, disregarding whether this makes coherent sense of *Capital* as a whole.) And although I am convinced that simultaneist interpretations perform more poorly when one considers the contested passages as a whole and in relation to the rest of *Capital*, I am sure that I shall not be able to demonstrate even this much to the satisfaction of simultaneist interpreters.

To refute the charges of inconsistency leveled against Marx's value theory, however, it is unnecessary to show any of this. That simultaneism and Marx's value theory are inherently incompatible has already been demonstrated. Moreover, several specific examples of incompatibility have been exhibited, and more will follow in subsequent chapters. In light of this body of evidence, it is quite implausible that Marx himself was a simultaneist. Since his actual theoretical conclusions so often contradict the physicalist conclusions to which simultaneous valuation leads, it is highly unlikely that he employed simultaneist premises but somehow reached non-simultaneist conclusions.

In the first place, it is improbable that his deductive powers were so limited that he repeatedly—in case after case, and year after year—drew invalid conclusions from simultaneist premises. Even a theorist of average caliber would be unlikely to blunder so consistently, and Marx was arguably somewhat above average.

To accept the claim that he was a simultaneist, moreover, we would also have to believe something even more implausible: Marx again and again deduced conclusions that were not only invalid, but *diametrically opposed* to those that actually follow from his simultaneist premises. We would have to believe, for instance, that he maintained that

- the rate of profit falls under circumstances in which his own, simultaneist premises imply that it must rise;
- surplus labor is the exclusive source of profit, although his simultaneist premises imply that it is not;

- value is determined by labor-time, although his simultaneist premises imply that labor-time is redundant;

and so on. That Marx drew valid (though not necessarily true) conclusions from non-simultaneist premises is simply far more plausible.

As chapter 4 emphasized, such considerations are what underlie the hermeneutic principles that tell us to reject interpretations, such as the simultaneist interpretations of Marx, under which the text becomes internally inconsistent. They are too implausible to be accepted. Of course, if alternative interpretations have continually failed to eliminate the inconsistencies, then it becomes considerably more likely that these inconsistencies are genuine. But if an interpretation that removes the appearance of inconsistency is available, interpretations that find the text inconsistent should be rejected as implausible.

Such interpretations should be rejected even if they at first seem (to some readers) to result in more natural readings of this or that contested passage, taken in isolation. If the alternative interpretations were truly arbitrary and forced, they could explain away one or another *individual* case of inconsistency. Yet because it is so difficult to make the various parts of a text fit together into a coherent *whole*, it is highly implausible that an interpretation that establishes textual coherence is a congeries of ad hoc apologetics on the author's behalf.

I am reiterating key arguments of chapter 4 here in order to emphasize that our examination of contested passages does not proceed *ab initio*. The only point still at issue is whether a non-simultaneist interpretation of the contested passages is indeed available. That it is *possible* to construe many of these passages in a simultaneist manner is undeniable—if only because simultaneist interpretations do happen to exist—but such construals should be rejected as long as an alternative is available. Thus, to refute the charges of inconsistency leveled against Marx's theory, only one thing remains to be shown: the contested passages *need not be* construed in a simultaneist (or dual-system) manner. I hope to show, to the satisfaction of disinterested readers, something more than this—namely that a temporal single-system interpretation of these passages is at least equally plausible—but no more is actually required.[1]

6.3 The Static Equilibrium vs. the Average Rate of Profit

As we saw in chapter 2, Marx held that actual market prices in a competitive environment tend to fluctuate around prices of production, and that actual rates of profit tend to fluctuate around the general rate of profit. Thus prices of production are *average* prices and the general rate of profit is the *average* rate.

There is no disagreement about this. However, many simultaneist authors, especially Sraffians, argue in addition that Marx's prices of production and general rate of profit are **static equilibrium** magnitudes—the prices and rate of profit that would prevail in a situation in which there is no tendency for anything in the economy to change. But if prices are not changing, then input and output prices are equal. Thus, on this interpretation, Marx's prices of production are simultaneously determined.

For instance, Mongiovi (2002: 399, 400, emphasis in original), a Sraffian, holds that the static equilibrium or "long-period *method* . . . was utilized by the classical economists and, *pace* the Temporal Single System view, by Marx"; his prices of production and general rate of profit are "static positions of central gravitation." Moseley (1999, section 3.2), a proponent of one of the simultaneous single-system interpretations, argues similarly that "Marx's prices of production are long-run center-of-gravity prices," and that the existence of such prices "require[s] that the prices of inputs are equal to the prices of outputs."[2]

Now, there is no evidence that Marx said anything like this. In the two passages that Mongiovi (2002: 401) quotes in support of his position, Marx (1991a: 478, 489) simply says that prices of production are the average prices around which market prices fluctuate. Moseley reviews a great deal more textual evidence, but the passages he quotes all say the same thing as well. Nowhere does Marx say or imply that prices of production are static equilibrium or simultaneously determined magnitudes.

So what is going on? The answer is that Mongiovi, Moseley, and other simultaneists are *equating* "average" and "static equilibrium." This is why they characterize Marx's references to the former as references to the latter. But if the two concepts are different—and I intend to show that they are very different— then their argument collapses. The fact that Marx understood prices of production and the general rate of profit as the average magnitudes around which actual magnitudes fluctuate does not make him an implicit simultaneist.

What I am about to show is by no means a new insight. More than sixty years ago, Joan Robinson (1967: 11–12, emphasis added) pointed out that in Marx's value theory, as developed in volume III of *Capital*, "There is no tendency to long-run equilibrium and *the average rate of profit is not an equilibrium rate*, or a supply price of capital. It is simply an average share in the total surplus which at any moment the capitalist system has succeeded in generating."

In 1984, near the start of the new controversy over Marx's value theory, Alan Freeman (1984: 232, emphasis added) returned to this point, and also explained the difference between "average" and "[static] equilibrium" quite clearly:

> [Marx's] concept of long-term average is precisely what it says: the average of a varying quantity. In no sense is this identical or even comparable to the notion of an equilibrium price. This is scientifically correct, because *in all but the simplest of oscillating systems the two magnitudes are numerically different*. In mechanics they are different, for example, in any system in which energy of oscillation is transformed into energy of motion, that is, in which net mechanical work is performed. Thus the average behaviour of a surfboard being pro-

pelled by a wave is quite different from the behaviour of the same board in a calm sea.

The reason why simultaneist authors still continue to characterize Marx's references to average magnitudes as references to static equilibrium ones is not, at least not entirely, that they have failed to take note of the difference. Mongiovi, for instance, is aware of the difference. Sandwiched in between his reference to "static positions of central gravitation" and his quotes from Marx is a sentence that lets the cat out of the bag. "*If* a theory is sound, the deviations between actual and theoretical magnitudes will tend to counterbalance one another over time, so that the averages of the observed magnitudes will be close to those established by the theory" (Mongiovi 2002: 401, emphasis added).[3] Yes, but if the theory has a static equilibrium character while reality does not, then the actual average magnitudes and the "established" static equilibrium magnitudes will simply be different.

To get a clearer sense of the difference, and how great the difference can be, consider the following equation, an example of what mathematicians call a "chaotic system":

$$r_{t+1} = r_t(1 - a[r_t - r^*]) \qquad (6.1)$$

r_t and r_{t+1} are the general rates of profit at times t and $t + 1$, r^* is some "benchmark" rate of profit and a, a positive constant, is a reaction coefficient. It measures the intensity of capitalists' reactions to deviations of the actual rate of profit from the benchmark rate.

Now if $r_t < r^*$, then $r_{t+1} > r_t$. In other words, if the actual rate of profit at time t is less than r^*, then capitalists react to this situation in such a way as to make the rate of profit rise. Conversely, if $r_t > r^*$, then $r_{t+1} < r_t$; capitalists react to the fact that the actual rate of profit is greater than the benchmark rate in such a way as to make the rate of profit fall. Finally, note that if $r_t = r^*$, then $r_{t+1} = r^*(1 - a[r^* - r^*]) = r^*$ as well. It follows that r_{t+2}, r_{t+3}, etc. will also equal r^*.[4] Thus r^* is the *static equilibrium* rate of profit. (More precisely, it is one of two static equilibrium rates; the other is $r = 0$.)

The *average* rate of profit, however, may be quite different. If a is greater than $2/r^*$ but less than or equal to $3/r^*$, the average rate is always less than r^*. When $a = 3/r^*$, the average rate of profit is one-third smaller than the static equilibrium rate. If, for example, the static equilibrium rate of profit is $r^* = 0.15$ (i.e. 15%) and $a = 3/0.15 = 20$, the average rate of profit is only 0.10 (i.e. 10%).[5] Moreover, the actual rate is generally not even close to the static equilibrium rate; r is either more than 18%, or less than 12%, more than three-fourths of the time.

It should also be noted that, despite Moseley's and Mongiovi's references to the "long run" and "long period," there is a great difference between the actual

long-run rate of profit—if one happens to exist—and its static equilibrium counterpart. Imagine that output prices have a systematic tendency to be lower than
(or higher than) input prices, and that rates of profit fluctuate around or converge
upon some fixed equilibrium value in the long run. *This* long-run equilibrium
rate of profit will be systematically lower than (or higher than) the *static* equilibrium long-run rate of profit to which Moseley and Mongiovi refer—the rate of
profit that would prevail if input and output prices were equal.

Figure 6.1 illustrates this point.[6] If input and output prices were equal, the
rates of profit of both sectors would continually be 25%. (If input and output
prices differed, but there were no trend to prices, then the rates of profit would
fluctuate around the 25% level.) However, the prices of both sectors' products
tend to fall, on average, by about 2% per year in the long run, and this causes
their rates of profit to fluctuate around a long-run equilibrium value of 22.5%, a
figure 10% below the static equilibrium rate. As we shall see in the next chapter,
this distinction between the actual long-run rate of profit and the static equilibrium rate of profit is of considerable significance in the controversy over the
internal consistency of Marx's law of the tendential fall in the rate of profit.

Figure 6.1. Static Equilibrium and Average Rates of Profit

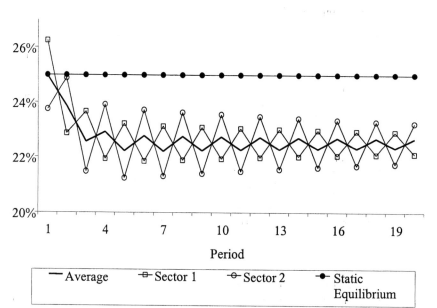

6.4 The Replacement-Cost Interpretation

6.4.1 Conceptual Distinctions

The interpretation of Marx as a static equilibrium theorist discussed above is compatible with the idea that his theory permits input and output prices to differ when rates of profit are unequal. In contrast, another simultaneist interpretation maintains that, even though input and output prices differ in the real world, the input and output prices relevant to Marx's theory are necessarily equal (see, e.g., Wolff *et al.* 1984: 129–31; Moseley 1993a: 168). Given that Bortkiewicz recognized that his seminal revision of Marx's value theory along simultaneist lines departed sharply from the original theory's "successivist" understanding of determination (see section 3.5, above), this interpretation is quite surprising.

The textual support most commonly offered on behalf of this interpretation consists of passages in which Marx is said to have stipulated or implied that the sum of value that used-up inputs transfer to products is the post-production *replacement cost* of the inputs. If, for instance, an apple costs $0.50 at 1 p.m. today, when it is used to make applesauce, but newly harvested apples cost $0.45 each at 2 p.m., when the applesauce is completed, then $0.45 is the post-production replacement cost of the $0.50 apple (see Table 6.1). Proponents of the replacement-cost interpretation hold, therefore, that this apple transfers a

Table 6.1. Changes in the Cost of an Input

Time	Yesterday, 2 p.m.	Today, 9 a.m.	Today, 1 p.m.	Today, 2 p.m.
Event	The apple is produced	The apple is sold	The apple becomes an input into applesauce	The applesauce is produced
Cost of Newly-Produced Apple	$0.60	$0.55	$0.50	$0.45
Cost Concept	Historical Cost		Pre-Production Reproduction Cost	(Post-Production) Replacement Cost

value of $0.45, not $0.50, to the applesauce. It follows that the input and output prices (or input and output values) relevant to Marx's theory of value determination must be equal: $0.45 is both the sum of value transferred to the applesauce from the input apple that entered into the production process at 1 p.m. and the price (or value) of a new output apple harvested at 2 p.m.

Since Marx often stressed that a commodity's value depends on the amount of labor currently needed to reproduce it, not the amount of labor actually used to produce it, the replacement-cost interpretation initially appears plausible, if not compelling. Once some important distinctions are brought to light, however, I find most of the evidence that supposedly supports this interpretation to be irrelevant, and the rest to disconfirm it.

Let us first distinguish between *historical cost* and pre-production *reproduction cost*. In the example above, the input apple's pre-production reproduction cost is $0.50, the cost (inclusive of profit) of producing an apple at the moment when this apple became an input into the production of applesauce. Imagine, however, that originally—when it was produced—this input apple cost $0.60. Then $0.60 is its historical cost.

Most of the textual evidence cited on behalf of the replacement-cost interpretation consists of passages in which Marx repudiates historical-cost valuation. Holding that commodities' values are determined by the amount of labor *currently* needed to reproduce them, he seems consistently to have denied the relevance of historical cost to value determination. Passages in his texts that make this point have long been construed as evidence in favor of the replacement-cost interpretation, but they count in its favor only if one overlooks the existence of a third alternative—the TSSI's pre-production reproduction-cost interpretation.[7] This interpretation is likewise compatible with the passages in question.

We also need to distinguish between the revaluation of *previously* produced commodities and the revaluation of *newly* produced commodities. The continual revaluation of previously produced commodities is an undeniable and essential feature of Marx's value theory. It follows immediately from the notion that a commodity's value is determined by the amount of labor currently needed to reproduce it (i.e., by the average amount of labor needed to produce new commodities of the same kind). Thus if the value of a newly produced apple is $0.60 when our input apple is produced, $0.55 when the input apple is sold, and $0.50 when it finally enters into the production of applesauce, then our input apple's value is also is $0.60, $0.55, and $0.50 at these three moments. Moreover, any apples that were harvested at the same time as this input apple, but that still remain in existence after it is turned into applesauce, will continue to be revalued thereafter. If, for example, the value of a newly produced apple is $0.45 when the applesauce is completed, the value of these previously produced apples is $0.45 as well.

As we shall see, Marx also held that the sum of value transferred from inputs to outputs that were *produced in the past* can change retroactively. Imagine that the price of apples falls, causing the value of applesauce to fall from $3/jar to $2.85/jar. Since the value of a previously produced commodity is determined by the value of new commodities of that kind, a jar of applesauce that was worth $3 when it was produced is now worth only $2.85. It follows that the apples used to produce this applesauce have transferred $0.15 less value to it than they transferred originally.

None of this is in dispute, but none of it favors the replacement-cost interpretation either. The controversy between the temporalist and replacement-cost interpretations concerns the valuation of *newly produced* commodities only, an issue that none of the preceding points addresses. The preceding points all reduce to the proposition that the values of previously produced commodities, and the sum of value transferred to them, are determined by the values of newly produced commodities. None of them pertain to how the value of these newly produced commodities is *itself* determined. Does the sum of value transferred from an input to a newly produced commodity depend upon the input's price when it enters production, as the TSSI holds, or upon the cost of replacing the input when the new commodity is completed, as the replacement-cost interpretation holds? Passages that refer to the revaluation of previously produced commodities shed no light on the answer.

The controversial issue is extremely narrow, and for that reason it may appear trivial. After all, even if the value transferred from an input apple to applesauce is $0.50 at 1 p.m., not its replacement cost of $0.45, $0.45 will be the sum of value transferred from apples that enter production at 2 p.m. How can minor delays in revaluation possibly matter? The answer is that minor delays matter because they can have persistent and mounting effects. If your bathtub faucet leaks, the eventual difference between fast- and slow-draining water is the difference between an empty tub and a flooded bathroom. And as the whole of this book shows, the difference between simultaneous and delayed revaluation is the difference between internal inconsistency and physicalist conclusions on the one hand, and internal consistency and Marx's own conclusions on the other.

6.4.2 Evidence of Simultaneous Valuation in Marx's Work?

In contrast to the substantial body of evidence that Marx rejected historical-cost valuation, there is little that can be construed as directly supporting the replacement-cost interpretation. A few passages have, however, been read as offering such direct support. The three strongest candidates are discussed below.

The first two passages, from volumes I and III of *Capital*, read as follows:

> Suppose that the price of cotton is one day sixpence a pound, and the next day, as a result of the failure of the cotton crop, a shilling a pound. Each pound of

the cotton bought at sixpence, and worked up after the rise in value, transfers to the product a value of one shilling, and the cotton already spun before the rise, and perhaps circulating in the market as yarn, similarly transfers to the product twice its original value. [Marx 1990a: 317–18]

If the price of a raw material rises—cotton for example— . . . cotton that has not yet been worked up, but is still in the warehouse, rises just as much in value as cotton that is still in the course of manufacture. As the retrospective expression of more labour-time, this cotton adds a higher value to the product which it goes into as a component than it possessed originally and the capitalist paid for it. [Marx 1991a: 207]

These passages clearly repudiate historical-cost valuation, but that is not in dispute. As discussed above, both the simultaneist interpretations *and* the TSSI deny that already existing stocks of commodities retain their original values after the change in the price of cotton. They both hold that the change in the cotton's price causes a revaluation of the already existing stocks (the "cotton spun [into yarn] before the rise" in the price of cotton, and the cotton that is "still in the warehouse" prior to being employed in production as a raw material). The previously spun yarn and the warehoused cotton now have the same values as the most recently produced yarn and cotton, respectively.

The TSSI may at first seem incompatible with the end of the first passage, since Marx states that the value transferred from the cotton to the yarn rises retroactively, after the cotton entered production. Yet since the yarn was *previously* produced, "spun before the rise" in value, while the sole controversial question is how the value of *newly* produced commodities is determined, there is actually no incompatibility.

If anything, these two passages seem to support the TSSI rather than the replacement-cost interpretation. They seem to suggest that more value is transferred from cotton to yarn *because* the cotton is worth more when it enters production; it is "worked up after the rise in value." In order to specify the amount of value the cotton transfers, Marx tells us its price when it is worked up. The information that the replacement-cost interpretation deems necessary—the cotton's price when the yarn is completed—is never mentioned.

The final candidate-passage, from the preparatory Economic Manuscript of 1861–1863, must unfortunately be quoted at some length, since so much of it seems controversial.

[1] But the values of the material and means of labour only re-appear in the product of the labour process to the extent that they were preposited as values, i.e. were values before they entered into the process. . . . [2] If later on more or less labour time were to be required to manufacture these particular use values, . . . their value would have risen in the first case and fallen in the second . . . . [3] Hence although they entered the labour process with a definite value, they may come out of it with a value that is larger or smaller . . . . [4] But this

change in the value of the material and means of labour involves absolutely no alteration in the circumstance that in the labour process into which they enter as material and means they are always preposited as given values, values of a given magnitude. [5] For in this process itself they only emerge as values in so far as they entered as values. . . . [6] If their general conditions of production have changed, this reacts back upon them. [7] They are an objectification of more or less labour time, of more or less value than they were originally; but only because a greater or smaller amount of labour time is now required than originally for their production. . . . [8] If [their] value changes before the new product of which they are the elements is finished they nevertheless relate to it as independent, given values preposited to it. [9] Their change of value stems from alterations in their own conditions of production, which occur outside and independently of the labour process into which they enter . . . . [10] For it they are always values of a given, preposited magnitude, even though . . . they are now preposited as of greater or smaller magnitude than was originally the case. [Marx 1988: 79–80; numbering added]

Emphasizing sentences 2, 3, 6, 7, and 10, Moseley (2000a) contends that this passage explicitly upholds replacement-cost valuation. Marx supposedly wants to affirm, on the one hand, that when inputs' values change during the course of production, so does the amount of value they transfer, and, on the other hand, that the value transferred nonetheless remains "given" or "preposited." This reading of "preposited" is in conflict with the definition given in sentence 1, which says that value is preposited if the pre-production value "re-appear[s]" in the product. Sentence 5 also states that the sum of value that goes into the production process is the sum that comes out. So do 4 and 8, once we decline to follow Moseley in stripping "preposited" and "given" of all quantitative significance.

Moreover, the TSSI is compatible with the sentences that Moseley emphasizes if we read the passage (as I do) as distinguishing between the inputs' own values and the amount of value they transfer. The value of a particular kind of input can change during the course of production; what does not change, however, is the amount of value transferred from a unit of that input which was used up in the production process prior to the change in value (see especially sentences 4–5 and 8). If "originally" in sentence 10 is construed as a reference to the start of production, the sentence suggests that the preposited value changes, as Moseley holds, but then we have to ignore sentence 1's definition of "preposited." Sentences 1 and 10 are no longer in conflict if, instead, "originally" is understood to refer to the inputs' own, original cost. On this reading, sentence 10 contradicts the historical-cost interpretation but not the TSSI.

In sum, the replacement-cost interpretation might make sense of this passage—*if* we employ idiosyncratic definitions of "given" and "preposited" in order to subdue sentences 4 and 8, and *if* we pretend that 1 and 5 do not exist. On a contrary construal that I find wholly plausible, the TSSI is compatible with all elements of the passage.

6.4.3 Disconfirming Evidence

We have seen that the case for the replacement-cost interpretation is quite shaky at best, even when we limit our evaluation to the passages that supposedly confirm it. It becomes far shakier when we consider these passages in a broader context.

At least from the 1857–1858 *Grundrisse* onward, Marx held that the production process results in "the preservation of the amount of labour already objectified" in used-up means of production (Marx 1973: 363), and "thus preserves the previously existing value of the capital" (Marx 1973: 365). The previously existing values of means of production "reappear" in the product (Marx 1973: 356). Subsequent works, including the chapter on "Constant Capital and Variable Capital" in *Capital* I that develops this notion systematically, also refer quite frequently to the preservation and reappearance (and synonymously, the transfer) of the existing value. Such terminology is explicitly temporal. It suggests that a sum of value, already in existence before production, emerges from production unchanged. I do not see how this can be reconciled with the replacement-cost interpretation.

Many passages in the Economic Manuscript of 1861–1863, almost all of them from the earlier notebooks (I through VII), state explicitly that the amount of value transferred depends upon inputs' pre-production value. "The value of the material and means of labour only re-appears in the product because the material and means of labour possess this value *before* the labour process and independently of it" (Marx 1988: 92, emphasis in original). Raw materials and means of labor "add to the labour time contained in the product only as much labour time as they themselves contained *before* the production process" (Marx 1988: 177, emphasis in original). The using-up of an input in production "increases the product's, the commodity's, value to the amount of its own value"; Marx further specifies that this means, "to be precise, the value it has when it enters the process of production" (Marx 1988: 322–23). A means of production "does not add more value to the product than it possessed before production. . . . As value, this part of capital therefore enters unchanged into the production process and emerges from it unchanged" (Marx 1989b: 362).

Finally, there is yet another passage in the 1861–1863 Manuscript that discusses how the value transferred from means of production is determined when an input's value changes:

> This *change in value*, however, never alters the fact that in the process of production, into which it enters as a condition of production, it is a postulated value which must reappear in the value of the product. Therefore this change of value of the constant capital can here be ignored. In all circumstances it is a definite quantity of *past, objectified* labour, which passes into the value of the product as a determining factor. [Marx 1988: 413, emphases in original]

This passage is quite similar to the one quoted at length earlier. It, too, suggests that the amount of value that goes into production is the amount that comes out. One might choose to read "postulated value which must reappear" in a way that deprives it of quantitative import, but the final sentence does not yield to this strategy. Marx regards the constant-capital value "as a determining factor" of the product's value, which is simply incompatible with simultaneism. Under the replacement-cost interpretation, the constant-capital value becomes a determined factor, not a determining one. The sum of value transferred is determined simultaneously with the product's value, and "physical quantities" do all of the determining, as the corn-model case makes especially clear.

Marx's subsequent economic writings contain fewer, and typically briefer, discussions of how the sum of value transferred is determined. The reason is perhaps that he had already worked matters out to his own satisfaction, so that he was able to state his results compactly and without duplication of effort. The evidence in these later texts suggests that his position remained unchanged.

The chapter in *Capital* I on "Constant Capital and Variable Capital" reiterates at length the temporal notion that constant-capital value is preserved in production and reappears in the product. As we saw above, the statement at the end of the chapter that might seem to suggest that Marx was a simultaneist does not in fact do so. Moreover, a couple of passages in this chapter also contain more explicit evidence that the inputs transfer their pre-production value to the product. The first states that "means of production never transfer more value to the product than they themselves lose during the labour process by the destruction of their own use-value" (Marx 1990a: 312). In the other, Marx (1990a: 313–14) writes, "The maximum loss of value the means of production can suffer in the process is plainly limited by the amount of the original value with which they entered into it . . . . [A means of production cannot] transfer any value to the product unless it possessed value before its entry into the process."

These passages contradict the replacement-cost interpretation. Imagine, for instance, that a good was worthless when some of it entered production as an input, but it has a positive value when the output emerges. The passages imply that no value is transferred in this case, but according to the replacement-cost interpretation, a positive sum of value is transferred.

At least one passage in volume II reiterates the idea that the value "the means of production already possessed . . . before the production process" is the sum of value they transfer (Marx 1992: 463). And one in volume III, resolving the commodity's value into constant capital, variable capital, and surplus-value, defines the constant capital portion of its value as "the value or price at which these means of production went into the commodity's production process" (Marx 1991a: 992).

6.4.4 Marx's Examples of Value Determination

The 1861–1863 Manuscript also contains a few passages in which Marx provides numerical examples of the valuation process, under conditions in which values are changing. These passages disconfirm the replacement-cost interpretation in an especially striking way. Purely verbal texts always permit multiple interpretations, and an imaginative interpreter can always explain away an embarrassing set of words, but little wiggle room remains when an interpretation must replicate the author's numerical results in order to be deemed correct.

The passages appear in some of the later notebooks of the Manuscript. In one, Marx discusses Ramsay's early formulation of a replacement-cost conception of the profit rate. Ramsay maintained that if productivity rises, so that a smaller share of total output is needed to replace inputs, the profit rate must rise. Marx challenged this conclusion by constructing a few numerical examples. The most relevant one is summarized in Table 6.2. All figures in boldface are Marx's; the others are inferred from the context.

Marx considers a capitalist farmer who produces corn by means of seed corn and other inputs. All costs are measured in terms of both money and corn. Marx assumes that "work was carried on in the same conditions" in both years, using "the same amount of labour," but that the output of Year 2 is double that of Year 1. The total value of this output, however, does not increase. "Since the 200 qrs [produced in Year 2] are the product of the same amount of labour [as in Year 1], then once again they are likewise = only £200. Thus, only £80 profit remains, which is now, however, = 140 qrs" (Marx 1991b: 267).[8] Marx thus

Table 6.2. Marx After Ramsay

Year	Input Price	Capital Advanced				Output	Profit	Output Price	Rate of Profit (%)
		Total	Constant		Variable				
			Seed Corn	Other					
1	£2 qr	**£120**	£40	£40	£40	**£200**	**£80**	**£2** qr	66.7
		60 qrs	20 qrs	20 qrs	20 qrs	100 qrs	40 qrs		66.7
2	**£2** qr	**£120**	£40	£40	£40	**£200**	**£80**	**£1** qr	66.7
		60 qrs	20 qrs	20 qrs	20 qrs	**200** qrs	**140** qrs		233.3

suggests that, contrary to Ramsay's claim, both the amount of profit and the rate of profit are the same in Years 1 and 2, despite the rise in productivity.

These conclusions are incompatible with the replacement-cost interpretation. If we use the seed corn's replacement cost in Year 2, £1/qr, to compute the value it transfers to the product, profit would exceed £80. Used-up constant capital would constitute a smaller share of the output's total value of £200, and thus surplus-value or profit would constitute a larger share, even if variable capital is assumed not to change. Marx's conclusion that profit remains £80, despite the rise in the physical surplus from 40 qrs to 140 qrs, is valid only if the value transferred from the seed corn is determined by its pre-production value of £2/qr.

The other numerical examples are similar, albeit shorter, and Marx draws similar conclusions from them. One passage examines Torrens' argument that "The farmer expends 100 qrs of corn and obtains in return 120 qrs. In this case, 20 qrs constitute the profit" (quoted in Marx 1989b: 268). In response, Marx (1989b: 268–69, emphases in original) agrees that "120 qrs of corn are most certainly more than 100 qrs," but he denies that this

increase in quantity constitutes *profit*, which is applicable solely to exchange value, although exchange value manifests itself in a surplus produce.

As far as exchange value is concerned, there is no need to explain further that the value of 90 qrs of corn can be equal to (or greater than) the value of 100, that the value of 100 can be greater than that of 120, and that of 120 greater than that of 500.

Thus, on the basis of one example which has *nothing* to do with profit, with the surplus in the *value* of the product over the *value* of the capital outlay, Torrens draws conclusions about profit.

Marx holds that Torrens' example "has *nothing* to do with profit" because the fact that the product exceeds the capital outlay in physical terms—that is, the fact that "120 qrs of corn are most certainly more than 100 qrs"—is irrelevant. Value is what matters, and "the *value* of the capital outlay" can be greater than "the *value* of the product"—"the value of 100 can be greater than that of 120." According to the replacement-cost interpretation, however, the 100 qrs of input could not have a greater value than the 120 qrs of output. Since the replacement-cost interpretation holds that each quarter of corn, whether input or output, must have the same value, it follows that "the value of 100 must always be only 100/120ths as much as the value of 120."

Although some reconstruction was necessary in order to elucidate the meaning of this passage, any doubts concerning the above interpretation should be dispelled once it is considered together with a passage from later in the Economic Manuscript that refers back to Marx's critique of Torrens.

All *surplus value* is expressed in *surplus produce* . . . . On the other hand, not all of the *surplus product* represents surplus value; this is a confusion found in Torrens and others. Assume, for example, that the year's harvest is twice as large this year as the previous year, although *the same* amount of objectified and living labor was employed to produce it. The *value* of the harvest . . . is the same. If the same acre produces 8 qrs of wheat instead of 4 qrs, 1 qr of wheat will now have half as much value as before . . . . Thus a qr of seed would have to be paid for with 2 qrs of wheat, and all the elements of capital as also surplus value would remain the same (similarly the ratio of the surplus value to the total capital). [Marx 1994: 219–20, emphases in original]

This passage reveals that Marx has applied a consistent line of thought throughout the three examples we have considered. He refers again to Torrens' "confusion" (at which point an editor's note directs us to the passage discussed above), and the present example is almost identical to the one Marx used in order to criticize Ramsay. So is Marx's conclusion: despite an increase in the physical surplus, both absolutely and in relation to the physical input, surplus-value and the profit rate are unchanged.

Once again, the same product serves as both input and output, and productivity doubles, so that the value of wheat declines by one-half. Consequently, one qr of input (seed) employed before the productivity increase is worth as much as two qrs of output (wheat). One "qr of seed would have to be paid for with 2 qrs of wheat" in the sense that two quarters of output would have to be sold, at value, to recover the sum of value that was advanced for each quarter of input. Hence, "not all of the surplus product represents surplus value": some portion of the physical excess of output over input would need to be sold, not to realize a profit, but merely to recover the full value of the capital advanced.

Marx argues that "the elements of capital . . . remain the same" in value terms. This is possible only if the capital value advanced at the start of this year remains unaffected by the subsequent decline in the wheat's value—only if, in other words, Marx is not revaluing the seed at replacement cost. And since the product's value and surplus-value remain unchanged, so does the amount of value transferred, contrary to what the replacement-cost interpretation holds.

6.4.5 Summary

Our review of the textual evidence has shown that the passages which purportedly confirm the replacement-cost interpretation are irrelevant in most cases and ambiguous if not disconfirming in the rest. Against this, a wealth of evidence supports the TSSI's pre-production reproduction cost understanding of value transfer.

More than one proponent of simultaneism has tried to dismiss most of this evidence on the ground that, when Marx discusses how the sum of value transferred to the product is determined, he frequently does not refer explicitly to the case in which the inputs' values change during the production period. Supposedly, a general statement applies to no particular case that it does not refer to explicitly. It is worth reiterating a point made in section 4.9: this method of reading would prevent us from regarding "vitamins are good for you" as a generally applicable statement unless it were followed by an infinitely long string of cases to which it applies (". . . in months ending in 'r,' and in years in which Brazil wins the World Cup, and when it is sunny, and if you stop liking reggae . . ."). In any case, this gambit cannot be used to dismiss the passages in which *Marx repudiates replacement-cost valuation even when inputs' values change during the period.* Such passages include not only the three examples reviewed in section 6.4.4, but also the "determining factor" passage and, I submit, the long "preposited" passage.

In sum, the preceding survey of the evidence has shown, at the very minimum, what it needed to show. The contested passages need not be construed as the replacement-cost interpretation construes them.

6.5 One System or Two?

This section briefly discusses the textual evidence that pertains to whether Marx was a single- or dual-system theorist. The main issue considered below is whether or not he held that prices are determinants of commodities' values and surplus-value, as the single-system interpretation maintains. This issue is important because Marx's value theory can be acquitted of the charges of internal inconsistency only if he was a single-system theorist as well as a temporalist.

Let us again begin with a conceptual distinction, this time between the *value of means of production and subsistence* and the *value advanced as constant and variable capital.* "[T]he capital advanced . . . is made up of two components, one the sum of money . . . *laid out on* means of production, and the other the sum of money . . . *expended on* labour-power" (Marx 1990a: 320, emphases added). In other words, the capital value advanced is the sum of money paid for inputs, and its magnitude therefore depends upon the inputs' prices, not their values.[9] If the value of an apple is $0.40 while its price is $0.50, a business must pay $0.50 in order to make applesauce out of it, and so the constant-capital value advanced is $0.50, not $0.40.

This distinction makes sense of otherwise inexplicable passages in *Capital,* such as "It is particularly apparent in the case of agriculture how the same causes that raise or lower the *price* of the product also raise or lower the *value of the capital,* since this consists to a large extent of that product itself, e.g. corn or cattle" (Marx 1991a: 209, emphases added). The distinction also has an important implication: the many passages in which Marx says things like "the value of the constant capital is transferred to the product, and merely re-appears in it"

(Marx 1990a: 321) offer *prima facie* support for the single-system interpretation, not the dual-system interpretation, notwithstanding the fact that "value of the constant capital" contains the word "value."

Since prices are assumed to equal values throughout most of *Capital,* the difference between the value of inputs and the value of capital advanced is not really discussed until chapter 9 of volume III. Yet a few passages earlier in the work do indicate that the constant-capital component of commodities' values depends upon inputs' prices. We have already encountered two such passages— the first two quoted in section 6.4.2, above. It might be argued that Marx was able to speak of the input's price rather than its value because he was still assuming that prices equal values, but the context in which the second passage appears strongly suggests otherwise. On the next page, he writes, "since we are dealing here with the effect that these price fluctuations have on the profit rate, it is actually a matter of indifference what their basis might be. The present argument is just as valid if prices rise or fall not as a result of fluctuations in value, but rather as a result of the intervention of the credit system, competition, etc." (Marx 1991a: 208).[10]

Traditionally, the notion that Marx was—or at least wanted to be—a dual-system theorist was based on Bortkiewicz's (1952: 11) claim that, in chapter 9 of *Capital,* volume III, Marx recognized that his account of the value-price transformation contained an error. Sweezy (1970: 115–16) seconded this claim in 1942, citing the following passage as evidence that Marx was aware of his error:

> It was originally assumed that the cost price of a commodity equaled the *value* of the commodities consumed in its production. But . . . [just] [a]s the price of production of a commodity can diverge from its value, so [can] the cost price of a commodity, in which the price of production of other commodities is involved . . . . It is necessary to bear in mind this modified significance of the cost price, and therefore to bear in mind too that if the cost price of a commodity is equated with the value of the means of production used up in producing it, it is always possible to go wrong. [Marx 1991a: 264–65, emphasis in original]

The reason why Marx's critics construe this passage as an admission of error is that they fail to distinguish between the value of *means of production* and the sum of value advanced as *capital.*[11] In the absence of that distinction, he seems to be admitting that there is a difference between the value of capital and the "price of capital"—a difference that leads directly to two separate value and price systems. Yet once we distinguish between the value of inputs and the value of capital, it becomes apparent that the main function of the passage is to make that very distinction! Rather than admitting error, Marx is anticipating that readers might "go wrong" if they overlook the distinction, as they now have for almost a full century.

A passage in the 1861–1863 Manuscript also discusses how commodities' values are determined when inputs are bought at their prices of production rather than their values; "the difference between [price of production] and value . . . is incorporated into the value of the new commodity as a presupposed element" (Marx 1989b: 352). In other words, the constant-capital component of the commodity's value is no longer equal to the value of the inputs, but to their value *plus* the price-value difference. And since value + (price − value) = price, this suggests that the sum of value transferred depends upon the inputs' prices.

Prior to chapter 9 of volume III, where he relaxed his assumption that prices equal values, Marx frequently stated that the variable capital, the value of labor-power, and workers' necessary labor are determined by the *value* of the means of subsistence needed to reproduce their labor-power. This seems to support the dual-system interpretation. We have already seen, however, that Marx actually defined "variable capital" more precisely as the amount of money spent to hire workers. Moreover, once he relaxed the assumption that prices equal values, Marx pointed out that it is really the *price* of means of subsistence that determines the value of labor-power and necessary labor. "[T]he average price of labour, i.e. the value of labour-power, is determined by the production price of the necessary means of subsistence" (Marx 1991a: 1008). Thus if workers consume "commodities whose prices of production are different from their values [they] must work for a greater or lesser amount of time in order to buy back these commodities (to replace them) and must therefore perform more or less necessary labour" (Marx 1991a: 309; cf. p. 261). Monopoly prices also have an effect. "If the commodity with the monopoly price is part of the workers' necessary consumption, it increases wages and thereby reduces surplus-value, as long as the workers continue to receive the value of their labour-power" (Marx 1991a: 1001). As the last sentence indicates, these passages are also incompatible with the dual-system interpretation of "surplus-value."

What follows from all of this is that commodities have a single cost price. There is no separate cost price that depends upon the values of means of production and subsistence. Indeed, Marx seems invariably to have referred to "the" cost price (see, e.g., the passage about the "modified significance of the cost price" quoted above), never to two separate cost prices. Moreover, Alejandro Ramos (1998–1999) has called attention to a passage left out of *Capital*, volume III by Frederick Engels, its editor, which expresses the value of a commodity as K + s (cost price + surplus-value) and the price of a commodity as K + p (cost price + profit). Marx's use of the same symbol, K, in both expressions makes it especially clear that values and prices share the same cost price. Basically the same symbol (k) appears throughout volume III as edited by Engels. That k does not represent a "value" magnitude in some places and a "price" magnitude in others is clear from two passages that use k in connection with both the price and the value of the commodity (Marx 1991a: 309, 897).

In recent decades, an additional argument has been put forth in support of the dual-system interpretation. Marx's frequent statements that a commodity's value is determined by the amount of labor needed to reproduce it have been read as input-output analysts are inclined to read them. "Amount of labor needed to reproduce" has been translated as the workers' "direct" labor plus the labor needed to reproduce used-up inputs. Since the latter amount of labor is the *value* of the used-up inputs (as measured in labor-time), it follows, proponents of the dual-system interpretation maintain, that the sum of value transferred depends upon the inputs' values rather than their prices.

This interpretation cannot be accepted if we take seriously Marx's other frequent statements that the value of constant capital—the sum of money laid out on means of production—is what is transferred to the product. Moreover, the same paragraph in which he referred to the "modified significance of the cost price" ends by arguing that even though the cost price depends upon inputs' prices, not their values, a commodity's value is still determined by the amount of labor needed to reproduce it. "The cost price of a commodity simply depends on the quantity of paid labour it contains, while the value depends on the total quantity of labor it contains, whether paid or unpaid" (Marx 1991a: 265). If one maintains, as the input-output interpretation does, that the "quantity of labor it contains" has nothing to do with prices, then these two parts of the paragraph fail to cohere.

An alternative, single-system, reading eliminates the difficulty. To reproduce a commodity, living labor and means of production are needed. What then is the amount of labor needed to reproduce the commodity? Answer: the living labor plus the amount of labor that is needed to *acquire* the necessary means of production. The latter amount of labor is the amount represented by the money capital that purchases these means of production. If, for instance, a means of production costs $1000, and $50 is the monetary expression of one hour of labor (i.e., the MELT—the monetary expression of labor-time—is $50/labor-hour), then the amount of labor needed to acquire the means of production is 1000/50 = 20 hours of labor.

Some proponents of the dual-system interpretation have recently cited two passages that are supposedly incompatible with the single-system interpretation. One, from volume III of *Capital,* states that "the divergence of price of production from value arises" for two reasons (Marx 1991a: 308). The other, from the 1861–1863 Manuscript, states that "the conversion of value into [price of production] works in two ways" (Marx 1989b: 351). One "reason" or "way" is that profit differs from surplus-value. The other is that inputs' prices differ from their values.

The single-system interpretation is supposedly incompatible with these passages because it denies that differences between inputs' prices and values cause a commodity's price to differ from its value.[12] Note, however, that Marx does not refer to "the divergence of *a commodity's* price of production from *its* value" or "the conversion of *a commodity's* value into *its* [price of production]." He might instead be contrasting an *economy* in which commodities exchange at values to an *economy* in which they exchange at prices of production. This reading eliminates the apparent problem, since the single-system interpretation affirms that prices in the latter economy will differ from prices (= values) in the former for two reasons—because profit differs from surplus-value *and* because inputs' prices and values differ.

It is also noteworthy that the two passages under consideration contain three of the pieces of evidence cited above in support of the single-system interpretation, and that Marx repeatedly refers to "the" cost price in one of these passages.

Notes

1. From a logical perspective, those who allege inconsistency and error bear the burden of proof. They need to show that the passages *must be* construed in a simultaneist manner. Yet since logical considerations have little to do with the outcome of this debate, I have decided to bear an otherwise unnecessary burden.

2. Moseley (1999, section 3:2) also gives a second argument for why Marx's prices of production are implicitly determined simultaneously: if prices of production were determined temporally, they could change for reasons other than changes in "productivity" and real wages, but Marx denies that they can. This argument does not succeed unless Marx and Moseley mean the same thing by "productivity," which Moseley fails to show. In the passage to which he refers, Marx (1991a: 307–308) used "change . . . in productivity" and "change in value" synonymously. And as Moseley himself agrees, Marx held that a commodity's value depends in part on the *prices* of the inputs needed to produce it (see, e.g., Marx 1991a: 264–65). It thus seems reasonable to conclude that a "change . . . in productivity" in the above sense can result from a change in input prices. On this interpretation, temporalist prices of production do *not* change for reasons other than changes in productivity and real wages.

3. Another cat nearly escaped a few paragraphs earlier: "theorists . . . need to ascertain *the conditions under which* the solutions to their [simultaneous] equations will function as centers of gravitation for the actual variables of the economy" (Mongiovi 2002: 400, emphasis added).

4. Here is why it follows. Denote the rate of profit of times 0, 1, and 2 as r_0, r_1, and r_2. Then at time 0, $t = 0$, so r_t is r_0 and r_{t+1} is r_1. But when we move on to time 1, $t = 1$, r_t is r_1, and r_{t+1} is r_2. So the r on the *left-hand* side of Equation (6.1) in one period becomes the r on the *right-hand* side in the next period. Now, if we start with r^* on the right-hand side, we get r^* on the left as our result. But when we move on to the next period, the r^* that we got as a result on the *left-hand* side gets plugged into the *right-hand* side, and we again get r^* on the left as our result. So we keep plugging in r^* on the right and getting it back on the left *forever*. It is this property of r^* that makes it a static equilibrium value.

5. More precisely, 10% should be very close to the average value of the rates of profit one gets if one computes the rate of profit over a *very* long time span, and if the initial r, r_0, is a rational number greater than 0, less than 0.20, and not *exactly* 0.05, 0.10, or 0.15. The computations are easily performed on a spreadsheet.

6. The data were generated as follows. In period t, x_{jt}, p_{jt}, p_{jt+1}, and r_{jt} are the output of good j, its input and output prices, and Sector j's temporal rate of profit. To produce a unit of output, Sector 1 uses $a_1 = 0.6$ units of good 1 and $l_{1t} = 0.4(0.98)^{t-1}$ units of living labor. Sector 2's requirements are $a_2 = 0.3$ and $l_{2t} = (0.98)^{t-1}$. The real wage rate per unit of living labor is $b_t = 0.5/(0.98)^{t-1}$ units of good 2. The monetary expression of labor-time is $m = 1$. Each good's initial (period 1) input price is 1.275. Initial output is 99 in Sector 1 and 101 in Sector 2. The equations governing the *temporal* system's motion are

$$p_{1t+1}x_{1t} = p_{2t+1}x_{2t},$$

$$x_{jt+1} = x_{jt}(1.04 + 0.6[r_{jt} - r_{kt}]),$$

$$r_{jt} = \frac{p_{jt+1}}{p_{1t}a_j + p_{2t}b_t l_{jt}} - 1,$$

$$p_{1t+1}x_{1t} + p_{2t+1}x_{2t} = p_{1t}(a_1 x_{1t} + a_2 x_{2t}) + m(l_{1t}x_{1t} + l_{2t}x_{2t}).$$

The first equation follows from the assumptions that aggregate expenditure is divided equally between the two goods (implying unitary elasticity of demand for each) and that prices adjust to equate demands with supplies. The second states that output would be increased in each sector by 4% per period if rates of profit were equal, but that output is also adjusted in response to the difference between the two sectors' rates of profit. The third equation is the temporal rate of profit, and the last equation is the TSSI equality of total price and total value.

The *static equilibrium* rate of profit is computed in the usual manner: the two rates of profit are equated and output prices replace input prices in their denominators. This yields a solution for p_{1t+1}/p_{2t+1}, from which the solution for the rate of profit follows.

7. Mirowski (1989: 180–85) argues that Marx flip-flopped between historical- and replacement-cost (which he calls "real-cost") valuation. He arrives at this conclusion by construing evidence against each method of valuation as evidence in favor of the other, overlooking the possibility that both are wrong and that Marx *consistently* held that the value transferred from inputs to the output is the inputs' pre-production reproduction cost. To my knowledge, all proponents of the TSSI subscribe to this latter view. On Freeman's (1996) interpretation, in which new commodities' values are determined in part by the current pre-production prices of inputs and other assets that are not used up during production, it remains the case that inputs transfer their pre-production reproduction cost. (I reject this interpretation, not because it is a historical-cost interpretation, but because I think it contradicts Marx's statements that an article's value is determined by the amount of labor needed to produce new articles of that kind, and because explicit textual support for it is lacking.)

8. Because "the same amount of labour" yields the same amount of value in *monetary* terms in both years, Marx is implicitly assuming that the monetary expression of labor-time (MELT) remains constant.

9. Carchedi's (1984) distinction between the "individual value" and "social value" of the inputs is very similar to my distinction between the "value of the inputs" and the "capital value advanced." Since Marx (1990a: 434–36) uses the same terms as Carchedi to make a quite different distinction, I have chosen to employ other terms in order to avoid possible confusion.

10. A passage in the 1861–1863 Economic Manuscript similarly holds that, if the price of cotton falls below its value due to an imbalance between supply and demand, this raises the rate of profit of a business that uses cotton as an input (Marx 1989a: 65).

11. Recall that a commodity's cost price equals the sum of value transferred (the constant-capital portion of its value) plus variable capital.

12. This follows from the fact that the inputs' values are irrelevant to the determination of both the price and the value of a commodity.

Chapter 7

The Falling Rate of Profit Controversy

7.1 Introduction

Since the 1970s, the core issue in the controversy surrounding Marx's law of the tendential fall in the rate of profit (LTFRP) has been whether increases in productivity resulting from labor-saving technological change can cause the general rate of profit to fall. Marx argued that they can,[1] but the Okishio (1961) theorem has widely been held to have proved him wrong. Indeed, the very suggestion that Marx, not the theorem, might be correct has regularly been contemptuously dismissed. It continues to be dismissed despite the publication of numerous disproofs of the Okishio theorem by temporalists during the last quarter-century (see, e.g., Ernst 1982, Kliman 1988, Freeman and Kliman 2000, Ramos 2004).

In the second volume of their *History of Marxian Economics*, for instance, Howard and King (1992: xiii) stated that "To reassert[,] in the face of [the Okishio theorem and related demonstrations,] the relevance of the falling rate of profit, as analyzed by Marx, has done much damage to the intellectual credentials of Marxian political economy." Several years later, Robert Brenner (1998), the noted Marxist historian, was able to dispose of the LTFRP in a single footnote of a 265-page work on economic crisis and stagnation. He simply invoked the Okishio theorem—and, for good measure, "common-sense":

> [Marx's] theory of the fall of the rate of profit . . . flies in the face of common-sense. For, if, as Marx himself seemed to take for granted[,] . . . capitalists . . . adopt technical changes that raise their own rate of profit . . . , it seems intuitively obvious that the ultimate result of their innovation . . . can only be . . . to *raise* the average rate of profit . . . . Formal proofs of this result can be found in N. Okishio . . . as well as in J. Roemer. [Brenner 1998: 11–12, n1]

The most recent such dismissal, as of this writing, is that of Hahnel (2005: 58, emphasis in original), a radical economist:

Despite a number of attempts by die-hard Marxists during the 1970s and 1980s to rescue the falling rate of profit crisis theory from being relegated to the dust bin of history by the Okishio theorem, by the end of the century virtually all open-minded political economists recognized that this supposed *internal contradiction* within capitalism had been nothing more than a lengthy intellectual red herring.

The main objective of this chapter is to argue that political economists and others who desire to be open-minded, who truly care about their intellectual credentials rather than their professional ones, would do well to consider the issue anew. Marx's LTFRP does indeed contradict what may seem intuitively obvious, especially to physicalists whose common sense tells them that rising productivity translates into rising profitability. Yet much else in economics—and nearly the whole of modern physics—also flies in the face of common sense.

The next section explains why the Okishio theorem is logically invalid and therefore fails to refute the LTFRP. Yet logically invalid arguments can have true conclusions (Socrates was a man; all men are mortal; therefore Socrates was a philosopher). The fact that the theorem is unproved will therefore not, by itself, shake the intuitive conviction that it is impossible for productivity improvements to depress the rate of profit. Thus I argue in the third section that this conclusion should not be regarded as obvious, for indeed it is implausible.

That physical output rises in relation to physical input as a result of increasing productivity is undeniable, as is the fact that this tends to boost profitability. Yet these same increases in productivity also tend to reduce the rate of increase in the *price* of the output relative to the price of the input. As we shall see, the price effect can cancel out, or more than cancel out, the physical effect—even when it is only the rate of inflation, not the absolute level of prices, that declines.[2] *The reason why the Okishio theorem appears to prove that rising productivity cannot lead to a falling rate of profit is that it overlooks the price effect, or, more precisely, spirits it away by valuing inputs and outputs simultaneously.* What remains is only the physical effect; the rate of profit is transformed into a physical relationship, a relation between output and input, and productivity increases do of course boost *this* "rate of profit."

Proponents of simultaneism have long been aware that their models prevent falling prices from lowering the rate of profit. Critiquing Marx's LTFRP in 1907, Bortkiewicz (1952: 40) wrote, "it is wrong to connect a change in the rate of profit with a change in prices, since, as can be seen from our formulae, . . . price movements affect the capitalist's product to the same degree as they do his outlay." In other words, falling prices cause costs as well as revenues to decline, and by the same percentage, and thus the rate of profit remains unchanged when prices fall. Instead of treating this far-fetched conclusion as a sign that his simultaneist formulae were seriously flawed, Bortkiewicz treated it as a solid fact about the real world, and one that showed that Marx had been wrong. This is not only disturbing, but ironic as well, since, earlier in the same essay, Bortkiewicz

(1952: 13) had charged that it is "characteristic of the author of *Das Kapital* . . . [to] hold the nature of the object to which his theoretical construction refers, responsible for the inner contradictions afflicting this construction."

What happens when we jettison the simultaneist theoretical construction and bring the disinflationary or deflationary impact of rising productivity—in other words, the determination of value by labor-time—back into the picture? As I shall show in the fourth section, a tendential fall in the rate of profit becomes possible, indeed plausible. This is because a decline in the rate of inflation causes the actual rate of profit to fall, necessarily and systematically, in relationship to the Okishio theorem's physicalist rate.

At this point, some critics' intuition will convince them that there must be some error in, if not outright trickery behind, these demonstrations. As I discuss in the final section, however, no one has yet discovered such an error. Indeed, physicalist-simultaneist authors have recently acknowledged, however tacitly, that the Okishio theorem does not in fact disprove the LTFRP; productivity-enhancing technological change *can* cause the rate of profit to fall.

It is often asked why this controversy cannot be settled by finding out whether the rate of profit does in fact fall. There are two main reasons why it cannot. First, as I noted in section 2.1.14, Marx's LTFRP does not predict that the rate of profit exhibits a long-term falling trend; much less does it predict the eventual collapse of capitalism. It predicts recurrent economic crises, by means of which the *tendency* of the rate of profit to fall is constantly overcome. Second, the issue here is not whether the rate of profit tends to fall, but why. The Okishio theorem does not deny that the rate of profit can fall. What it holds is that, if a fall does occur, Marx's theory cannot possibly explain correctly why it occurs.

Furthermore, the fact that the theorem denies that Marx's theory can ever, even in a single instance, provide a correct explanation for why the rate of profit fell, implies that the controversy cannot be settled by any empirical means whatsoever. It cannot be settled even by sophisticated econometric studies that do try to explain *why* the rate of profit fell. If the Okishio theorem is true, then—as Roemer (1981: 113), a prominent advocate of the theorem, correctly stressed—no facts or data analysis can vindicate the LTFRP. They may seem to do so, they may be quite convincing, but if the theorem has truly proved that Marx's law cannot possibly hold, that ends the matter once and for all. Disproof of the Okishio theorem on logical grounds is therefore an absolutely necessary precondition to any attempt to appeal to the data in order to demonstrate that technological change tends to lower the rate of profit.

7.2 Why the Okishio Theorem Has Not Been Proved

7.2.1 Marx's Equilibrium Rate of Profit

The LTFRP has a seemingly paradoxical implication: capitalists "kill[ ] the goose that was laying their golden eggs" (Hahnel 2005: 58). They introduce technological innovations that boost their *individual* rates of profit, but these innovations end up lowering the *general* rate of profit in the economy as a whole. It might seem intuitively obvious that this must mean that the LTFRP is false, since "what is true in the individual case must be true in the general case," but it is actually this latter statement—known as the "fallacy of composition"— that is false. First-year economics students are regularly cautioned not to fall prey to this fallacy (see, e.g., McConnell and Brue, 2005: 11).

Although Marx explained, at the end of his presentation of the LTFRP, why capitalists engage in what seems at first to be self-destructive behavior, the Okishio theorem holds that his explanation is internally inconsistent. According to the theorem, Marx's premises actually lead to the contrary conclusion: technological innovations which boost the innovating firm's rate of profit can *never* lower the "equilibrium rate of profit." In most cases, they cause it to rise.

To understand why the proofs of this theorem are logically invalid—why the theorem's conclusion does not in fact follow from Marx's actual premises— one needs to pay careful attention to the meaning of "equilibrium rate of profit" in this context. Marx, too, refers to an equilibrium rate of profit in his presentation of the LTFRP. As we shall see, however, the reason why the Okishio theorem seems to disprove the LTFRP is that it subtly replaces the equilibrium rate to which he referred with a different one.

Marx (1991a: 373–74, emphasis added) resolved the apparent paradox arising from his law in the following way:

> No capitalist voluntarily applies a new method of production, no matter how much more productive it may be . . . , if it reduces the rate of profit. But every new method of production of this kind makes commodities cheaper. . . . He pockets the difference between their costs of production and the market price of other commodities, which are produced at higher production costs. . . . But competition makes the new procedure universal and subjects it to the general law [of value]. *A fall in the profit rate then ensues—firstly perhaps in this sphere of production, and subsequently equalized with the others*—a fall that is completely independent of the capitalists' will.

In other words, the innovating firm's own rate of profit does rise initially, because it produces at lower cost than its competitors but sells its product for the same price. Once the competitors adopt the new technology, however, the product's cost of production falls generally, and thus its value and price of production fall as well. This causes the rate of profit to fall throughout the industry. Since this industry's rate of profit is "subsequently equalized with the others," the general, or average, rate of profit also falls. Note that if we apply the term "equilibrium rate of profit" to what Marx is discussing here, what it means is simply the equalized rate of profit, nothing more.

This explanation makes sense of the capitalists' apparently self-destructive behavior. The innovating firm acts its own interest; the innovation does increase its rate of profit, even if only temporarily. And although its rate of profit later falls, the innovator would have fared even more poorly had it not been the first to introduce the new technology. When competitors adopt it subsequently, they are also acting in their own interest. Because the innovator produces at lower cost, it can sell its product more cheaply than the competitors (while still realizing a higher rate of profit) and thereby steal customers away from them, perhaps even drive them out of business. To prevent this from happening, they too must now adopt the new technology.

7.2.2 The Okishio Theorem's Equilibrium Rate of Profit

Okishio's (1961) original theorem, as well as Roemer's later extension of the theorem to allow for the presence of fixed capital, are based on the passage quoted above (see esp. Roemer 1981: 108–109). For the most part, they replicate its premises tolerably well. The rate of profit is initially equalized throughout the economy. A new technology then appears in some industry. Firms in the industry adopt the new technology because, given current prices and the current real wage rate (the wage rate in physical terms), they will raise their own rates of profit by doing so. The economy-wide rate of profit is therefore no longer equalized. Later, however, a new "equilibrium" rate of profit is established. Unless the real wage rate happens for some reason to have risen in the meantime, the theorem says that the new "equilibrium" rate of profit is *always* higher than the original one (or equal to it, if the technological innovation occurred in a luxury-producing industry).

The secret behind this result is that Okishio and Roemer not only assume, along with Marx, that rates of profit are equalized after the innovation is adopted. They also take the liberty of equalizing input and output prices. *Their* "equilibrium" rate of profit, in other words, is the simultaneist or static equilibrium rate, a rate that spirits away the disinflationary or deflationary effect of the technological change. Yet *Marx* did not assume the equalization of input and output prices, either in the above passage or, to my knowledge, anywhere else.

It is true that if the rate of profit is equalized, then firms in all industries obtain the average rate of profit and sell their output at its average price (price of production). As was shown in section 6.2, however, average and static equilibrium magnitudes are quite different things, conceptually and often quantitatively as well. There is therefore no mathematical reason why the average rate of profit must coincide with the static equilibrium rate, and no one has discovered any economic reason.[3] It is therefore not permissible to infer the equality of input and output prices from Marx's assumption that the rate of profit is equalized. Thus the Okishio theorem fails to show that Marx's LTFRP is logically invalid —inconsistent with *his own* premises, premises that do not include, explicitly or implicitly, the equalization of input and output prices.

The theorem fails on its own terms as well. Starting from the premise that rates of profit are equalized after the technological innovation, what it supposedly *deduces* is a new, static equilibrium rate of profit that exceeds the original one. That the new rate of profit is a static equilibrium rate is, in other words, a conclusion of the theorem, not a premise. This is quite clear from Roemer's (1981: 97–98) statement that "what the theorem says is that after prices have readjusted to equilibrate the rate of profit again, the new rate of profit will be higher than the old rate." The readjustment of prices that causes the rate of profit to equilibrate is what Roemer, faithfully following Marx in this regard, takes as his premise. That this leads to the establishment of a new static equilibrium rate of profit is clearly part of Roemer's *conclusion*. But this feature of the conclusion does not follow from the premise that rates of profit are re-equilibrated. Nor does Roemer show by other means that the newly equalized rate of profit must be his static equilibrium rate. The theorem is therefore logically invalid; its conclusion has not been deduced, but only asserted.

7.2.3 Simultaneist Critiques of the Okishio Theorem

A number of works, critiquing the Okishio theorem from within the simultaneist framework, have shown that its physicalist rate of profit can fall for a variety of reasons. Yet these works do not vindicate Marx's LTFRP, since they do not show that the rate of profit can fall because labor becomes more productive. Rising productivity can never cause the *physical* rate of profit to fall. Nor do these works disprove the Okishio theorem; they obtain their contrary results only because they alter one or another of the theorem's premises.[4]

For instance, some authors (e.g., Laibman 1982; Foley 1986, chap. 8; Lipietz 1986) have altered the theorem's assumption that the real wage rate remains constant. If a real wage increase happens to accompany technological progress, the physicalist rate of profit may fall. Yet it falls because of the increase in the real wage, not because of the technological progress; the latter actually lessens the amount by which the rate of profit falls. This result does not confirm the LTFRP, much less disprove the Okishio theorem.

Similarly, Alberro and Persky (1981) show that the physicalist rate of profit can fall if new machines are prematurely scrapped—replaced, while still serviceable, when even better machines unexpectedly come along. Because they are prematurely scrapped, the new machines fail to produce all of the output they were expected to produce. Thus the physicalist rate of profit falls because the scrapped machines prove to be less, not more, productive in the end. This is clearly not a confirmation of the LTFRP.

Whereas Marx and the Okishio theorem assume that innovations are adopted voluntarily, because they raise the innovator's own rate of profit at least temporarily, Shaikh (1978) and Nakatani (1979) assume the opposite. Innovation in their models is a defensive response to cutthroat competition. The technologies that firms adopt are not those which yield the highest rate of profit, given current prices and wages, but those which will best allow them to survive when cutthroat competition in the industry forces down the price of the product. Adoption of such technologies can cause the physical rate of profit to fall. But since it falls because the new technologies are less, not more, productive, these models do not vindicate the LTFRP.

Another way of putting the point is that these models identify cutthroat competition, not rising productivity, as the cause of falling profitability. In his presentation of the LTFRP, on the other hand, Marx (1991a: 361) argued that falling profitability is what causes the cutthroat competition, not the reverse. Elsewhere, he explicitly rejected the view that competition can be the cause of a permanent fall in the rate of profit (Marx 1973: 751–52).[5]

It has often been suggested that the physicalist implications of the Okishio theorem can be circumvented by abandoning its, and Marx's, assumption that the rate of profit is equalized after technical innovation occurs. In the absence of a uniform rate of profit, supposedly "anything can happen." Yet Farjoun and Machover, who studied this possibility very carefully, came to the contrary conclusion: there are definite laws governing the *distribution* of rates of profit (Farjoun and Machover 1983: 17–19, 169–71). Since by rates of profit they meant physicalist rates—the physically-determined rates of the simultaneous dual-system interpretation—Farjoun and Machover (1983: 171) concluded: "The continued viability of capitalism . . . will depend on the ability of continual innovation in the methods of production to keep pace with the merely quantitative expansion of the economy." In other words, physicalism implies that technological progress boosts profitability whether or not the rate of profit is uniform.

7.3 Physical Determination of
Profitability: Obvious or Implausible?

Perhaps the primary reason why Marx's LTFRP is so often dismissed out of hand is that it runs counter to the physicalist notion that greater productivity must translate into greater profitability. This notion is regarded as obviously correct, not only by Sraffian and simultaneist-Marxist economists, but by economic policymakers, politicians, and the news media. However, I intend to show here that this notion is far from self-evident and is actually highly implausible.

Specifically, I will show that although the Okishio theorem appears to prove that rising productivity does translate into rising profitability, this is because the theorem mis-measures the rate of profit by valuing inputs and outputs simultaneously. As we saw in sections 5.6 and 5.7, the revaluation of inputs at output prices produces a spurious reduction in the capital value advanced when output prices are falling in relation to input prices. This boosts the rate of profit artificially, and it is because of this artificial boost that the Okishio theorem concludes that technological progress cannot cause the rate of profit to fall. Once the rate of profit is measured correctly, however, Marx's real rate of profit *always* falls in relationship to the physicalist rate if productivity growth accelerates, and the nominal rate of profit tracks the physicalist rate *only* if rising productivity fails to have a disinflationary effect—that is, only if it fails to lower the rate at which prices are rising.

7.3.1 A Simple Example

Let us examine the simplest case possible: a one-sector ("corn") economy, without fixed capital, in which all of the year's output is plowed back—literally—into production, as seed corn planted at the start of the next year. Since all output is invested as seed, the farmworkers and farm owners consume none of it.

Because fixed capital and wages are assumed away in this example, the seed corn (SC) is the whole of the capital advanced in physical terms, and the physical surplus (PS) equals the net product (NP)—corn output (CO) minus seed corn. The physical rate of profit (ROP) equals the physical surplus divided by the physical capital advanced (seed corn).

Let us also assume that, between Years 1 and 2, the seed corn, the output, and the amount of living labor (LL) performed by the farmworkers all increase by 25%. The economy is growing, but there is no productivity growth. Output per unit of living labor and output per unit of corn input both remain unchanged. Given the physical quantities of Year 1 presented in Table 7.1, the figures for Year 2 follow from the assumption of 25% growth.

Table 7.1. Physical Quantities

Year	SC	NP = PS	$CO = SC + NP$	$ROP = PS/SC$	LL
1	64	16	80	**25.0%**	80
2	80	20	100	**25.0%**	100
3	100	30	130	**30.0%**	100
4	130	45	175	**34.6%**	100

In Years 3 and 4, technological progress commences. The net product now increases by 50% per year, while employment no longer increases—100 hours of living labor are performed each year. Both output per unit of living labor ("labor productivity") and output per unit of seed corn ("capital productivity") rise in Years 3 and 4. Another important feature of the example is that the technological changes are labor-saving in Marx's sense; the ratio of means of production (seed corn) to workers, which he called the **technical composition of capital**, increases in both years. (The seed corn figures for Years 3 and 4 are based on our assumption that all output is invested as seed; for instance, CO = 100 in Year 2, so SC = 100 in Year 3.)

Of course, this is an extremely unrealistic set of assumptions. I do not pretend to be modeling the process of accumulation in any actual economy here. The Okishio theorem can be, and has been, disproved without making *any* of these assumptions.[6] I make them here only for the sake of simplicity: because all output becomes input, we can easily track the flows of corn and labor without getting bogged down in the complications that arise when the output is divvied up in different ways. Since there is only one industry, there are no inter-industry differences in profitability to worry about; the rate of profit is continually equalized. And because of our extreme growth-rate assumptions, we have mostly "easy" numbers to work with.

7.3.2 The Simultaneist Value/Price Rate of Profit

As a result of the technological progress, the physical rate of profit rises from 25% to 30% and then to 34.6%. According to all simultaneist interpretations of Marx's value theory—the New Interpretation and the simultaneous single-system interpretations, as well as the simultaneous dual-system interpretation—the value rate of profit follows precisely the same trajectory, as does the nominal price rate of profit. Since these are general results, not by-products of the present example, these interpretations imply that Okishio was right and Marx was wrong: rising productivity tends to raise, not lower, the rate of profit.

Yet as all simultaneists recognize, the technological progress causes productivity to increase, and therefore causes the per-unit value of corn to decline. It would seem that this decline would necessarily lower the value rate of profit, the ratio of surplus-*value* to capital value advanced, in relation to the physical rate. How is it possible for simultaneist interpretations to reach the opposite conclusion? The answer, as I noted above, is that simultaneous valuation produces an incorrect measure of profitability, one that systematically undervalues the capital advanced when values are falling.

To see this, let us assume that the monetary expression of labor-time (MELT) always equals $1/labor-hr. (This is purely a simplifying assumption; the simultaneist value and price rates of profit are always equal in a one-sector context, no matter how the MELT changes over time.) Since the MELT equals 1, the new value (NV) added equals the living labor performed and the money price (p) of a bushel of corn equals its labor-time value (v). In the present case, all simultaneist interpretations hold that the per-unit value of corn is the ratio of new value to the net product and, of course, that each year's input and output values are the same. Given these assumptions and the physical data above, we obtain the simultaneist value tableau, Table 7.2.[7]

The constant capital (c) is the total value of the seed corn, its per unit-value times the amount of it invested. Since there are no wages or fixed capital, the constant capital, the total capital advanced (C), and the sum of value transferred (VT) are all equal, and surplus-value (s) equals the new value added. As always, the total value of output (TV) equals the value transferred plus the new value added, and the value rate of profit is surplus-value divided by capital advanced.

We see that although the technological change causes the per-unit value of corn to fall by one-third in Year 3 and again in Year 4, this has absolutely no effect on the relationship between the value and physical rates of profit. The two rates are always equal, and both rise as a consequence of the increases in productivity.

Since s fails to grow after Year 2, the value rate of profit, s/C, would have to fall if capital accumulation were taking place—that is, if C were growing. But capital is being dis-accumulated in Years 3 and 4, and this is why the value rate of profit rises.

Why, however, is capital dis-accumulation occurring? Since all output of one year becomes the seed corn invested in the next, the total value of output in one year should become the next year's capital advanced. And since the total value in each year consistently exceeds the capital advanced in that same year, the capital advanced *should* be increasing year after year. Consider, for example, what occurs between Years 1 and 2, when capital accumulation does take place. The output at the end of Year 1, 80 bushels of corn, becomes the physical capital advanced at the start of Year 2. *Since the 80 bushels are sold for $400, they are*

Table 7.2. Simultaneist Value/Price Rate of Profit

Year	$p = v =$ LL/NP	$C = c = VT$ $= p \times SC$	$NV =$ $LL = s$	$TV =$ $VT + NV$	ROP $= s/C$
1	5.000	320	80	400	25.0%
2	5.000	400	100	500	25.0%
3	3.333	333	100	433	30.0%
4	2.222	289	100	389	34.6%

bought for $400, and thus the capital value advanced at the start of Year 2 is $400 as well. And since the total value of Year 1's output, $400, exceeds that year's capital advanced, $320, the capital advanced increases from $320 to $400 between Years 1 and 2.

Once technological progress begins, however, the capital advanced of one year falls below the previous year's total value of output—even though all of that output is still being invested as seed. For example, *the 100 bushels of output of Year 2, all of which are planted as seed in Year 3, are sold for $500 and bought for $500, yet what is recorded in the simultaneist books is an advance of only $333!* In effect, one-third of the purchase price has vanished into thin air. The miracle of simultaneous valuation has caused it to disappear. Since a bushel of corn is worth $3.33 at the end of Year 3, a bushel of corn purchased at the start of the year for $5 is retroactively revalued at $3.33, and this is what causes the rate of profit to rise.

I am not suggesting that the decline in the value of the seed corn should actually cause the rate of profit to *fall*. As Marx (1991a: 342–43) recognized, the cheapening of means of production does reduce the capital value advanced, and thus it tends to counteract the tendency of the rate of profit to fall. My point is simply that it cannot do so *retroactively*. Owing to the fall in the value of corn during Year 3, the capital advanced in *Year 4* will be smaller than otherwise and, all else being equal, *Year 4's* rate of profit will consequently be greater than otherwise. But the fall in the value of corn during the course of Year 3 cannot retroactively reduce the capital value that was advanced at the start of *Year 3*; what's done is done.

The same thing holds true in the case of fixed capital. When declining prices cause the value of fixed assets to fall, a company cannot simply declare that it invested less to acquire those assets than it actually invested. The size of its investment can only be reduced by taking a loss or by increasing the company's depreciation expense, both of which lower its rate of profit.[8] Here again, it is only the rate of profit of *subsequent* years, not the *current* year's rate, which tends to rise as a result of the cheapening of means of production.

7.3.3 The Simultaneist Defense of Retroactive Revaluation

In spite of these facts, many simultaneist authors have defended retroactive re-valuation of the advanced capital and the rate of profit that results from it—the so-called "replacement-cost rate of profit." They have claimed that the "re-placement-cost rate" is a meaningful measure because it is the "*potential* profit rate*" (Laibman 1999a: 223, emphasis in original) and therefore the rate that governs investment decisions.

For example, if a business invested $2000 for the purchase of a machine, and the investment has yielded a profit of $100 each year, the annual rate of profit has actually been $100/$2000 = 5%. However, the simultaneists' argument goes, if the machine can be replaced for just $1000 today, then the potential rate of profit—the rate that can be obtained by investing in the replacement machine—is $100/$1000 = 10%. A business or investor whose other alternative is an investment that yields 6% would decide to invest in the machine instead, even though machines of this kind have only yielded a 5% rate of profit in the past.

In a rebuttal that has gone unanswered,[9] Alan Freeman and I pointed out that the "replacement-cost rate of profit" does not actually govern investment decisions, because it is not actually the potential rate of profit:

> Businesses and investors make their investment decisions on the basis of meas-ures such as the internal rate of return and net present value. Whereas the "re-placement cost profit rate" values current investment expenditures and future receipts simultaneously, using a single set of prices, these measures use current prices for the former but expected future prices for the latter.
>
> Capitalists employ these measures because what they seek, must seek, to maximize is the rate of self-expansion of their value, not the rate of self-expansion of use-value that the material rate [i.e., the physical rate of profit] measures. Consider a firm that produces computers by means of computers. Computer prices plummet markedly year by year. In computing its potential profit rate, only the most naïve firm would overlook or be indifferent to the fact that a unit of its output will be worth less than a unit of its input, physically identical though they may be. [Kliman and Freeman 2000: 287–88]

Yet even if we were to grant the legitimacy of the "replacement-cost rate of profit" for the sake of argument, the issue here is whether simultaneist interpre-tations are adequate as interpretations of Marx's LTFRP. Is the "replacement-cost rate of profit" a correct measure of the rate of profit to which the law refers? It clearly is not. One cannot deduce the LTFRP from Marx's premises when the replacement-cost rate is used; it never tends to fall as a result of rising productiv-ity. Hence, the replacement-cost interpretation creates an avoidable inconsistency in the text. This alone strongly suggests that the rate of profit to which the law refers is determined temporally, not simultaneously.

More direct textual evidence leads to the same conclusion. According to the replacement-cost concept, profit is the difference between the value of output and the cost of replacing inputs at the end of the period. However, Marx measured profit and the rate of profit in essentially the same way that businesses and investors do. When first introducing the concept of surplus-value in *Capital*, he defined it as the difference between the sum of money that "is finally withdrawn from circulation" and the original sum "thrown into it at the beginning," the "excess over the original value" (Marx 1990a: 251). He also regularly defined profit as "an excess over and above the total capital advanced" (Marx 1991a: 133), rather than as an excess over and above the replacement cost of means of production.

Other passages, from Marx's Economic Manuscript of 1861–1863, indicate perhaps even more clearly that by "profit" he meant the increase in the value of capital at the end of a period over the sum of value advanced at the start:

> The point of departure . . . is the independent form of value which maintains itself, increases, measures the increase against the original amount . . . . The relation between the value preposited to production and the value which results from it—capital as preposited value is capital in contrast to profit—constitutes the all-embracing and decisive factor in the whole process of capitalist production. [Marx 1989b: 318]

> Profit . . . expresses in fact the increment of value which the total capital receives at the end of the processes of production and circulation, over and above the value it possessed before this process of production, when it entered into it. [Marx 1991b: 91]

7.3.4 Consistent Physicalist Valuation

In simultaneist interpretations of Marx's theory, value is purportedly determined by labor-time. Yet these interpretations arrive at the paradoxical conclusion that Marx's rate of profit is identical to the physical rate. As we have seen, the source of this paradox is that simultaneous valuation causes a portion of the capital advanced to be conjured away. The following question then arises: Might it be the case that, after this error is corrected, the rate of profit still turns out to be physically determined?

To answer this question, let us assume the conclusion—the rate of profit is determined temporally, so no capital value is being conjured away, yet it always equals the physical rate—and see what conditions are needed in order for this conclusion to hold true. Beginning with the same initial advance of capital as before, $320, we multiply this figure by Year 1's physical rate of profit to obtain the surplus-value (= new value added). Adding the new value to the sum of value transferred, we obtain the total value. Since all of the year's output is invested as seed, and valuation is now temporal, the value of the output of Year 1 becomes the capital advanced in Year 2. We then multiply the new capital advanced by Year 2's physical rate of profit to obtain the new value of that year, and so forth. The result is a series of rates of profit which are physically determined, even though no capital value is mysteriously disappearing between one year and the next (see Table 7.3).

We see that a temporally determined rate of profit that mirrors the physical rate is indeed a possibility. However, *value is no longer determined by labortime*. If we divide the new value by the living labor figures of Table 7.1, we find that the new value created per hour of living labor, initially $1/hr, rises once technological progress commences, to $1.50/hr in Year 3 and $2.25/hr in Year 4. In contrast to Marx's (1990a: 137) theory, which holds that an hour of average labor "always yields the same amount of value, independently of any variations in productivity," rising productivity is causing each hour of average labor to yield a greater amount of value.

Indeed, if we divide the new value added by Table 7.1's net product figures, we find that the new value is a constant $5 per bushel of net product. A bushel of net product always yields the same amount of value, independently of any variations in the amount of labor needed to produce it. *Physical output has replaced labor-time as the determinant of value.*

We can see the same thing from a different angle by computing the per-unit prices. Dividing the capital advanced by our seed corn figures, and total value by the corn output figures, we obtain the input and output prices, respectively. We find that the price (= value) of corn is constant, $5/bushel, even though productivity is rising, and in fact rising at an increasing rate. This result makes clear that *the actual rate of profit mirrors the physical rate only if increases in productivity do not tend to lower values or prices.*[10] Physicalism is therefore incom-

Table 7.3. Consistent Physicalist Value/Price Rate of Profit

Year	$p_{in} =$ C/SC	$C = c$ $= VT^*$	$NV = s =$ $C \times$ (Phys. ROP)	$TV =$ $VT + NV$	**ROP** $= s/C$	$p_{out} =$ TV/CO
1	5.000	320	80	400	**25.0%**	5.000
2	5.000	400	100	500	**25.0%**	5.000
3	5.000	500	150	650	**30.0%**	5.000
4	5.000	650	225	875	**34.6%**	5.000

* The capital advanced equals the total value of the prior year. Year 1's advance of capital is a given datum.

patible with the fact, widely recognized even by non-Marxists like Alan Green-span (2000), that prices do tend to fall as a result of increasing productivity:

> [F]aster productivity growth keeps a lid on unit costs and prices. Firms hesitate to raise prices for fear that their competitors will be able, with lower costs from new investments, to wrest market share from them.
>   Indeed, the increased availability of labor-displacing equipment and software, at declining prices and improving delivery times, is arguably at the root of the loss of business pricing power in recent years.

7.4 The Law of Value and the Rate of Profit

I shall now challenge the notion that the LTFRP is obviously wrong in a more direct fashion. We shall see that, when value is determined by labor-time and capital value is not spirited away by means of simultaneous valuation, it follows naturally, indeed inescapably, that labor-saving technological progress can cause the rate of profit to fall.

The discussion will consider both the real and the nominal rates of profit (even though, to repeat, movements in the nominal rate have no bearing, strictly speaking, on the internal coherence of the LTFRP). Nominal prices have tended to rise for many decades even though labor-time-determined (i.e., constant-MELT) values have consistently fallen. Under such circumstances, it may be thought, productivity growth cannot cause the nominal price rate of profit to fall. I shall show that this belief is mistaken. Whether productivity increases tend to lower prices themselves, or whether they tend to lower only the rate of inflation, their effect on the nominal rate of profit is essentially the same.

7.4.1 The Constant-MELT Value/Price Rate of Profit

Let us now compute the rate of profit in the same manner as we did in section 7.3.4, introducing only one modification: the new value added will now be determined directly by labor-time, in the sense that each hour of labor adds a constant amount of nominal, as well as real, value. In other words, the MELT, which expresses the relationship between nominal and real value, remains constant over time. If we assume that the MELT is $1/hr, the new value is always equal to the living labor figures of Table 7.1, and the nominal price of corn equals its value. The resulting flow of value is given in Table 7.4.

The value/price rate of profit is initially equal to the physical rate, and the two rates remain equal as long as productivity is not growing. Once techno-

**Table 7.4. Temporalist Value/Price Rate of Profit,
Given the Law of Value & Constant MELT**

Year	$p_{in} = v_{in}$ *	$C = c = VT = p_{in} \times SC$	$NV = LL = s$	$TV = VT + NV$	$ROP = s/C$	$p_{out} = v_{out} = TV/CO$
1	5.000	320	80	400	25.0%	5.000
2	5.000	400	100	500	25.0%	5.000
3	5.000	500	100	600	20.0%	4.615
4	4.615	600	100	700	16.7%	4.000

* The input price equals the prior year's output price. Year 1's input price is given.

logical progress occurs, however, the value/price rate of profit falls, even though the physical rate rises.

It is very easy to see why. Since the total value of output increases by $100 each year and all output is invested, the capital advanced also increases by $100 each year. But employment is no longer increasing, so surplus-value is a stagnant $100. And since surplus-value is the numerator of the rate of profit while capital advanced is its denominator, the rate of profit falls. To those not habituated to physicalist thought, this result might even be—dare I say it—intuitively obvious.

Another way of explaining the fall is that, because value is determined by labor-time here, the increase in productivity causes the price of corn to fall, which in turn causes the rate of profit to fall. This effect is offset, to some degree, by the fact that the productivity increase also causes the ratio of physical output to physical input (and thus the physical rate of profit) to rise. Yet since the price of corn falls faster, in percentage terms, than the output/input ratio rises, the rate of profit falls.

Where is the internal inconsistency? Marx's premise that the amount of new value created is determined by labor-time leads naturally, indeed inescapably, to the conclusion that labor-saving technological progress can cause the rate of profit to fall. One may surely reject the premise, but that is not relevant here. If the conclusion follows from the premises, the argument is internally consistent.

Although the present example is quite unrealistic in most respects, one important result holds true generally. If value is determined by labor-time, an increase in the rate of productivity growth *always* causes the value/price rate of profit to decline in relationship to the physical rate. The greater the increase in the rate of productivity growth, the greater is the decline in the value/price rate of profit relative to the physical rate (Freeman and Kliman 2000: 254–55). Thus the reason why this example's value/price rate of profit falls so markedly in relationship to the physical rate is that the rate of productivity growth increases so sharply.

7.4.2 The Limited Influence of Inflation and a Rising MELT

In the real world, of course, we have experienced an almost continual rise in prices for many decades, despite the fact that increasing productivity has caused commodities' values (measured in terms of labor-time or a constant MELT) to decline. In other words, the MELT does not remain constant, but rises systematically. It is tempting to assume that this phenomenon negates the LTFRP, at least in the sense that the *nominal* price rate of profit must rise, not fall, when prices are continually increasing. Yet this is not the case.

Imagine that in our corn economy, the price of corn rises by 10% year after year. This year's output sells for 10% more than it would have sold for last year, but the seed corn advanced at the start of the year also costs 10% more than it would have cost last year. The rate of profit—the ratio of sales revenue to costs, minus one—is consequently the same whether we use this year's or last year's input and output prices to value the seed corn and output. In other words, inflation leaves the rate of profit unchanged if the rate of inflation remains constant.

What affects the rate of profit is therefore not inflation per se, but *changes* in the rate of inflation. A rising rate of inflation causes sales revenue to increase by a greater percentage than costs increase, and thus the nominal rate of profit rises. Conversely, when the rate of inflation is falling, sales revenue increases by a smaller percentage than costs, causing the nominal rate of profit to fall. *What matters is not whether prices are rising or falling—that is, whether the rate of inflation is positive or negative—but whether the rate of inflation is rising or falling.*

Hence, productivity growth need not lead to deflation, falling prices, in order to cause the nominal rate of profit to fall. It needs to lead to disinflation, a falling rate of inflation. If this occurs, then the nominal rate of profit, just like the real value rate, must fall in relationship to the physical rate of profit, regardless of whether prices are rising or falling. Unless the physical rate rises by an amount sufficient to offset this effect, both the nominal and the real value rates of profit will decline in absolute terms as well.

The point can also be expressed in the following way. A rising MELT does not cancel out the tendency of the rate of profit to fall. It is easy to show that the rate of inflation is approximately equal to the growth rate of the MELT plus the growth rate of values.[11] Thus if the MELT grows at a constant rate, but values fall at an increasing rate as a result of a rising rate of productivity growth, the rate of inflation must decline, and the nominal rate of profit will tend to fall. Assume, for example, that the MELT increases by 6% per year while values decline by 1%. The rate of inflation is approximately equal to 5% (= 6% + (−1%)). If faster productivity growth now causes values to decline by 4% per year, the rate of inflation falls to about 2% (= 6% + (−4%)) and, all else being equal, both the nominal and real rates of profit will fall.

It is of course possible, in principle, that the growth rate of the MELT will accelerate, canceling out or more than canceling out this effect. However, there is no inherent reason that it should do so.[12] A rising MELT reflects built-in or exogenous inflation, inflation that arises because of factors other than productivity growth.

7.4.3 A Rising-MELT Example

To see all of this more clearly, let us introduce one change into our example: the MELT increases by 20% per year. Since the MELT equals 1 at the start of Year 1, for instance, it equals 1.2 at the end. Instead of the constant-MELT prices of Table 7.4, we now have the new prices of Table 7.5 that reflect this 20% growth. (The nominal prices equal the values of Table 7.4 times the MELT. To obtain the total value figures, we multiply the corn output figures of Table 7.1 by the output price and, to obtain the nominal value added, we subtract the sum of value transferred from the total value.)

Through Year 2, there is no productivity growth, so the value of corn remains constant. Thus the nominal price of corn increases at the same rate as the MELT, 20%. This is exogenous inflation, unrelated to productivity growth. Once productivity growth commences in Year 3, the exogenous 20% inflation persists, but the falling value of corn partially offsets this effect, causing the overall rate of inflation to decline. However, the MELT rises more rapidly than the value of corn falls, so the nominal price of corn rises continually; the overall rate of inflation remains positive.

Although the *level* of the nominal rate of profit is significantly greater than the level of the real value rate of profit given in Table 7.4, its *trend* is essentially the same. Both rates are constant through Year 2, and both fall once productivity growth begins. The reason why both rates of profit fall is that, as I stressed above, the rate of inflation falls both when the MELT is constant and when it increases at a constant percentage rate. That the price of corn falls in one case and rises in the other is irrelevant.

The exact relationship between the nominal and real rates is

$$1 + r_{nom} = (1 + g_m)(1 + r_{real})$$

where r_{nom} and r_{real} are the nominal and real rates of profit and g_m is the growth rate of the MELT. In Year 1, for instance, we have 1.50 = (1.20)(1.25), while in Year 4 we have 1.40 = (1.20)(1.167). This relationship holds true in all cases in

Table 7.5. Temporalist Value/Price Rate of Profit, Given the Law of Value & 20% Annual Growth of MELT

Year	p_{in} *	$C = c$ $= VT =$ $p_{in} \times SC$	$NV = s =$ $TV - VT$	$TV =$ $p_{out} \times CO$	ROP $= s/C$	$MELT_{out}$	$p_{out} =$ $MELT_{out} \times v_{out}$	Rate of Inflation $(p_{out} - p_{in})/p_{in}$
1	5.000	320	160	480	**50.0%**	1.200	6.000	20.0%
2	6.000	480	240	720	**50.0%**	1.440	7.200	20.0%
3	7.200	720	317	1037	**44.0%**	1.728	7.975	10.8%
4	7.975	1037	415	1452	**40.0%**	2.074	8.294	4.0%

* The input price equals the prior year's output price. Year 1's input price is given.

which there is no fixed capital, and a similar relationship obtains when fixed capital is present. Thus, if the MELT increases at a more or less constant rate, the nominal price rate of profit will closely track the real value rate. Whether the *level* of the MELT is constant or not makes no difference.

7.5 Recent Physicalist-Simultaneist Responses

Although temporalist critiques of the Okishio theorem were published as far back as 1982 (Ernst 1982), it was not until fifteen years later that they generated a response from simultaneist authors. This section surveys and comments upon the major responses that have appeared in recent years—contributions by David Laibman and Duncan Foley in two successive symposia published in *Research in Political Economy*,[13] and a more recent paper by Roberto Veneziani (2004). I shall first focus on the economic issues, and then on the debate over the logical status of the Okishio theorem.

7.5.1 The *Research in Political Economy* Symposia

In his lead paper in the first symposium, Laibman's (1999a: 216–17) key argument was that the falling rate of profit exhibited in Kliman (1996) depended crucially on the paper's assumption that there is fixed capital which lasts forever. Laibman claimed that if there is any depreciation or premature scrapping of old, less productive, fixed capital: (1) productivity will increase, which will cause the value rate of profit to *rise*; (2) the value rate of profit will therefore "converge toward" the physical rate of profit; and thus (3) the value rate "is governed by" the physical rate. He also argued that (4) there is only one case in which the failure of employment to increase will cause the value rate to fall toward zero over time, the case in which "capitalists continually accumulate capital stocks that . . . produce no output" (Laibman 1999a: 222).

Foley's paper opened with the statement that "I find David Laibman's thoughtful critique . . . convincing and clarifying. . . . [T]he TSS arguments cannot sustain some of the more extreme conclusions claimed for them, particularly the 'refutation' of Okishio's Theorem" (Foley 1999: 229). He then presented an algebraic example, and concluded from it that "[c]ontinuing technical change can depress the monetary rate of profit below the material [i.e. physical] rate of profit" (Foley 1999: 232). This conclusion is of course the essence of the temporalist case against the Okishio theorem. Yet Foley (1999: 232) held that it "confirms Laibman's analysis," since "the two [rates of profit] do not diverge asymptotically."

What "do not diverge asymptotically" means is that there is a maximum amount by which the two rates will differ. For instance, if rising productivity growth causes the physical rate of profit to rise from 25% to a maximum level of 50%, while causing the value/price rate to fall from 25% to a minimum level of 0%,[14] the two rates have not diverged asymptotically. It is extremely difficult to see how this result (which is, in any case, specific to Foley's example) can possibly be construed as confirmation of the notion that the physical rate of profit governs the value/price rate, much less as a confirmation of the Okishio theorem. Since the theorem states that technological changes of a certain type can *never* cause the price rate of profit to fall, a single example that exhibits even the slightest, most ephemeral, fall in the price rate would be sufficient to disprove it.

These and other arguments were answered in Freeman and Kliman's (2000) lead paper in the next year's symposium. In his response, Laibman chose not to defend his claims (1) through (4) of the previous year. He instead put forward a "Temporal-Value Profit-Rate Tracking Theorem" that he described as "propos[ing] that r_v [the value rate of profit] must *eventually* follow the trend of r_m [the material rate of profit]" (Laibman 2000: 275, emphasis in original). However, his theorem itself says nothing of the sort. In fact, it constitutes an implicit acknowledgement that his earlier claims were incorrect.

The "Tracking Theorem" states, in part: "If the material rate [of profit] *rises* to an asymptote, the value rate either *falls* to an asymptote, or first *falls and then rises* to an asymptote permanently below the material rate" (Laibman 2000: 274, emphases added). This statement, which is very similar to Foley's "do not diverge asymptotically" conclusion, contradicts claims (1) through (3) as well as Laibman's characterization of the "Tracking Theorem." If the physical rate of profit rises forever, while the value rate of profit falls forever, the value rate is certainly not following the trend of the physical rate, not even eventually.[15]

Foley's response was quite different. He now accepted the crux of the temporalist refutation of the Okishio theorem—the price and value rates of profit can fall under circumstances in which the theorem says that "the" rate of profit cannot fall: "I understand Freeman and Kliman to be arguing that Okishio's theorem as literally stated is wrong because it is possible for the money and labor rates of profit to fall under the circumstances specified in its hypotheses. I accept their examples as establishing this possibility" (Foley 2000b: 282).

7.5.2 Veneziani's Critique

More recently, Veneziani (2004: 107–12) has also challenged the temporalist disproofs of the Okishio theorem. From a logical point of view, his critique is an advance over earlier ones. Laibman and Foley (and others, in unpublished works) had put forward examples which showed, on the basis of the theorem's premises, that labor-saving technological changes *need not always* cause the rate of profit to fall. Yet since the theorem states that such technological changes *cannot ever* cause the rate of profit to fall, the exhibition of even a single falling-rate-of-profit example is sufficient to refute it. Subsequent rising-rate-of-profit examples are irrelevant, as Veneziani (2004: 109) recognizes. Thus, instead of offering such an example, he tries to demonstrate that the temporalist refutations of the Okishio theorem are not robust, that they depend crucially upon scenarios that are impossible, or almost impossible.

Two of his four objections are criticisms of the assumption in Kliman (1996) that the MELT remains constant. Veneziani (2004: 110–12) suggests that this assumption plays a critical role in the temporalist refutation of the Okishio theorem. As I showed in section 7.4, this is not the case.

Veneziani (2004: 109, emphasis in original) also contends that "Kliman's (1996) conclusions may have some analytical support *only* in the implausible, singular case" assumed in my paper: the case in which the amount of living labor needed to produce a unit of output approaches zero over time. Although Veneziani calls this case implausible, *any other assumption implies that labor productivity cannot increase beyond a certain point*. If, for example, the amount of labor needed to produce a unit of output continually falls over time from 1000 hours to 1 hour, but cannot decline any further, then an hour of labor can never yield more than 1 unit of output—not now, and not at any time in the future. It seems to me that this is the implausible, singular case. There is certainly no evidence that the level of aggregate productivity has ever run up against such an insurmountable barrier.

Veneziani's (2004: 109) remaining objection is that my paper assumed that capitalists are "compelled to invest according to a fixed rule, regardless of what happens to the price of output and to the profitability of investment." He does not elaborate further, and his point is unclear. If he is claiming that I assumed that capitalists introduce new technologies regardless of profitability considerations, he is incorrect. I employed the Okishio theorem's own decision rule: they introduce those new technologies that will boost their rates of profit if prices and the real wage rate remain constant (Kliman 1996: 219).

Yet Veneziani may be suggesting that if the rate of profit falls, capital accumulation will slow down, which in turn will cause the rate of profit to rise. This is quite possible, but it is difficult to see how it affects "the robustness of TSS results" (Veneziani 2004: 109). Slower accumulation causes a slowdown in productivity growth, and the latter slowdown is what leads to the subsequent rise in the rate of profit. There is nothing here to support the notion that the rate of profit is physically determined; as before, the rate of productivity growth and the rate of profit tend to move in *opposite* directions. Moreover, the cyclical behavior of the rate of profit accords with the LTFRP. As I discussed in chapter 2 and reiterated earlier in this chapter, Marx did not predict a falling long-run trend in the rate of profit. He argued that the falling tendency of the rate of profit leads to economic crises, which in turn create conditions that cause the rate of profit to rise (see Marx 1991a, chap. 15, esp. pp. 362–64).

7.5.3 The Logical Status of the Okishio Theorem

I noted above that Foley has come to accept the *substance* of the temporalist disproofs of the Okishio theorem. Yet he refrained from drawing the conclusion that the theorem is false, because "I personally think Okishio thought he was stating and proving" that the *physical* rate of profit cannot fall unless real wages rise (Foley 2000b: 281). Laibman (2000: 275, emphases in original) defended the logical status of the Okishio theorem in the same way, though more forcefully: "If a viable technical change is made, and the real wage rate is constant, *the new MATERIAL rate of profit must be higher than the old one.* That is all that Okishio, or Roemer, or Foley, or I, or anyone else has ever claimed!" In other words, the proponents of the Okishio theorem have always been talking about the simultaneist rate of profit, and nothing else. They have simply told us how the rate of profit *would* behave in the imaginary special case in which input and output prices happened for some reason to be equal.[16]

I find all of this extremely implausible, to say the least. As Freeman and I noted in our rejoinder (Kliman and Freeman 2000: 290), these claims seem simply to be "an effort to absolve the physicalist tradition of error." The LTFRP is clearly not based on an imaginary case in which input and output prices are equal. In his presentation of the law, Marx (1991a : 332–38) analyzes the fall in prices resulting from productivity growth at considerable length. Moreover, the law clearly assumes continuous technological progress (Marx: 1991a: 318–19), a factor that continually counteracts any tendency of input prices and output prices to equalize.

Let us therefore ask:

- Could Okishio have intended his theorem to refer exclusively to what would happen under imaginary conditions that differ so radically from those that Marx's law assumes?
- Could he have thought that such a theorem had any bearing upon the LTFRP, much less that it constituted a refutation?
- Have commentators throughout the last three decades really been claiming that failure to accept such an irrelevant theorem as a definitive refutation of the LTFRP "has done much damage to the intellectual credentials of Marxian political economy"? (Howard and King 1992: xiii).
- Have Brenner (1998: 11–12, n1) and many others really invoked the Okishio theorem as "proof[ ]" that Marx's theory of the falling rate of profit is false, while knowing perfectly well that the theorem is irrelevant?

- Have the commentators really been claiming that the LTFRP deserves to be "relegated to the dust bin of history" (Hahnel 2005:58) by a theorem that pertains only to a different rate of profit from Marx's?

Here is a far more plausible explanation. Okishio and others set out to prove a theorem on Marx's actual LTFRP. They noted that he had assumed the re-establishment of an equilibrium rate of profit after a technological innovation occurs. They recognized that the tendency of prices to adjust to their equilibrium levels is what gives rise to the tendency of rates of profit to equilibrate as well.[17] They then concluded, reasonably but wrongly, that if an equilibrium rate of profit is to be re-established after a technological change, an "equilibrium" price level (the equality of input and output prices) must also be achieved. This error then went mostly undetected and uncorrected—and later, the corrections were ignored—probably because of factors such as ignorance, physicalist intuitions, political opposition to the LTFRP, the quest for academic respectability, etc. And all along, everyone has understood that "the equilibrium rate of profit cannot fall" refers to *Marx's* equilibrium rate of profit.

Yet even if we suppose, for the sake of argument, that the Okishio theorem was not originally meant to be a theorem on Marx's rate of profit, that is certainly what it is now, for that is how it is now understood. And as a theorem on Marx's rate of profit, the Okishio theorem is simply false; the recent debates have made this clear. The record should be set straight, and Marx's critics should do their part to help set it straight.

Notes

1. "The progressive tendency for the rate of profit to fall is thus simply *the expression, peculiar to the capitalist mode of production*, of the progressive development of the social productivity of labour" (Marx 1991a: 319, emphasis in original). "The profit rate does not fall because labour becomes less productive but rather because it becomes more productive" (Marx 1991a: 347). "The rate of profit . . . falls, not because labour becomes less productive, but because it becomes more productive" (Marx 1989b: 73).

2. I am referring here to the fact that increases in productivity can cause the nominal rate of profit to fall. Strictly speaking, the LTFRP pertains to the real rate of profit (i.e., the value or price rate of profit based on the prices that would exist if the MELT were to remain constant). Thus, although I shall exhibit a falling nominal rate of profit, it is *unnecessary* to do so in order to vindicate the internal coherence of the LTFRP as formulated by Marx.

3. Models which show that, in some case, rates of profit converge to a static equilibrium level do not address this issue. When the rates of profit converge, so do the rates at which commodities exchange for one another, but this does not mean that input and output prices equalize. If, for instance, all prices continually rise or fall by the same percentage, then the rates at which commodities exchange will be constant over time. Some general equilibrium models do yield an equality of input and output prices, but only by

making some extremely implausible assumptions (perfect foresight, perfect forward markets for everything, and no time preferences), not by demonstrating that economic behavior leads to this result.

4. There is arguably an exception: in the Sraffian model of joint production, an increase in productivity can cause the physicalist-simultaneist rate of profit to fall (Salvadori 1981). It is highly doubtful, however, that joint production exists in the Sraffian sense. For example, the production of beef and the production of beef by-products split off, after a certain stage, into two distinct processes (see Mirowski 1988: 182). In any case, Salvadori's work does not vindicate Marx's LTFRP, since it does not show that a fall in the rate of profit can result from a decline in prices or in the rate of inflation.

5. See Kliman (1996: 209–210, 219–20) for further discussion of this issue.

6. On the other hand, the theorem precludes none of these assumptions, so the example will in fact disprove it. For a disproof of the theorem in the context of fixed capital, see Kliman (1996). For a disproof in the context of multiple sectors, see Kliman and McGlone (1999). The examples in both papers assume that workers' and capitalists' consumption is positive. Moreover, neither of those examples assumes that all output is invested, a feature of the present example that increases the extent to which the actual rate of profit falls below the physical rate.

7. Here and below, value and price figures are rounded to the nearest dollar.

8. The reason why profit is reduced when the depreciation expense is increased for this purpose is that the product's price remains unchanged, all else being equal. In other words, the increase in the depreciation expense does not cause more value to be transferred to the product. This is because the value and the price of the product depend upon its *currently necessary* cost of production. A portion of the original cost of an asset, bought in the past at one price, is not currently necessary if the asset's price has since fallen.

9. Milios et al. (2002: 154; 157, n9) endorse Laibman's claim, without explaining why and without responding to our rebuttal, even though they cite the paper that contains it. Yet Laibman's argument is the sole basis for their conclusion that the temporalist refutation of the Okishio theorem is "of low significance."

10. In section 7.4.3, I will show that even if increases in productivity growth only lead to a fall in the rate of inflation, not a fall in the actual price level, the actual rate of profit will still decline relative to the physical rate.

11. If $A = B \times C$, the growth rate of A is approximately equal to the growth rate of B plus the growth rate of C. Since the level of prices equals the MELT times the level of real values, it follows that the growth rate of prices, i.e. the inflation rate, is approximately equal to the growth rate of the MELT plus the growth rate of real values.

12. Even if the growth rate of the MELT does increase enough to cancel out the tendency of the nominal rate of profit to fall, it does not follow that the LTFRP has been negated. It is possible, even likely, that some combination of rising government debt burdens and easy credit conditions is what is causing the MELT to rise more quickly. In that case, I have suggested, the crisis tendencies that result from productivity growth have not been negated, but only displaced. Instead of crises in which goods cannot sell, or can sell only at reduced prices, we are likely to experience debt crises and fiscal crises of the state (Kliman 2003: 127–28).

13. Laibman (1999a, 1999b, 2000), Foley (1999, 2000b). The temporalist contributions to the symposia are Freeman (1999), Kliman (1999b), Freeman and Kliman (2000), and Kliman and Freeman (2000).

14. This is what would eventually occur in the example of sections 7.3 and 7.4 if net output always continued to rise by 50% per year while employment always remained constant and all output was always invested.

15. Claim (4) is implicitly contradicted by the "Tracking Theorem's" next point, which says nothing about capital stocks that produce no output: "The value rate falls to zero only under extreme and unlikely assumptions: all output invested, constant labor force, material rate rising to an asymptote, and the production turnover period equal to the technical change period" (Laibman 2000: 274). This claim was subsequently refuted as well (see Kliman and Freeman 2000: 292).

16. Veneziani (2004: 107) gives a different reason for not accepting that the Okishio theorem has been disproved: "all TSS 'refutations' are based on patent violations of the formal assumptions of [the Okishio theorem]." Curiously, he does not bother to tell us which assumptions he is referring to, nor why he thinks they have been violated.

17. As we saw above, Roemer (1981: 97–98) wrote that "what the theorem says is that after prices have readjusted to equilibrate the rate of profit again, the new rate of profit will be higher than the old rate."

Chapter 8

The "Transformation Problem" (1): Marx's Solution and Its Critics

8.1 Significance of the "Transformation Problem" and the Value-Price Relationship

The term "transformation problem" generally refers to the alleged internal inconsistency in Marx's account of the transformation of commodity values into production prices in chapter 9 of *Capital*, volume III. All too often, Marx's account and his critics' objections have been presented in a needlessly abstruse and technical fashion that obscures, rather than illuminates, their real significance. Partly because of this, the controversy has frequently been dismissed as a tempest in a teapot. Before proceeding further, I wish to indicate briefly why I believe that it should not be so dismissed.

First, the transformation controversy is important because the internal inconsistency issue is important. The claim that chapter 9 of volume III contains a demonstrated error that invalidates Marx's results is one of the most potent weapons in the arsenal of those who seek to suppress his work. This alleged error is also the basis upon which his Marxist and Sraffian critics claim that their simultaneist-physicalist models are corrected versions of his account of the transformation, rather than alternative accounts. Thus the transformation controversy has a profound ideological significance, quite apart from the substantive theoretical issues at stake.

As I noted in section 3 of chapter 1, the "transformation problem" has often been dismissed on the ground that Marx had little interest in explaining how prices are determined. I agree that he was not very interested in this issue *per se*, yet price determination is inseparable from other matters that were certainly of great concern to him. For instance, he wished to explain where profit comes from and what determines its magnitude. But since price is cost plus profit, and profit is price minus cost, the theory of price determination is essentially the same as the theory of profit determination. Thus, if Marx's argument that total price equals total value is logically invalid, so is his argument that total profit equals total surplus-value, and this seriously jeopardizes his theory that the exploitation of workers in capitalist production is the exclusive source of profit.

Marx's law of the tendential fall in the rate of profit (LTFRP) is also inseparable from price determination. The rate of profit depends upon prices just as much as the absolute magnitude of profit does. As we saw in chapter 7, the LTFRP depends crucially upon the tendency of prices (or the rate of inflation) to fall as productivity increases. As Marx explicitly noted, moreover, his account of the transformation—particularly its conclusion that the average "price" and "value" rates of profit are equal—is the basis upon which he derived the LTFRP:

> But it was also shown that considering the sum total of the capitals . . . the total capital of the capitalist class, the average rate of profit is nothing other than total surplus value related to and calculated on this total capital . . . . Here, therefore, we once again stand on firm ground, where, without entering into the competition of the many capitals, we can derive the general law directly from the general nature of capital as so far developed. This law, and it is the most important law of political economy, is that the rate of profit has a tendency to fall with the progress of capitalist production. [Marx 1991b: 104, emphasis omitted.]

Thus Marx's account of the transformation of values into prices of production is the "firm ground" upon which the LTFRP rests. But if that account is not in fact firm ground—if, as a century of criticism has supposedly proved, it is logically invalid—then so is the LTFRP.

At the most basic level, the issue of transformation has to do with how values are related to real-world prices. One might ask why this is even worth discussing. Why not jettison the "metaphysical" notion of value altogether, as neoclassical, Sraffian, and analytical Marxian economists do? Why not simply explain how real-world prices are determined, and theorize in terms of them?

Part of the answer is that Marx's value theory does address how real-world prices are determined. As I have noted, when Marx argued that productivity increases cause commodities' values to fall, this was his way of singling out changes in productivity as a key determinant of changes in real-world prices. One can, of course, dispense with the *word* "value" and still theorize the inverse relationship between prices and productivity. Yet if one abandons Marx's *concept* of value in favor of physicalism, then, as section 7.3.4 showed, one must also abandon the notion that productivity increases tend to reduce prices (or the rate of inflation).

Another part of the answer is that value is not "metaphysical" in the sense that the critics mean. The distinction between value and price exists in real life.

Whenever we ask whether we've gotten our money's worth, or gotten a "good value," we are asking whether the value of the thing we've bought was not, in fact, less than the price we paid.

But am I not resorting to clever wordplay? Doesn't the term "value" here refer to utility, use-value, rather than what Marx meant by value—something akin to but distinct from and regulative of price? To see that this is not the case, consider Marx's (1989b: 336) observation that "The most ordinary merchant does not believe that he is getting the same value for his £1 when he receives 1 qr of wheat for it in a period of famine and in a period of glut." Even this "ordinary merchant" realizes that he has received more value in exchange for his £1 in a period of famine, and less value in a period of glut, *even though he has received the same amount of wheat and the utility of the wheat is the same in both cases.* Since the value of the wheat varies, though its price and utility do not, it is clear that value is distinct from both price and utility.

One might perhaps argue that we only think of them as distinct, that the unobserved "value" exists only in our minds. Actually, Marx himself affirmed that value is a mental construct.[1] But our mental constructs are part of the real world. We base many of our actions on the value construct, for instance when we buy items if and only if they "are worth as much" or more than they cost. (As much or more *what?*) Moreover, the mere fact that value is unobserved does not imply that value relations lack a constitutive or regulatory role. The nature, causes, and effects of this mental construct are thus worthy of theorization and explanation.

8.2 Marx's Resolution of the Classicists' Problem

The classical political economists subscribed to what Marx called the "law of value," yet they also subscribed to the notion that competition tends to equalize rates of profit. These two notions seem at first to be incompatible. Since the law of value implies that the amount of value generated depends upon the amount of labor performed, it also seems to imply that rates of profit do not tend to equalize. Instead, it seems to imply that industries which employ a relatively large number of workers will tend to reap above-average rates of profit, while industries which employ a relatively small number of workers will tend to suffer from below-average profitability.

The classical school did not resolve this conundrum. Marx (1989b: 258–373) argued that its failure to do so led to its "disintegration." Given the immense importance of the law of value to his own critique of political economy, he realized that it was his task to come up with a "solution of this apparent contradiction" (Marx 1990a: 421).

Marx solved it in a simple, straightforward manner. The essence of his solution is that the total amount of profit in the economy is the same when prices adjust to equalize rates of profit as when they reflect commodities' actual values (i.e. the amounts of labor required to produce them). The total profit is simply distributed differently. Accordingly, the total amount of sales revenue received throughout the economy—total price—is also unchanged, merely distributed differently, in the two cases. Thus, although the law of value would seem to be falsified if we were to confine our attention to individual industries, it holds true as a law pertaining to the *aggregate* economy.[2]

Chapter 9 of volume III contains little explanation or justification of Marx's claim that the total amount of profit is unchanged. However, a passage in a subsequent chapter provides a key to his thinking. Arguing that interest, the profit of industrial capitalists, and the profit of commercial firms all stem from the same source—surplus labor—he writes, "The ratio in which profit is divided, and the different legal titles by which this division takes place, already assume that profit is ready-made and presuppose its existence. . . . Profit is produced before this division takes place, and before there can be any talk of it" (Marx 1991a: 503–504). The temporalist character of Marx's reasoning is striking. If profit is produced *before* outputs go to market, then competition, whether between lending institutions and other kinds of capitalist firms, or between capitalists in different industries, cannot alter the total amount of profit that already exists. What's done is done. (A downturn in the economy may prevent all of the profit from being realized, of course, but that is a different matter, since it is the downturn in the economy, not competition, that has prevented all of the profit from being realized.)

Chapter 5 of volume I provides another key to Marx's thinking. He argued there and earlier (Marx 1990a: 260; cf. Marx 1973: 213, Marx 1990a: 220) that a commodity's price, and not only its value, is determined "before it enters into circulation"—that is, before it goes to market. The sale of the commodity realizes the price but does not determine its magnitude. (I take this to mean that production and demand conditions determine the "real" price, but haggling in the market does not.) Given this premise, Marx shows that exchange is a zero-sum game. If a commodity is sold for more than its "real" price, the seller's gain is exactly offset by the buyer's loss. The total amount of value in existence remains unchanged. This is so even if all commodities sell for more than they are worth. In the aggregate, the amount of value that commodity owners gain as sellers is the amount that they lose as buyers.

In order to understand Marx's solution to the classicists' problem, the above is sufficient. However, familiarity with some of the details is necessary in order to understand and evaluate the charges of internal inconsistency that have been leveled against his solution.

Marx constructed an example in which the economy consists of five branches (industries) and production requires fixed capital, means of production that last more than one production period. Although the following example, of a two-branch economy without fixed capital, is somewhat simpler, it alters none

Table 8.1. Marx's Solution

Branch	c	v	s	w	π	p	$s/(c+v)$	$\pi/(c+v)$
1	54	6	12	72	15	75	20%	25%
2	16	4	8	28	5	25	40%	25%
Total	70	10	20	100	20	100	25%	25%

of the controversial features of Marx's solution. Since there is no fixed capital, the capital advanced in each branch equals the cost price of its output. As in Marx's example, the figures refer to a particular "year, or . . . any other period of time" (Marx 1991a: 258), and the rate of surplus-value is the same in both branches.

Chapter 9 of volume III does not indicate explicitly the units in which price and value figures are measured. This has given rise to a controversy that I shall discuss below. In order not to prejudge the issue, the present example does not specify whether the value and price figures are sums of money or sums of labor-time.[3] In Table 8.1 and below, c, v, and s stand for constant capital, variable capital, and surplus-value, $w \equiv c + v + s$ is the value of output, π is average profit, and $p = c + v + \pi$ is the output's price of production. $s/(c + v)$ and $\pi/(c + v)$ are the value and price rates of profit.

It is important to stress that, in keeping with Marx's solution, the sums of constant and variable capital (and the surplus-values) are *data*, specified at the start. The only derived magnitudes are the prices, profits, and price rates of profit. As we shall see below, this is a key difference between Marx's solution and his critics' "corrections" of it.

If the year's outputs were sold at their actual values, then $s/(c+v)$ would be the rate of profit, and the two branches would obtain unequal rates of profit. But if competition has resulted in an equalized rate of profit, Marx argues—and this is the crux of his solution—that the total surplus-value produced throughout the economy is distributed among the branches in proportion to the sizes of their capital advances $(c + v)$. Each branch thus receives what he calls an average profit. Since the capital advanced in Branch 1 is $54 + 6 = 60$, and this is three-fourths of the total capital advanced throughout the economy $(70 + 10 = 80)$, Branch 1 receives a profit equal to three-fourths of the twenty units of surplus-value produced in the economy as a whole—that is, fifteen units rather than the twelve units of surplus-value actually produced in Branch 1. Similarly, the capital advanced in Branch 2 is one-fourth of the economy-wide total, and so Branch 2 receives a profit of five units, one-fourth of the total surplus-value, though it produced a surplus-value of eight units. The rate of profit based on the profit actually received is thus $\pi/(c + v) = 25\%$ in both branches.

Marx's *three aggregate value-price equalities* follow immediately from his conception that competition leads to a different distribution of the surplus-value without altering the total amount already produced:

- total profit equals total surplus value
- total price equals total value
- the aggregate "price" rate of profit equals the aggregate "value" rate of profit

In Marx's view, these aggregate equalities were immensely significant. They confirmed both the law of value and his theory that all profit has its origin in the exploitation of workers:

> the law of value [is not] affected by the fact that the equalization of profit . . . gives rise to governing average prices for commodities that diverge from their individual values. This . . . affects only the addition of surplus-value to the various commodity prices; it does not abolish surplus-value itself, nor the total value of commodities as the source of these various price components. [Marx 1991a : 985]

8.3 Böhm-Bawerk's Critique

Two years after volume III appeared, Böhm-Bawerk, a prominent member of the Austrian school of economics, polemicized against Marx's solution. Böhm-Bawerk's critique has been very influential among mainstream economists, since it reflects their view that only price and profit, not value and surplus-value, matter in the real world. It has also been very influential among non-economists, probably because it is simpler than the subsequent critiques put forth by physicalist-simultaneist authors. Particularly since Samuelson (1971: 423) dismissed it, however, the specialist literature has all but ignored Böhm-Bawerk's critique. I take it up here for two reasons. First, non-specialists frequently conflate and confuse it with the critiques of Bortkiewicz and later simultaneists, so it is important to uncouple them. Second, I shall use Böhm-Bawerk's critique and Postone's (1993) counter-critique to illustrate a point I made in section 1.3: allegations of a "transformation problem" cannot properly be waved away by arguing that the critics misunderstand Marx's intentions.

Böhm-Bawerk's critique differs from subsequent ones, above all, because he did *not* claim that Marx's solution was internally inconsistent. On the contrary, he wrote that "it is quite true that the total price paid for the entire national produce coincides exactly with the total amount of value or labor incorporated in it" (Böhm-Bawerk 1984: 36). When he claimed that *Capital* is self-contradictory, he instead meant that "Marx's third volume contradicts the first"

(Böhm-Bawerk 1984: 36). The alleged contradiction to which he refers is not within chapter 9 of volume III, but between it and volume I.

Böhm-Bawerk (1984: 28) argued that Marx had claimed in volume I that commodities tend to sell at their values, at least in the long run, and he had promised to reconcile this proposition with the proposition that commodities tend to sell at their prices of production. (This was Böhm-Bawerk's reading of Marx's (1990a: 421) reference to his forthcoming "solution of this apparent contradiction.") But chapter 9 of volume III simply reproduced the contradiction between these propositions, reconciling nothing.

It is important to stress that Böhm-Bawerk was discussing contradictory propositions because, as we shall see, Postone overlooks this fact. Near the start of his chapter on "The Question of the Contradiction," Böhm-Bawerk (1984: 28–29) refers to "the actual incompatibility of these two propositions" and calls them "two irreconcilable propositions."

The reason why Böhm-Bawerk denied that Marx had reconciled the law of value with real-world prices was that he believed that the deviation of individual prices from values is all that matters. The equality of the aggregates does not. "[T]he chief object of the 'law of value' . . . is *nothing else than* the elucidation of the exchange relations as they actually appear to us. . . . It is plain that Marx himself so conceives the explanatory object of the law of value" (Böhm-Bawerk 1984: 34, emphasis added). Although it is "quite true" that total price equals total value, it is also irrelevant, because it has nothing to do with "the exchange relations," the rates at which goods exchange. Böhm-Bawerk's point was that Marx tells us that goods A and B together sell for $3, while the question here is instead whether A sells for $2 and B sells for $1, or whether A sells for $1 and B for $2.

Moreover, Böhm-Bawerk (1984: 35) argued, Marx's solution is not even an answer to a different question, but a "simple tautology." The statement that the total price of A and B is $3 is meaningless, since "commodities do eventually exchange with commodities—when one penetrates the disguises due to the use of money." Once we abstract from money, we see that the total price of A and B is nothing other than A and B themselves.

Böhm-Bawerk's interpretive practice was unsound. His interpretation of what Marx meant when he promised to solve the "apparent contradiction" was very implausible. Could Marx, who held a doctoral degree in philosophy, really have promised to show that "commodities tend to sell at their values" and "commodities do not tend to sell at their values" are not really, but only apparently, contradictory propositions? Given the implausibility of this interpretation, and especially its inability to make sense of Marx's solution, Böhm-Bawerk should have searched for a more successful interpretation. There is no evidence in his text that he did so.

The direct textual evidence also indicates that his interpretation was quite weak. He quoted several snippets—never even a complete sentence—of volume

I out of context and paraphrased a few others (Böhm-Bawerk 1984: 12–13, 29–30), interpreting them as claims that commodities tend to sell at their values. I could provide alternative interpretations of these snippets that I find much more plausible, but the better part of a chapter would be required.

There are, moreover, two passages in volume I—pointed out by Hilferding (1984: 156–57) in his 1904 response to Böhm-Bawerk—in which Marx states categorically that commodities do not sell at their values, even on average. At the end of chapter 5, when he first invokes the assumption that commodities sell at their values, Marx cautions that they do not do so in reality, even in the long run. "How can we account for the origin of capital on the assumption that prices are regulated by the average price [price of production], i.e. ultimately by the value of commodities? I say 'ultimately' because average prices do not directly coincide with the values of commodities, as Adam Smith, Ricardo, and others believe" (Marx 1990a: 269, n24).

In chapter 9 he notes, "We have in fact assumed that prices = values. We shall, however, see in Volume 3 that even in the case of average prices the assumption cannot be made in this very simple manner" (Marx 1990a: 329, n9). These statements strongly suggest that the alleged contradiction between what Marx claimed in volume I and what he conceded in volume III is nonexistent.

Another aspect of Böhm-Bawerk's critique is seriously flawed as well. His conclusion that the equality of total price and total value is tautological rests entirely on his very controversial premise that money is an inessential veil. Marx did not accept that premise, nor did Keynes, nor do his followers. Böhm-Bawerk put forth an argument to support it, but did not really prove it, especially because the fact that commodities "eventually" exchange with other commodities does not mean that money and value play no other essential roles, apart from the exchange process. Consider the gross domestic product (GDP). If it is a meaningful concept—and in some sense it must be, since businesses and governments respond to its ups and downs—then so is total price, since the GDP is simply the difference between total price and expenditures on "intermediate inputs." Böhm-Bawerk was entitled to his theory that money is a veil, but in the absence of conclusive proof that Marx's contrary theory was false, he was not entitled to declare Marx's solution tautological.

8.4 Postone's Counter-Critique

Postone presents the whole of the transformation controversy as a controversy surrounding Böhm-Bawerk's critique. This creates the impression that Postone's rebuttal is a response to both the allegation of internal inconsistency *within* chapter 9 of volume III and the allegation of contradiction *between* volumes I and III. In fact, Postone does not discuss the former allegation directly, nor does he refer to anything written on the transformation controversy after 1942. He says only that much of the controversy "has suffered from the assumption that Marx intended to write a critical political economy," especially the assumption that he "intended to operationalize the law of value in order to explain the workings of the market" (Postone 1993: 133). The remainder of Postone's discussion consists of his contrary interpretation of Marx's intentions.

By itself, a discussion of Marx's intentions does not refute the internal inconsistency allegation. Postone does not call his discussion a refutation, but what then is its actual purpose? An internally inconsistent argument is no more consistent after the author's intentions are clarified than it was before. And if, because of such inconsistency, the intended conclusion cannot be sustained, why do the author's intentions matter?[4] The claims that *Capital* is internally inconsistent need to be taken seriously, and taken for what they actually are—not elements of a discourse on Marx's *intentions* or *method*, but an attempt to discredit his *arguments*.

Even when Postone's discussion is read exclusively as a response to Böhm-Bawerk, it fails to address his actual charge of contradiction. Postone emphasizes the importance of the distinction between essence and appearance to Marx's understanding of the value-price relationship. Marx wished to show that price is the form of appearance of an essence, namely value. Since appearances "both express and veil" the essence, express it in a distorted form, the "divergence of prices from values should . . . be understood as integral to, rather than as a logical contradiction within, Marx's analysis" (Postone 1993: 134).[5]

This is all true, I believe, but it completely misconstrues Böhm-Bawerk's critique. He did not claim that Marx's analysis was logically contradictory because prices diverge from values. Rather, as we saw above, Böhm-Bawerk claimed that it was logically contradictory because Marx, in volume I, had *both affirmed and denied* the proposition that prices diverge from values. In other words, Marx had asserted that the proposition and its negation were only apparently contradictory, and he had promised to substantiate that assertion, but he failed to do so.

It is very doubtful, moreover, that Böhm-Bawerk's charge of contradiction stems from a failure to appreciate the distinction between essence and appearance, or its importance to Marx's value theory. Böhm-Bawerk (1984: 101) complained that while Marx's "formal dialectic[al] . . . system runs in one direction, facts go in another." He also stressed that the chief object of the law of value is to elucidate prices "*as they actually appear to us*" (Böhm-Bawerk 1984: 34, emphasis added).

What is at issue, then, is whether or not the law of value actually elucidates the real-world facts. Postone shows that Marx intended to demonstrate that it does so, but no one questions that point. To answer Böhm-Bawerk, one needs to show that Marx actually demonstrated what he intended to demonstrate. Postone does not even try to show this, since he completely overlooks the controversies over the significance and validity of the aggregate equalities.

Putting the matter in philosophical terms, what is at issue is whether value is actually an essence that underlies price. Böhm-Bawerk in effect claimed that it is not. Postone's critique fails to refute this claim, since all he really tells us is that price differs from value. He says that this difference is a difference between appearance and essence, but that doesn't make it so. After all, price also differs from orange juice, but that does not make orange juice an essence that underlies price. To show that value is indeed the essence of price, Postone would have needed to show that Marx's understanding of the significance of the aggregate equalities was right—and that, *pace* Bortkiewicz and his successors, the aggregate value-price equalities do hold true—but he simply ignores the issue.

The crux of the problem, once again, is that Postone is discussing Marx's intentions and method when the point at issue is instead the logical consistency of his arguments. Of course, these two things may be connected: a central theme of the present book is indeed that the allegations of logical inconsistency stem from misinterpretation of Marx's intended meanings. But one must demonstrate that such a connection exists, and Postone does not.

I suspect that the misplaced emphasis on intentions and method is due in part to the influence of relativism within much of the humanities and social sciences. If our presuppositions fully determine the conclusions at which we arrive, as relativism holds, then the logic of our arguments is irrelevant; presuppositions lead to conclusions *directly*, not through logical argument.[6] If that were so, one could bypass the logic of Marx's arguments and acquit him of error simply by explaining "where he was coming from." It seems to me that this is the methodology of Postone's discussion. I do not mean to suggest that he is a relativist; his text indicates otherwise. My point is simply that, if Postone had been working in a different milieu, he might have been more cognizant of the need to respond to allegations that Marx's arguments are logically flawed.

8.5 Bortkiewicz's Proof of Internal Contradiction

Whereas Böhm-Bawerk argued that Marx's solution was tautological, simultaneist critiques hold that it is internally inconsistent; Marx's conclusions fail to follow from his theoretical premises in chapter 9 of *Capital*, volume III. The source of the supposed internal inconsistency is Marx's "failure" to value inputs—the means of production and subsistence underlying his constant and variable capital figures—and outputs simultaneously.[7] As we shall see below, the key result of Marx's solution—the three aggregate equalities—would necessarily be incorrect if this critique were sound.

8.5.1 The Proof

To this day, Bortkiewicz's (1952, 1984) papers of 1906–1907 are the only works that have really tried to *prove,* not merely assert, that the non-simultaneous character of Marx's solution leads to internal inconsistency. The difference is crucial. Advocates of a theory can ignore an assertion of inconsistency, but not a proof. If the proof turns out to be valid, they are not entitled to advocate the theory any longer.

In the second of his four essays, Bortkiewicz (1952: 7–9) constructed a numerical example of Marx's solution, on the assumption that **simple reproduction** (production on the same scale, without growth) would occur if inputs and outputs were bought and sold at their actual values. Marx himself did not assume anything about reproduction conditions, but Bortkiewicz's modification is unexceptionable, since Marx's solution was meant to hold true universally. It must therefore be viable in the special case of simple reproduction. Bortkiewicz set out to prove, to the contrary, that Marx's solution leads to a spurious breakdown of the reproduction process. In a 1942 work that endorsed Bortkiewicz's "proof" and brought it to the attention of the English-speaking world, Sweezy (1970: 113–14) explained the reasoning behind it as follows:

> If the procedure used in transforming values into prices is to be considered satisfactory, it must not result in a disruption of the conditions of Simple Reproduction. Going from value calculation to price calculation has no connection with the question [of] whether the economic system as a whole is stationary or expanding. It should be possible to make the transition without prejudicing this question one way or the other.

Table 8.2 presents an example similar to Bortkiewicz's. The only significant difference is that it depicts two consecutive periods rather than one. The physical quantities are the same in both periods. In keeping with Bortkiewicz's interpretation of Marx's solution, I assume that the per-unit values of inputs equal the per-unit values of outputs, and that Period 1's inputs are bought at their values. In other words, Period 1's constant and variable capital figures represent the *values* of means of production and means of subsistence. Departments I, II, and III produce the material elements of constant capital (means of production), the material elements of variable capital (workers' means of subsistence), and luxury goods, respectively.

For simplicity, let us assume that the value of each type of good equals $1 per unit in Period 1. Thus, the figures for w, the value of output (400, 240, and 160), are also the physical amounts of means of production, means of subsistence, and the luxury good produced in Period 1. Similarly, since inputs are bought at their values in Period 1, the figures for c, the constant-capital value

Table 8.2. Bortkiewicz's Proof of Internal Contradiction

Period	Dept.	r	c	v	s	w	π	p	$s/(c+v)$	$\pi/(c+v)$
1	I		280	72	48	400	88	440	13.6%	25.0%
	II		80	96	64	240	44	220	36.4%	25.0%
	III		40	72	48	160	28	140	42.9%	25.0%
	Total		400	240	160	800	160	800	25.0%	25.0%
2	I	66	308	66	54	428	102	476	14.4%	27.3%
	II	44	88	88	72	248	48	224	40.9%	27.3%
	III	30	44	66	54	164	30	140	49.1%	27.3%
	Total	140	440	220	180	840	180	840	27.3%	27.3%

(280, 80, and 40), are also the physical amounts of the means of production employed in each department, and the figures for v, the variable-capital value (72, 96, and 72), are also the physical amounts of the means of subsistence consumed by the workers of each department. Thus, Department I produces 400 units of the means of production, just enough to replace the 400 units used up as constant capital throughout the economy, and Department II produces 240 units of the means of subsistence, just enough to replace the 240 units that workers throughout the economy consumed.

According to Bortkiewicz, simple reproduction would take place here if the input and output prices were equal—that is, if the outputs of Period 1, like the inputs, were bought and sold at their values. He implicitly reasoned as follows. The value of Department I's output, 400, equals the total value of the means of production that were used up as constant capital (Total c), so the used-up means of production could be exactly replaced in Period 2. Similarly, the value of Department II's output, 240, equals the total value of the means of subsistence that workers consumed (Total v), so the same number of workers could be rehired, at the same wages, in Period 2. Finally, the value of output in Department III equals Total s, which means that Period 1's surplus-value is exactly enough to purchase all of the luxury goods produced in that period.

But what would happen if, as Marx assumed in chapter 9 of volume III, the outputs of Period 1 are sold at their prices of production instead of at their values? Given our assumption that the inputs were bought at their values, input and output prices would differ. Bortkiewicz claimed that this difference would prevent simple reproduction (in physical terms) from taking place.[8] If Department I's output were priced at Marx's price of production, 440, some would go unsold, since constant capital expenditures total only 400 (Total c). Thus fewer means of production would be employed in Period 2 than in Period 1, and this would cause output to contract. Conversely, there is excess demand for the output of the other two departments; Total v and Total s exceed the price of output of Departments II and III, respectively. On the basis of this argument, Bortkiewicz (1952: 9) concluded that "We have thus proved that we would involve ourselves in internal contradictions by deducing prices from values in the way in which this is done by Marx."

Bortkiewicz's (1984: 212–13) fourth essay contains a related demonstration: unless inputs and outputs are valued simultaneously, each industry's sales and purchases will fail to coincide. This implies that supplies and demands will be unequal, which is incompatible with Marx's assumption that rates of profit are equal. If exchanges took place at Marx's prices of Period 1, then, according to Bortkiewicz's argument, Department I would sell means of production to the other departments priced at 120 (IIc + IIIc), but its workers and capitalists would buy means of subsistence and luxury goods from the other departments that are worth 160 (Iv + Iπ). Department II's sales of 144 (Iv + IIIv) and purchases of 124 (IIc + IIπ), and Department III's sales of 132 (Iπ + IIπ) and purchases of 112 (IIIc + IIIv), would also fail to match.

8.5.2 The Refutation

If these arguments were valid, I would regard them as having decisively demonstrated that Marx's account of the value-price transformation, and thus his theories of value and economic crisis, are insupportable. But neither argument is valid. Simple reproduction and uniform profitability do require that supplies equal demands, but they can be equal even if the input and output prices *of Period 1* are unequal. Since the outputs of one period are the inputs of the next, what is needed in order for supplies to equal demands is that the output prices of Period 1 equal the input prices *of Period 2*. But they are always equal; the end of one period is the start of the next, so the output prices of one period necessarily equal the input prices of the next period. Once this is recognized, Bortkiewicz's proofs immediately fail, as was first demonstrated in Kliman and McGlone (1988).[9]

Recall that the physical quantities of Table 8.2 are the same in both periods. This means that simple reproduction *does* occur. The reason why the value magnitudes change is that Period 1's inputs are bought at their values, but Period 2's inputs are bought at prices that differ from these values—the prices of production that prevail at the end of Period 1. Thus Total c increases from 400 to 440 because, although the same 400 units of means of production are again employed, they now cost 440 instead of 400. Similarly, Total v falls from 240 to 220, although workers once again receive 240 units of the means of subsistence, because these means of subsistence now cost 220 instead of 240.

After advancing sums of value (c and v) sufficient to obtain the same inputs as before, but at these new prices, capitalists have residual proceeds (which Marx calls revenue, here denoted as r) left over from the sale of Period 1's outputs, which they spend on luxury goods. Since Total c, Total v, and Total r in Period 2 exactly equal the Period 1 prices of the outputs of Departments I, II, and III, respectively, the whole social product has been bought and sold at the new, changed prices. Moreover, the inputs of Period 1 have been exactly replaced, so production can resume on the same scale as before. This refutes the first of Bortkiewicz's proofs.

Also note that, in Period 2, Department I's sales (IIc + IIIc) and purchases (Iv + Ir) both total 132, as do Department II's sales (Iv + IIIv) and purchases (IIc + IIr). Department III's sales (Ir + IIr) and purchases (IIIc + IIIv) both total 110. This refutes Bortkiewicz's second proof.

We thus see that equality of input and output prices is not necessary for reproduction to take place or for supplies to equal demands. Since one period's output prices are the next period's input prices, supplies and demands in monetary terms must always be equal whenever supplies and demands are equal in physical terms, no matter how prices may have changed over the production period.

This refutation of Bortkiewicz's attempted proofs has not itself been refuted. Laibman (2004: 10), the only critic of Marx to have addressed it in print, acknowledges that Kliman and McGlone demonstrated that "Reproduction equilibrium exists between periods" even though the input and output prices differ. In other words, Bortkiewicz's proofs are invalid. Laibman's acknowledgement of this fact, embedded in a mass of objections to temporal valuation, is easy to miss, but it is there.[10]

8.6 Modern Simultaneist Critiques of Marx's Solution

During the last few decades, many simultaneist critics have put forth other reasons why the non-simultaneous character of Marx's solution supposedly renders it inconsistent. In contrast to Bortkiewicz, none of them have tried to prove their claims. They often seem to think that no proof is necessary, because the inconsistency is immediately obvious. Brewer (1995: 120), for instance, writes that it is "immediately obvious . . . that costs have to be calculated in terms of prices, not values" if outputs are sold at prices of production. Marx needed to revalue the inputs at output prices, but failed to do so.

One reason why some critics find this obvious is evidently that they presume that the dual-system interpretation is self-evident. If the constant- and variable-capital value figures of Marx's solution are based upon the values of means of production and subsistence, not their prices, these figures are no longer correct when means of production and subsistence sell at their prices of production instead of at their values. As we have seen, however, it is far from self-evident that the dual-system interpretation is right.

Another reason why Marx's solution has been judged inconsistent is that, since sale prices and purchase prices must be equal, it is supposedly obvious that input and output prices must also be equal (see, e.g., Steedman 1977: 31). Yet this notion is fatuous, as Carchedi (1984: 434–41; 2002: 169–72) has repeatedly stressed. It seems to stem in part from ignorance of the fact that Marx's solution refers to a particular accounting period ("year"), and is not a "static once-for-all equilibrium solution," as Desai (1988: 307) asserts.[11] Sale prices and purchase prices must be equal because sale and purchase occur *simultaneously*. Yet input and output prices can and usually do differ, because inputs are usually acquired *before* outputs are produced. If the price of coal changes during the day, coal bought as an input at the start of the day, and coal sold as an output at day's end, will have two different prices.

Even worse, if one denies that inputs can enter production at one price while outputs exit at a different price, one is implicitly *denying* that sale and purchase prices must be equal. Imagine that a ton of coal sells for $10 at the end of Day 1 but only $9.75 at the end of Day 2. If coal must have the same price, upon becoming an input at the start of Day 2, as coal that exits production at the end of Day 2, then its price as an input at the start of Day 2 must also be $9.75/ton. But the start of Day 2 is the end of Day 1. Hence, at the end of Day 1, a ton of coal is sold for $10 but bought for $9.75!

It also seems obvious to some critics that Marx's solution suffers from dimensional inconsistency. They take the fact that his outputs sell at *prices* of production, while the sums of *value* advanced as constant and variable capital remained unchanged, to mean that the outputs were measured in *money* terms while the inputs were measured in *labor-time* terms (e.g., Steedman 1977: 30–31). This objection is also fatuous. It seems to have arisen because, particularly from the 1970s onward, many Marxian economists began to measure prices exclusively in money terms but values exclusively in labor-time terms.[12] Yet as we saw in section 2.1.7, Marx (1990a: 188) himself noted early in volume I that there are two measures of value, labor-time *and* money. Thereafter, he regularly measured sums of value in money terms. To take just one example, from *Capital* volume I, chapter 7: "the value of the product is one-ninth greater than the value advanced to produce it; 27 shillings have been turned into 30 shillings; a surplus-value of 3 shillings has been precipitated" (Marx 1990a: 301).

Moreover, there is no evidence that Marx mixed and matched his units of measurement in chapter 9 of volume III—he did not specify any units of measurement. The very fact that he derived equalities between value and price magnitudes should suffice to demonstrate that he was implicitly measuring them in the same units; one cannot equate apples and oranges. Finally, it is worth noting that early critics of his solution, such as Böhm-Bawerk and Sweezy, did not complain about any mixing and matching of money and labor-time figures, and

Bortkiewicz (1952: 11) explicitly recognized that "Marx thought of values and prices in terms of money."

The interpretive practice of those who have called the alleged inconsistency in Marx's solution "immediately obvious" is quite shoddy. Their interpretations make his solution seem not just wrong but silly, contrary to facts that are self-evident to all. Given this problem, and given that Marx's solution had previously been understood very differently, even by its staunch critics, proponents of these interpretations should have abandoned them and searched for more plausible ones. The idea that a serious theorist could commit such ridiculous errors and *never* notice that his sale and purchase prices differ, or that his values and prices are dimensionally inconsistent, is so implausible that it is sufficient reason to reject these interpretations.

Notes

1. "[T]he basis of value is the fact that human beings relate to each other's labour as equal . . . . *This is an abstraction, like all human thought, and social relations only exist among human beings to the extent that they think, and possess this power of abstraction from sensuous individuality and contingency.* The kind of political economist who attacks the determination of value by labour-time on the ground that the work performed by 2 individuals during the same time is not absolutely equal (although in the same trade), doesn't even yet know *what distinguishes human social relations from relations between animals.* He is a beast. As beasts, the same fellows then also have no difficulty in over-looking the fact that no 2 use values are absolutely identical (no 2 leaves, Leibniz) and even less difficulty in judging use values, which have no common measure whatever, as exchange values according to the degree of utility" (Marx 1988: 232; emphases altered). I thank Alan Freeman for bringing this passage to my attention.

2. As Dunayevskaya stresses, Marx's solution implies that the real-world phenomena ultimately confirm, not contradict, the essential laws of capitalist production developed in volume I of *Capital*. "How have [the real facts discussed in volume III] changed the laws that arise from the strict process of production which the academic economists call 'abstract'? . . . [Marx] shows us that in the final analysis the sum of all prices is equal to the sum of all values. Where the worker has created nothing, the capitalist manipulator can get nothing. Profit, even as surplus value, comes not from 'ownership' but from production. . . . Nothing fundamental has changed; nothing whatever" (Dunayevskaya 2000: 141).

3. In either case, both values and prices are measured in the same units; otherwise, comparison of value and price aggregates would be impossible.

4. That they do not matter was made clear in the early 1970s. A well-known main-stream economist (Baumol 1974) claimed that Samuelson's (1971) work on the "trans-formation problem" had misconstrued what Marx was trying to say. In response, Samuelson (1974a: 64, 66) pointed out, correctly, that the objection had nothing to do with his paper, which dealt with whether Marx had succeeded in demonstrating what he intended to demonstrate.

5. Postone (1993: 132–33) also repeats the old myth that Böhm-Bawerk claimed, incorrectly, that Marx failed to realize that prices deviate from values until after volume I was published. The claim is indeed incorrect, but it does not appear in Böhm-Bawerk's text. The myth apparently arose because Hilferding (1984: 155) discussed the claim in his critique of Böhm-Bawerk.

6. More precisely, reason is a sham. Presuppositions fully determine what is considered rational as well.

7. As I will discuss in the next chapter, proponents of the simultaneous single-system interpretations hold that Marx *did* value inputs and outputs simultaneously, and for this reason do not object to his solution.

8. Although Marx sometimes discussed reproduction in value terms, his core definitions of simple and expanded reproduction are also physical. For instance, he noted that if means of production and subsistence become cheaper, expanded reproduction can occur without an increase in the sum of value advanced (Marx 1992: 174).

9. See also Kliman and McGlone (1999), Carchedi (2005).

10. I have responded to most of Laibman's other objections in Kliman (2004a: 34–35, n3 and passim). In private correspondence, a friend has recently asked about a comment of Laibman's that immediately follows his acknowledgement that "Reproduction equilibrium exists between periods": "(although there is an infinite regress problem in illustrating this)." I did not respond to this originally because its meaning is unclear. Laibman may have been repeating an old saw of simultaneism: temporal valuation involves an infinite regress, since the input prices of one period depend upon the output prices of the previous period, which in turn depend upon the input prices of that period, ... Anyone who agrees with this objection must, to be consistent, object to the notion that the physical inputs of one period depend upon the physical outputs of the previous period, which in turn depend upon the physical inputs of that period, ...

11. In an electronic search of chapter 9 of volume III, I found twelve occurrences of the words "annual" or "annually," eleven of "period" or "periods," and three of "year," plus "produced in a given time."

12. This practice may have begun as a way of justifying the dual-system conception of values and prices.

Chapter 9

The "Transformation Problem" (2): If It Ain't Broke, Don't Correct It

9.1 Bortkiewicz's "Correction"

In the fourth of his 1906–1907 essays, Bortkiewicz (1984) put forth what he called a "correction" of Marx's solution. Yet since his attempted proof of internal contradiction is invalid, the term "correction" is a misnomer. If Marx's solution is not in error, there is nothing to correct. Thus the fact that Bortkiewicz's conclusions differ from Marx's does not imply that the latter are incorrect. Bortkiewicz is entitled to his theory of price determination, but Marx is equally entitled to his.

Having supposedly proved that non-simultaneous valuation leads to a spurious breakdown of the economy, Bortkiewicz "corrected" Marx's figures by valuing inputs and outputs simultaneously. In other words, the per-unit values of inputs and outputs are equal in Bortkiewicz's model, as are their per-unit prices. Since the sums of constant and variable capital that capitalists advance reflect the cost of inputs (means of production and workers' means of subsistence), it follows from this procedure that there are now two distinct sums of capital advanced, one based on the inputs' values, the other on their prices. In this respect, Bortkiewicz's "correction" differs sharply from Marx's own solution, in which there was a *single* set of capital advances, given as data at the outset.

There are thus two sets of price-value differences in Bortkiewicz's model. As in Marx's solution, the prices of production of the outputs differ from their values, but now, in addition, the capital advances "in price terms" differ from capital advances "in value terms." Since everything—all components of capital as well as output—now has a price that differs from its value, value and price are severed into wholly separate systems of determination. This is the origin of the dual-system conception of value and price.

To see how Bortkiewicz's uncoupling of price from value affects Marx's conclusions, let us consider a simple two-branch example without fixed capital.

Table 9.1. Physical Quantities

Branch	Input of Good 1	Real Wages	Output	Living Labor
1	96 MP	10 CG	120 MP	8 labor-hrs
2	12 MP	20 CG	60 CG	16 labor-hrs
Total	108 MP	30 CG		24 labor-hrs

In Table 9.1, Branch 1 produces means of production (MP) while Branch 2 produces a consumer good (CG) that both workers and non-workers consume. Branch 1 uses 96 units of the means of production and 8 hours of living labor to produce 120 units of the means of production; Branch 2 uses 12 units of the means of production and 16 hours of living labor to produce 60 units of the consumer good. In each branch, the real wage is 1.25 units of Good 2 per hour of living labor; thus the wages of the workers in Branches 1 and 2 allow them to buy 10 and 20 units of Good 2, respectively.

The above information is sufficient to derive Bortkiewicz's "value system" in labor-time terms. In order to compare his value aggregates with his money price aggregates, however, values and prices need to be measured in the same units. Let us thus assume that a labor-hour is equivalent to $3 *within* the value system.[1] With this additional assumption, we can express the value system as well as the price system in dollar terms.

In keeping with Bortkiewicz's dual-system conception, the constant-capital value is the value of the means of production and the variable-capital value is the value of the means of subsistence (the workers' real wages). And because Bortkiewicz's revision of Marx's solution is simultaneist, we assume that the value of each good as an output is equal to its value as an input. On the basis of these assumptions and the above data, we find (after some tedious but unimportant algebraic calculations) that the value of each good is $1 per unit. Using these values and the physical data, we obtain the Value System of Table 9.2.[2]

We can now derive Bortkiewicz's "price system." (Our procedures will differ somewhat from those he employed, but the results will be the same.) The physical quantities are the same as in the value system, and we again value inputs and outputs simultaneously. But the constant-capital value of the price system, c', is the *price* of the means of production, and the variable-capital value, v', is the *price* of the means of subsistence. To obtain these prices, we assume that rates of profit are equal and we assume, as Bortkiewicz did (though in a more roundabout manner), that total profit equals total surplus-value (in money terms). Given these assumptions, the price of Good 1 turns out to equal $1.75 per unit, while Good 2's price is $0.70. Using these prices in the same manner as we used the values above, we obtain Bortkiewicz's Price System of Table 9.2.[3]

Table 9.2. Simultaneous Dual-System Solutions*

Value System

Branch	*vpu*	*c*	*v*	*s*	*w*	*s*/(*c*+*v*)
1	1	96	10	14	120	13.2%
2	1	12	20	28	60	87.5%
Total		108	30	42	180	30.4%

Bortkiewicz's Price System

Branch	*ppu*	*c'*	*v'*	π	*p*	π /(*c'*+*v'*)
1	1.75	168	7	35	210	20%
2	0.70	21	14	7	42	20%
Total		189	21	42	252	20%

Moszkowska-Winternitz Price System

Branch	*ppu*	*c'*	*v'*	π	*p*	π /(*c'*+*v'*)
1	1.25	120	5	25	150	20%
2	0.50	15	10	5	30	20%
Total		135	15	30	180	20%

New and Improved Price System

Branch	*ppu*	*c'*	*v'*	π	*p*	π /(*c'*+*v'*)
1	1.50	144	6	30	180	20%
2	0.60	18	12	6	36	20%
Total		162	18	36	216	20%

* Value and price magnitudes are both measured in dollars. *vpu* is the value per unit and *ppu* is the price per unit.

Comparing the price and value systems, we see that they have very little in common. Total profit equals total surplus-value, by assumption, but Marx's other aggregate equalities are not preserved: total price deviates from total value, and the price and value rates of profit are unequal. Bortkiewicz and his successors have portrayed these discrepancies as proof that Marx was wrong about the aggregate equalities. Many of them have also claimed that these discrepancies disprove Marx's theory that surplus labor is the exclusive source of profit. None of them seem to have seriously considered the idea that their failure to deduce Marx's conclusions is *prima facie* evidence that they had misinterpreted the terms of his solution.

As Bortkiewicz (1952: 40, 32) was quick to note, his "correction" also implies that the law of the tendential fall in the profit rate is incorrect, as was Marx's rejection of Ricardo's claim that production conditions in luxury industries have no influence upon the economy-wide rate of profit. Marx's and Bortkiewicz's results are incompatible in other respects as well. The source of these incompatibilities is that, as we saw in chapter 5, simultaneous valuation makes technology and real wages the sole determinants of prices and profitability and is therefore incompatible with Marx's theory that value is determined by labor-time.

9.2 Theft vs. Honest Toil

Curiously, some Marxist economists construed the fact that Bortkiewicz's "correction" preserved the equality of total profit and total surplus-value as a confirmation of Marx's theory. Sweezy (1970: 123) went so far as to call Bortkiewicz's model the "final vindication of the labor theory of value, the solid foundation of [Marx's] theoretical structure"!

Other authors sought to vindicate Marx's theory with even greater finality, however, by choosing a different, presumably better, aggregate equality to preserve. Moszkowska (1929) was the first paper of this genre; she privileged the equality of total price and total value, as did Winternitz (1948). If we use this equality instead of the one that Bortkiewicz assumed, but retain all of his other assumptions, we obtain Table 9.2's Moszkowska-Winternitz Price System.

Such "solutions to the transformation problem" had certain advantages—the advantages of theft over honest toil (as Bertrand Russell remarked in a similar context). It was much easier to assume some aggregate value-price equality and declare that Marx was vindicated than to rethink the problem from the bottom up. As Samuelson (1971: 400, 425) stressed, however, none of these solutions actually vindicated Marx, because none of them *proved* anything. Their aggregate equalities were simply imposed arbitrarily, not deduced, and in all other respects the value and price systems of the dualistic solutions are simply different.

To see how arbitrary such solutions are, let us consider another possible aggregate equality: the total capital advanced of the price system $(c' + v')$ equals total value (w). Using this new equality rather than Bortkiewicz's, but retaining all of his other assumptions, we obtain Table 9.2's New and Improved Price System. Note that this system's total price exceeds the total value of the value system by $216 - 180 = 36$, and that this difference is exactly equal to total profit.

We have thus "proved" that profit is a pure markup over and above commodities' real values, a result completely antithetical to Marx's theory. By means of the same procedures that supposedly vindicate Marx, we have produced the "final refutation of the labor theory of value, the demolition of Marx's theoretical structure"!

Note also that all three price systems are essentially the same. The price rate of profit in all cases is 20%, which is quite different from the value rate. All other relationships between the various price components (the ratio of profit to wages, the ratio of constant to variable capital, etc.) are also the same. The only difference between the systems is that the figures in the Bortkiewicz Price System are all 40% greater, and the figures in the New and Improved Price System are all 20% greater, than those of the Moszkowska-Winternitz Price System. Governments often alter their nations' economies in the same way—not at all, that is—when they change their currency unit.

All simultaneous dual-system solutions necessarily share these properties. They preserve only one of Marx's aggregate equalities, and only by imposing it by fiat; none of them preserves the equality of the price and value rates of profit; they all arrive at exactly the same price rate of profit; and they differ from one another only by a scale factor.

9.3 The NI Solution

Largely because of the inadequacies of such solutions, several alternatives—the New Interpretation (NI), the simultaneous single-system interpretations (SSSIs), and the temporal single-system interpretation (TSSI)—finally emerged in the early 1980s. Proponents of the NI (Duménil 1980, 1983, Foley 1982) challenged the Bortkiewiczian interpretation of the value of variable capital. According to the NI, the variable-capital value is not the value of workers' means of subsistence, but the sum of value that workers actually receive as wages. Thus if workers are paid the value of their labor-power, their wages depend upon the prices, not the values, of the means of subsistence they need in order to reproduce their labor-power.

Proponents of the NI did not, however, rethink the dual-system notion that the "price" and "value" of constant capital differ. They justified their differential treatment by arguing that labor-power is a unique commodity because it is not produced capitalistically, and that workers are paid money wages, not physical goods.

In their solutions to the "transformation problem," adherents of the NI also employed a new aggregate value-price equality. They set the total value added in the price system (variable capital + profit) equal to the total value added in the value system (variable capital + surplus-value).

To illustrate the NI solution, let us use the same physical quantities as before. We thus assume (though the NI solution does not require such an assumption) that workers' wages enable them to buy the amounts of Good 2 specified in Table 9.1. Let us also assume the equality of rates of profit, simultaneous valuation, the NI's aggregate value-added equality, and a monetary expression of labor-time (MELT) equal to $3 per unit of living labor. Then the price of Good 1 turns out to equal $2 per unit, and the price of Good 2 equals $0.80. Multiplying the physical quantities by the appropriate prices, we obtain the NI price system of Table 9.3. It differs from those above only by a scale factor.

In most respects, the NI value system is also the same as the one above. This is because the NI retains the dual-system interpretation of constant capital. However, the NI maintains that workers' actual wages, the variable capital of the price system, is also the variable capital of the value system. Thus we use the v' figures of the NI price system as the v figures of its value system. Because these v figures differ from those of Table 9.2, so do the s figures.

We see that, because of its non-dualistic interpretation of variable capital, the NI preserves the equality of total profit and total surplus-value. In addition, value added in the price system ($v' + \pi$) equals value added in the value system ($v + s$) by stipulation. Proponents of the NI have claimed that this latter equality is an improved version of Marx's equality of total price and total value. If one accepts this claim, it is possible to conclude that "the equalities among aggregates obtain in a different manner" (Duménil and Lévy 2000: 120) under the

Table 9.3. NI Value and Price Systems*

NI Value System

Branch	vpu	c	v	s	w	s/(c+v)
1	1	96	8	16	120	15.4%
2	1	12	16	32	60	114.3%
Total		108	24	48	180	36.4%

NI Price System

Branch	ppu	c'	v'	π	p	$\pi/(c'+v')$
1	2.00	192	8	40	240	20%
2	0.80	24	16	8	48	20%
Total		216	24	48	288	20%

* By assumption, the MELT equals $3 per unit of living labor. Value and price magnitudes are both measured in dollars. *vpu* is the value per unit and *ppu* is the price per unit.

NI—but only if one ignores Marx's result, crucial to his law of the tendential fall in the rate of profit (LTFRP), that the aggregate price and value rates of profit are equal! Like other solutions based on a dualistic interpretation of constant capital, the NI solution fails to preserve this equality.

Moreover, the NI value-added equality is imposed in a manner no less arbitrary than other authors imposed other aggregate equalities. It is true that NI authors justified their choice, yet other dual-system theorists also justified their choices, often with equal validity. The equality of total price and total value, for instance, was surely regarded by Marx as a fundamental result of his own solution.

9.4 The SSSI Solution

The SSSIs construe variable-capital value as the actual sum of value that workers receive as wages, as the NI does. However, they also construe constant-capital value in an analogous manner, as the sum of value needed to acquire the means of production. The constant-capital value therefore depends on the prices of the means of production, not their values. Thus the SSSIs do away entirely with the notion of a distinct value system in which the constant and variable-capital value depend on the values of inputs (means of production and subsistence). As in Marx's own solution, there is only a single set of constant and variable capital figures. For this reason, all three of his value-price equalities are preserved by the SSSIs, at least in a formal sense.

To illustrate the SSSI solution, let us make the same assumptions we made in the case of the NI, with one exception. Instead of imposing the value-added equality, we assume that any one of Marx's original three value-price equalities holds true. Given these assumptions, the prices of Goods 1 and 2—which remain simultaneously determined—are $2/unit and $0.80/unit.

The c, v, π, and p figures in Table 9.4 are computed in the same way as before, except that c and v depend upon the *prices* of the two goods, not their values. Surplus-value is the difference between the new value added and variable

Table 9.4. Simultaneous Single System*

Branch	*ppu*	*c*	*v*	*s*	*w*	*π*	*p*	*s*/(*c*+*v*)	*π*/(*c*+*v*)
1	2.00	192	8	16	216	40	240	8%	20%
2	0.80	24	16	32	72	8	48	80%	20%
Total		216	24	48	288	48	288	20%	20%

* By assumption, the MELT equals $3 per unit of living labor. Value and price magnitudes are both measured in dollars. *ppu* is the price per unit.

capital. (The new value added is obtained by multiplying the living labor figures of Table 9.1 by the MELT.) The value of output, w, is the sum of c, v, and s.

We see that all three of Marx's aggregate equalities are preserved. Total price and total value both equal 288, total profit and total surplus-value both equal 48, and the general price and value rates of profit both equal 20%. These are extremely important results, since they disprove a longstanding claim of dual-system theorists that it is impossible to preserve all of these equalities at once.

Yet owing to the simultaneism of the SSSIs, the equalities are preserved in a formal sense only. The SSSI rate of profit, 20%, is the same as the price rate of profit in the price systems considered above. Moreover, all price and profit figures (c, v, π, and p) are identical to those of the previous price systems except for a scale factor—for instance, all SSSI price magnitudes are 60% greater than those of Moszkowska-Winternitz price system. Hence, what determines relative prices, profits, and the price rate of profit in the other simultaneist models—technology and real wages—is what determines them here as well.

Thus we have a curious paradox. The SSSIs preserve Marx's aggregate equalities, yet they imply that Marx's rate of profit is identical to the rate of profit of his physicalist critics! The voice is the voice of Marx, but the hands are the hands of Sraffa.

How can this be? The answer is that, because the SSSIs are simultaneist, their price rate of profit is physically determined. Their value rate of profit is then obtained by stipulating that it is equal to the price rate, and thus to the physical rate (or an analytically equivalent procedure is employed). Thus, although the aggregate equalities are preserved, the causal relationships differ markedly from those of Marx's theory. In the SSSIs, the physical rate of profit determines both the price rate and the value rate. In Marx's theory, the value rate of profit determines the price rate, and the physical rate plays no role at all.

9.5 The Temporal Single-System Interpretation

In a mathematical sense, the TSSI is almost identical to the SSSIs. The one difference is that the TSSI denies that Marx held that the prices of inputs are determined simultaneously with the prices of outputs. But this one difference makes a world of difference.

In order to compare the contrasting implications of these interpretations, let us assume that input and output prices do happen to be equal initially. In this case, the two interpretations arrive at the same results. Thus, given the above physical quantities and MELT, the TSSI values and prices of production are the same as those of Table 9.4.

Imagine that labor-saving technological progress now takes place in both branches. In the next period, the same amount of output is produced, using the same amount of means of production, but each branch uses only half as much living labor as before. Given that the real wage rate, the rate of surplus-value, and the MELT remain unchanged, we obtain the Temporal Single System of Table 9.5. Note that the temporal c and v figures are based on the *actual* input prices of the period, namely the output prices of the previous period ($2/unit and $0.80/unit).

Both branches' constant capital investments are the same as before, because the input price of Good 1 and the amounts of means of production they use are unchanged. Owing to the 50% reduction in employment, however, the variable capital investments and the surplus-values produced are 50% smaller than before. Thus the value of each branch's output falls. Since aggregate surplus-value declines by 50% while the aggregate capital value advanced declines by only 5%, the aggregate rate of profit falls sharply.

All three aggregate equalities hold true, and in a *substantive* sense. Because less living labor is performed, there is a fall in the amounts of value and surplus-value produced, which in turn causes a decline in total price and profit. And because less living labor is performed, the value rate of profit falls, which causes the price rate to fall as well.

The SSSI results in the lower half of Table 9.5 are quite different. Although all three of Marx's aggregate equalities are preserved once again, the labor-saving technological change causes the rate of profit to *rise*, which is of course contrary to his LTFRP. This occurs because simultaneist models retroactively revalue inputs at output prices, as was discussed in sections 5.7 and 7.3.2. When output prices are lower than the prices at which the inputs are actually bought, as is the case here, retroactive revaluation causes a portion of the capital advanced to be conjured away, and this boosts the rate of profit artificially. The SSSIs are no different from other simultaneist models in this respect.

Thus we see that although the TSSI and SSSIs both preserve Marx's aggregate equalities, their implications and results are radically different. The SSSIs, like other simultaneist interpretations, make value redundant, while the TSSI does not. Since the *only* mathematical difference between these interpretations is that the former are simultaneist while the latter is temporalist, it is this difference that is responsible for all differences in their implications and quantitative results.

9.6 Critics' Responses to the TSSI

Marx's physicalist critics have conceded, however grudgingly, that the TSSI undoes the appearance of internal inconsistency in his account of the value-production price transformation. Laibman (2004: 10) has acknowledged that, in TSSI examples of the transformation, "profit-rate equalization occurs within each period (complete with the much adored [aggregate] equalities)." Although Marx's simultaneist critics charged throughout all of the twentieth century that

Table 9.5. The Effect of Technological Progress*

Temporal Single System

Branch	Input ppu	c	v	s	w	π	p	$s/(c+v)$	$\pi/(c+v)$
1	2.00	192	4	8	204	20.63	216.63	4.1%	10.5%
2	0.80	24	8	16	48	3.37	35.37	50.0%	10.5%
Total		216	12	24	252	24.00	252.00	10.5%	10.5%

Simultaneous Single System

Branch	ppu	c	v	s	w	π	p	$s/(c+v)$	$\pi/(c+v)$
1	1.18	113.05	1.82	10.18	125.05	26.44	141.32	8.9%	23.0%
2	0.36	14.13	3.64	20.36	38.13	4.09	21.87	114.5%	23.0%
Total		127.19	5.47	30.53	163.19	30.53	163.19	23.0%	23.0%

* By assumption, the MELT equals $3 per unit of living labor. Value and price magnitudes are both measured in dollars. ppu is the price per unit. There are some errors due to rounding.

his solution failed on mathematical grounds, Mongiovi (2002: 413) has recently conceded "the absence of arithmetical error" in Marx's solution as interpreted by the TSSI. And Veneziani (2004: 98), acknowledging that the TSSI obtains Marx's results in this and other cases, admits that "the TSS approach . . . 'corresponds to the original [theory of Marx's] in a way that others do not.'"[4]

I have purposely quoted these authors out of context in order to highlight the facts they have acknowledged. If one does not read their works with extreme care, it is easy to overlook these very brief acknowledgements, which are tucked away within texts that divert the discussion from the question of internal inconsistency, even to the point of making it seem that this is not what the transformation debate is about. A thorough response to these works would require several chapters, since their critiques of the TSSI are marred by a great many misinterpretations, misrepresentations, and mathematical and factual errors. Here, I must limit myself to discussing a few of the ways in which the above authors try to lessen the impact of their concessions by diverting readers' attention elsewhere.

Although Laibman acknowledges that the TSSI deduces Marx's aggregate equalities in a logically consistent manner, he complains that "[t]he 'price' paid for this orthodox imagery, however, is substantial: . . . an apparently infinite number of sets of production prices, each set with its associated rate of profit . . . correspond to a *single* production schema, with its given inputs, outputs, techniques and flows of labor. This alone invites a reiterated charge of absurdity" (Laibman 2004: 10, emphasis in original). In other words, Marx should remain convicted of internal inconsistency because, on the interpretation that acquits him, his theory of price and profit determination is anti-physicalist, but anti-physicalism is absurd.

Had Laibman proved that physical quantities ("inputs, outputs, techniques and flows of labor") do in fact uniquely determine prices and rates of profit, his charge of absurdity would make sense. But he provides no argument at all. Instead, the charge of absurdity serves a purely diversionary function. Rather than simply admitting that Marx's solution can be interpreted in a manner that renders it internally consistent, Laibman changes the subject. Here, and throughout his paper, he makes it seem that the transformation controversy is not about the question of internal consistency, but about whether Marx's theory as understood by the TSSI satisfies Laibman's own standards of good economics. Thus Marx is not only guilty until proven innocent; he is guilty until proven a physicalist.

Mongiovi diverts attention away from the failure of Marx's critics to prove internal inconsistency in much the same way. Noting that proponents of the TSSI hold that "Marx's work should be debated on the basis of an interpretation that attributes coherence to his arguments," he responds: "The mere absence of arithmetical error does not render a model coherent, in the sense of providing a meaningful set of propositions about what the world is like" (Mongiovi 2002: 413). Of course not—but the mere absence of arithmetic error does indeed acquit Marx of the century-old charge of arithmetic error (i.e., of the charge that his aggregate equalities do not hold true).

Mongiovi substitutes one sense of the word "coherent" (meaningful) for another (internally consistent) in order to divert attention from the question of internal inconsistency. "Arithmetic error" is the overriding issue in the transformation controversy, and not because proponents of the TSSI say so, but because Marx's simultaneist critics have made it the overriding issue for a full century. Why has this suddenly become an issue that Mongiovi no longer wishes to discuss?

What he supposedly wishes to discuss instead are "meaningful . . . propositions about what the world is like." Yet Mongiovi's paper is diversionary in this respect, too, since it completely ignores the fact that Marx's theory arrives at anti-physicalist results, in case after case, when understood in accordance with the TSSI. This diversion is what allows Mongiovi to claim that it is meaningless. For instance, as we have seen, a key conclusion of Marx's account of the value-price transformation—the aggregate price rate of profit is determined by and equal to the value rate—is crucial to his conclusion that labor-saving technological change can cause the real-world rate of profit to fall. But since Mongiovi avoids any discussion of the LTFRP, and since he ignores the other important implications of the aggregate value-price equalities as well, he turns them into purely mathematical results. When the meaningful propositions that flow from Marx's value theory are ignored, it does of course become meaningless.

Veneziani diverts attention from the question of internal inconsistency by making the value theory controversy seem to be about whether Marx's value theory is true. Although he admits that the TSSI succeeds in deducing Marx's conclusions, Veneziani says that this is "unsurprising[ ]"; the conclusions are deduced only because "all [of] Marx's propositions [i.e. premises] are *assumed* to be correct" in TSSI works (Veneziani 2004: 98, emphasis in original).

If proponents of the TSSI claimed to prove that Marx's conclusions are true, as Veneziani asserts, his complaint would be legitimate. One cannot prove that conclusions are true simply by showing that they follow from the premises. Yet we have continually stressed that our demonstrations are not efforts to prove that Marx's theory is true, but efforts to prove that the theory can be interpreted in a manner that renders it logically consistent (see, e.g., Freeman and Kliman 2000: 260). And the way in which one proves this latter claim is *precisely* by showing that Marx's conclusions follow from his premises (as we interpret them). Once this is understood, Veneziani's revelation that the TSSI arrives at Marx's conclusions by deducing them from his premises no longer reads like an exposé of trickery or failure. His statement now seems to be what it actually is—an admission that the TSSI demonstrations have succeeded in refuting the century-old "proofs" of Marx's logical inconsistency.

Appendix to Chapter 9: The Loranger and Moseley Solutions

I have argued in this chapter that simultaneist interpretations cannot preserve Marx's aggregate equalities in a substantive sense. The SSSIs preserve the equalities in a formal sense only, and the other simultaneist interpretations fare even more poorly. This is crucial evidence that Marx's value theory is not simultaneist.

Yet a couple of simultaneist theorists—Loranger and Moseley—have claimed that their interpretations preserve all three equalities, and in a substantive sense. If these claims were true, they would disprove my contention that simultaneism is incompatible with the determination of value by labor-time, and they would suggest that Marx might have been a simultaneist after all. I shall show, however, that these claims are not true. My discussion of Loranger is of necessity a bit technical, but readers who skip the math should be able to follow the gist of the argument.

Loranger

Loranger (2004) succeeds in deriving all three of Marx's aggregate equalities, and his price rate of profit is indeed determined by, not only equal to, the value rate. Yet these results are meaningless because other results that emerge along with them are impossible. There are quite plausible cases in which Loranger's solution yields the aggregate equalities only because his wage rate and some of his prices are negative.

Whereas the standard, simultaneous dual-system solution takes real wages (workers' means of subsistence) as given, and solves for the price rate of profit, Loranger (2004: 38–41, 50–52) proceeds in the opposite direction. He takes the aggregate value rate of profit (of the dualist value system) as given, sets the price rate of profit equal to the value rate, and solves for the money wage rate. In the particular example he presents in his paper (Loranger 2004: 41–44), this procedure seems to work, but other, quite reasonable examples yield meaningless results.

Assume, for instance, that Branch 1 uses ten units of Good 1, a means of production, and two labor-hours to produce twelve units of Good 1, while Branch 2 uses two units of Good 1 and ten labor-hours to produce twelve units of Good 2, a consumer good. Also assume that the rate of surplus-value is 100% in both sectors. Thus half of the living labor expended, one and five hours, respectively, is surplus labor. If we assume, as Loranger (2004: 43) does, that the MELT is $1 per labor-hour, then the simultaneously determined per-unit value of each good is $1/unit, and we obtain the value system of Table 9.6.

Table 9.6. Loranger's Solution

Value System

Branch	c	v	s	w	$s/(c+v)$
1	10	1	1	12	9.1%
2	2	5	5	12	71.4%
Total	12	6	6	24	33.3%

Price System

Branch	c'	v'	π	p	$\pi/(c'+v')$
1	30	-3	9	36	33.3%
2	6	-15	-3	-12	33.3%
Total	36	-18	6	24	33.3%

Loranger's price equations are the usual simultaneist price of production equations, except that in his case the rate of profit is a datum and the wage rate is unknown, not vice-versa. He stipulates that the price of production rate of profit equals the aggregate value rate ($33.3\% = 1/3$), and thus his equations are

$$12p_1 = (1 + 1/3)(10p_1 + 2m)$$

$$12p_2 = (1 + 1/3)(2p_1 + 10m)$$

where p_1 and p_2 are the simultaneously determined per-unit prices and m is the money wage rate per unit of living labor. To obtain a determinate solution, Loranger also assumes that total price equals total value:

$$12p_1 + 12p_2 = 24$$

Each unknown has a unique solution: $p_1 = 3$, $p_2 = -1$, and $m = -1.5$. Using the prices in the same way as we did before to compute c' and p, and multiplying m by the living labor figures to compute v', we obtain Table 9.6's price system. We see that all three aggregate equalities are indeed preserved. Yet this is no great achievement, since Loranger's solution is clearly nonsensical.

Moseley

Moseley (1993a, 2000a, 2000b) contends that his interpretation yields Marx's results rather than Sraffian results because it starts from different "givens" (data). This is not the case. His interpretation can indeed sound quite Marx-like when he presents it, but words can be deceiving. With regard to its analytical content, Moseley's interpretation differs in no essential respect from the other SSSIs, which, as we saw above, obtain the same rate of profit (and the same relative prices of production) as other simultaneist models. Whereas Sraffians and other physicalists take technology and real wage rates as their fundamental data, and deduce prices and the rate of profit from them, Moseley claims to follow Marx's method:

> The total surplus-value for the economy as a whole is *taken as given*, as determined by the prior analysis of capital in general in Volume 1 [of *Capital*]. The ratio of the total surplus-value determined in Volume 1 to the total capital invested is the general rate of profit, which is also taken as given in the Volume 3 determination of prices of production. . . . *The same quantities of constant capital and variable capital are taken as given* in both of these stages. [Moseley 2000b: 287, 290, emphases in original]

So far, so good. Yet Moseley's givens are not given in any meaningful sense. Although he claims that his interpretation is non-simultaneist, because its value magnitudes are determined prior to its price magnitudes, "The constant capital that is taken as given and transferred to the price of the final product is the *current replacement cost* of the existing means of production" (Moseley 1993a: 168, emphasis in original). Thus the sum of value transferred is not the actual, given cost of the means of production when they entered into their production process, but what it would cost to replace them when the output is sold. In other words, the constant capital is retroactively revalued at post-production prices, as in every other simultaneist model.

Moseley maintains that his interpretation nonetheless takes the constant-capital value as given. When prices of means of production change during the production period,

> constant capital *continues to be taken as given*, but the precise magnitude of constant capital that is taken as given changes as a result of the change in the value of the means of production. *The fact that the magnitude of constant capital may change does not imply that the constant capital cannot be taken as given in the determination of output prices.* [Moseley 2000a, section 2.1, emphases in original]

But of course this fact implies exactly what he says it does not. If Moseley's salary is *given* by contract at the start of the year, but his employer pays him only half that amount during the year, only the "precise magnitude" of his salary changes, not the word "salary." Does this mean that his employer has not violated its *given* contractual obligation?

In any case, the implications of simultaneous valuation cannot be evaded by wordplay. If Moseley's interpretation seems to produce Marx-like results, that is only because his "given" sums of value mask the changes in technological and real wage coefficients that actually determine his rate of profit. Consider, for instance, the example in Table 9.7, which depicts a single-good economy in two consecutive years. Corn is the only output, produced by means of seed corn and living labor. Farmworkers use their wages to buy corn. The same amount of corn, ten bushels, is produced in both years.

Since the same constant capital, $8, is "given" in both years, it may seem that we can tell the following story. "In contrast to what occurs in the models of Sraffians and other physicalist theorists, technological progress has caused the rate of profit to fall. The same amount of constant capital is used in both years. But in Year 2, only one-sixth as many workers are needed to produce the same amount of corn as in Year 1, and since the real wage rate is unchanged, Year 2's surplus-value is also only one-sixth of what it was in Year 1. Thus the rate of profit falls."

This is a nice story, very Marx-like, but it is the exact opposite of the truth. Although Moseley's constant capital is supposedly "given," what has actually taken place is that twice as much seed corn is needed to produce the same output in Year 2 as in Year 1. And even though the variable capital falls to the same degree that employment falls, the real (i.e. physical) wage rate is not "given" either. It doubles as well. Thus, what causes Moseley's rate of profit to fall is a combination of technological regress—not progress—and a rise in the real wage rate. In other words, the rate of profit that falls here is the physical rate.

These results can be derived as follows. Since ten bushels of corn are produced during each year, the per-bushel value (= price) of corn is $20/(10 bu) = $2/bu at the end of Year 1 and $10/(10 bu) = $1/bu at the end of Year 2. But Moseley's input and output values are always equal, so the per-bushel value of the inputs (seed corn and workers' real wages) is also $2/bu in Year 1 and $1/bu in Year 2. Thus the same "given" constant capital, $8, which purchased four bushels of seed corn in Year 1, purchases eight bushels in Year 1. Since the amount of corn produced is the same, ten bushels, it follows that the amount of

Table 9.7. Moseley's Interpretation*

Year	c	v	s	w	s/(c+v)
1	$8	$6	$6	$20	42.9%
	(4 bu)	(3 bu)		(10 bu)	
2	$8	$1	$1	$10	11.1%
	(8 bu)	(1 bu)		(10 bu)	

* The figures in boldface are data. The remaining figures are derived from these data and Moseley's premise that valuation is simultaneous.

seed corn needed to produce a unit of output has doubled. Similarly, while in Year 1 the workers were able to buy three bushels of corn with their wages of $6, in Year 2 they can buy one bushel of corn with their wages of $1. Thus, although there are only one-sixth as many farmworkers in Year 2 as in Year 1, they can buy two-sixths (= one-third) as much corn. In other words, the real wage rate has also doubled.

A bit of algebra allows us to uncover the underlying physicalism of Moseley's interpretation even more clearly, and without having to assume that the amount of output remains unchanged. Note first that the physical rate of profit in a one-good model is

$$r = \frac{1-(a+b)}{a+b}$$

where a is the technical coefficient, the quantity of the means of production (seed corn) required to produce a unit of output, and b is the real wage coefficient, workers' real wages (means of subsistence) per unit of output. Now let us find the a and b coefficients that underlie Moseley's value figures. Because (but only because) his inputs and outputs have the same per-unit value, his value figures can be written as

$$c = \lambda \times (\text{means of production})$$

$$v = \lambda \times (\text{real wages})$$

$$w = \lambda \times (\text{physical output})$$

where λ is the simultaneously determined per-unit value of corn. Hence, if we divide c by w, the λ terms in the numerator and denominator cancel out, and we obtain a, the ratio of means of production to output. Similarly, dividing v by w, we obtain b, real wages per unit of output.

Thus a doubles from $8/$20 = 0.4 in Year 1 to $8/$10 = 0.8 in Year 2, while b falls from $6/$20 = 0.3 to $1/$10 = 0.1.[5] Substituting these coefficients into the above equation, we find that the physical rate of profit falls from

$$\frac{1-(0.4+0.3)}{0.4+0.3} = 42.9\% \qquad \text{to} \qquad \frac{1-(0.8+0.1)}{0.8+0.1} = 11.1\%\,.$$

These results are identical to Moseley's. It is possible (but much more tedious) to show that the same conclusions hold true in multisector examples in which prices and values differ.

Thus Moseley's rate of profit is determined by the same technological and real wage coefficients that determine all other simultaneist theorists' rate of profit, and in exactly the same manner. That he expresses his rate of profit as the ratio of surplus-value to capital value advanced, instead of as a ratio of physical coefficients, makes no difference. It is all value-form and no value-substance.

My purpose here has not been to expose the failures of Loranger and Moseley, but to show that their embrace of simultaneism makes failure inevitable. Simultaneous valuation necessarily leads to physicalist conclusions, not Marx's conclusions.

Notes

1. I emphasize "*within* the value system" because, in the dual-system interpretations, it is impossible to define a unique MELT that allows us to convert all labor-time magnitudes of the value system into the corresponding money magnitudes of the price system. For instance, the ratio of the money price of output to the value of output (in terms of labor-time) differs from the ratio of money profit to surplus-value (in terms of labor-time). This is a consequence of the dual-system interpretations' failure to preserve all of Marx's aggregate equalities.

2. The c figures are obtained by multiplying the inputs of Good 1 by its value, the v figures are obtained by multiplying the real wages by the value of Good 2, and the w figures are obtained by multiplying the output of each good by its value. Subtracting c and v from w, we obtain s.

3. The c', v', and p figures are obtained in the same way as the c, v, and w figures, though we now multiply the physical quantities by prices, not values. Subtracting c' and v' from p, we obtain π.

4. The interior quote is from Kliman and McGlone (1999: 43).

5. Since b falls to one-third of its original level, while employment falls to one-sixth of its original level, the real wage *rate*—the real wage per worker—has also doubled.

Chapter 10

The "Fundamental Marxian Theorem"

10.1 Introduction

Simultaneist authors have frequently sought to minimize the importance of the fact that their interpretations are unable to solve the "transformation problem" in a satisfactory manner. Although their general price and value rates of profit differ, and although it is only by fiat that they preserve one of Marx's other aggregate price-value equalities, we are told that "it is quite pointless" to worry about the precise numbers. What matters is the fact, which "remains absolutely unchanged[,] that the surplus labor of workers . . . is the unique source of profit" when these terms are defined in the simultaneous dual-system manner (Okishio 1993d: 45, 46).[1] This claim, which Okishio (1993b: 32–33; 1993c: 80–81) and subsequent authors have supposedly proved, was dubbed **the fundamental Marxian theorem** (FMT) by Morishima (1973: 53).

The FMT serves an enormous ideological function within mainstream Marxian and radical economics. It has continually been claimed that Marx's exploitation theory of profit has been vindicated by one or another interpretation or theory that makes use of the FMT.[2] These interpretations and theories have continually been hailed as embodiments of the very essence of Marx's theory, even though they arrive at his conclusions by somewhat different means. Thus the FMT, and the models from which it follows, are also said to demonstrate that Marx's own value theory is superfluous (or worse): "the Marxian theory of exploitation can be constructed quite independently of the labor theory of value" (Roemer 1981: 149).[3] "Profit . . . depends upon the degree to which workers can be made to produce more output than they and the production process consume. This surplus approach can be developed without reference to Marx's problematic value categories, as in Sraffa's [work]" (Mongiovi 2002: 394–95).

Yet if the theorem stated above — "the surplus labor of workers . . . is the unique source of profit" when surplus labor and profit are defined in the simultaneous dual-system manner—is false, then this line of argument collapses.[4] I wish to show that this theorem is indeed false. Simultaneist definitions imply

175

that total profit could be positive even though no surplus labor is extracted from workers, and total profit could be negative even though surplus labor is extracted. But this means precisely that surplus labor is not the unique source of profit. Even simultaneous single-system interpretation (SSSI) definitions imply this, notwithstanding the fact that the SSSIs preserve all three aggregate equalities in a technical sense. Only the temporal single-system interpretation (TSSI) yields the opposite result.[5]

It has long been known that the FMT fails to hold true in the case of joint production if the definition of surplus labor is not modified accordingly (see, e.g. Steedman 1977, Chs. 11–13). I will not try to exploit such quirks in order to refute the theorem. The FMT fails even when every industry produces only a single product, and for a much more basic reason. We have seen throughout this book that the physicalist character of simultaneist interpretations is what causes them to contradict Marx's conclusions. I wish to show that this is the source of the problem in the present case as well. The notion that surplus labor and profit "are no more than two sides of the same coin[,] . . . simply 'labour' and 'monetary' expressions of the physical surplus" (Steedman 1981: 17), is just not correct.[6] Physicalism *tries* to define surplus labor and profit in this manner, but its definitions do not work; "anomalies" arise that falsify the FMT. Things go awry because of two elementary facts: *surplus labor is not the sole determinant of physical surpluses*, and *there is no such thing as "the" physical surplus*. In light of these facts, there is simply no reason to expect a simultaneist FMT to hold true.

The interesting and peculiar thing is that simultaneist authors have even tried to replicate Marx's conclusions in this case. In other cases, a discrepancy between their conclusions and his is construed as an error or internal inconsistency on his part. When, for instance, Okishio found that his model contradicts Marx's theory that technological advances tend to lower the rate of profit, he did not try to resolve or conceal the contradiction, but simply declared that Marx's conclusion is impossible. Yet although his model also contradicts Marx's exploitation theory of profit—and for the same reason—in this case Okishio tried to patch up the problem and pronounced his effort a success.

Why are the two cases treated differently? I can think of no reason other than that simultaneist authors would *like* the one theory to be wrong and the other right. Marx's law of the tendential fall in the rate of profit has revolutionary implications—the abolition of economic crises requires the abolition of value production—and the idea that technological advances tend to reduce profitability runs counter to physicalists' intuition. The exploitation theory of profit, on the other hand, can seem to suggest the need for reform of an unfair distribution of income, and physicalists find it intuitively plausible or even obviously correct.

10.2 The Corn Model

One reason why the exploitation theory of profit may seem obvious is that profit always exists under capitalism and surplus labor presumably always exists as well. Yet their mere coexistence does not imply that surplus labor is any source of profit, much less the unique one. After all, other things always coexist with profit, too; apples and birds and cliffs, etc. have continually existed throughout the capitalist epoch.

It may also be obvious (to some people) that the more surplus labor workers perform, the more profit there is, but this is likewise not the issue. The more heart attacks people suffer, the more deaths occur, but heart attacks would be the *exclusive* cause of death only if (1) every case of heart attack necessarily resulted in death and (2) it would be impossible to die except by suffering a heart attack.[7] In precisely the same way, surplus labor is the exclusive source of profit only if, in the aggregate economy, (1') the performance of surplus labor necessarily results in profit in every case and (2') it is impossible for profit to arise except through the extraction of surplus labor. If there could be surplus labor without profit, then some other thing or things are needed in order for profit to exist. And if there could be profit without surplus labor, then some other thing or things would be the source of profit in that case.

There is also another—physicalist—intuition that makes the exploitation theory of profit seem obvious. Workers produce some stuff, but their wages allow them to buy back only part of this stuff, and capitalists get their profit by selling the rest of the stuff. The technical term for "stuff" is *corn*.

In the "Preface to the Second Edition" of her *Essay on Marxian Economics*, Joan Robinson (1967: vii) suggested that economists of her generation could not understand Marx's theory of profit, in part because they could not see that it was a corn model in disguise. "[H]is nineteenth-century metaphysical habits of thought" were alien to them. Her *Essay,* published in 1942, had "tried to translate Marx's concepts into language that an academic could understand," but "[t]he task of translation is now much easier than it was at that time." What made it easier, she implied, was that Piero Sraffa (1960), her Cambridge University colleague, had in the meantime revealed that underneath Marx's "metaphysical" concepts there lay concealed a "penetrating analysis of exploitation . . . derived from Ricardo" (Robinson 1967: viii):

> [C]onsider an economy consisting of capitalists and workers (land is free) whose only product is Ricardo's "corn". There are no prices of commodities, since there is only one commodity. The technical conditions of production determine the net product . . . —that is, the harvest minus seed corn . . . . The corn-wage . . . then determines the profit . . . . The ratio of profit, or surplus [corn], to the [corn-]wage is the rate of exploitation. . . .

> Now, it seems obvious that this analysis cannot be affected, in essence, by allowing for a variety of commodities. . . . [I]t does not alter the main line of the argument. [Robinson 1967: vii–viii]

We shall see that the introduction of a variety of commodities does indeed affect the argument. However, a more fundamental question pertains to the corn-model case as well: just how penetrating is this analysis of exploitation?

10.3 Intuitions Can Be Wrong

The main objective of this section is to challenge the intuition that the corn-model analysis must be right. I will therefore consider a couple of striking cases. My assumptions will be unrealistic—but so are those of the corn model. More realistic cases will be examined later.

First, imagine a farmworker who "live[s] on air" (Marx 1991a: 356) and thus receives no corn-wages, but nonetheless toils under the hot sun throughout the year. Clearly all of her labor is surplus labor—labor for which she receives no equivalent—as all simultaneist interpretations of Marx's theory acknowledge. Yet if the farmworker planted 100 bushels of seed corn at the start of the year but, owing to bad weather, only harvested 99 bushels at the end, then "profit, or surplus [corn]" is 99 bushels – 100 bushels = –1 bushel. Thus physicalism implies that there could be surplus labor but negative profit.[8]

Some simultaneists, disagreeing with Robinson's contention that there are no prices here, would prefer to express the profit in money terms. In this case, if the per-bushel price of corn is p dollars—both before and after the harvest, since we are valuing the corn simultaneously—then profit is $99p$ dollars – $100p$ dollars = $-p$ dollars. Once again, surplus labor has been performed, but physicalist-simultaneist definitions imply that the capitalists have not gotten profit. (p cannot be negative. That would mean that the capitalists would pay you to take the corn off their hands, which is clearly not the case.) Thus all simultaneist interpretations—the dual-system interpretation, the NI, and the SSSIs—come to the same conclusion.

Second, consider the case of fully automated production, which Dmitriev (1974)—Sraffianism's foremost predecessor—put forth in order to demonstrate that there can be profit without surplus labor. That he sought to use his physicalist model to *disprove* Marx's exploitation theory of profit is important, for it underscores the point that the intuitions of physicalists and the implications of physicalism are two different things.

Let us assume, as we did in section 3.2 when we first considered Dmitriev's demonstration, that there is one kind of machine that produces replicas of itself, without any human labor. Imagine that the year begins with ten machines, which produce thirteen machines, at which point the original ten machines have worn out and become unusable. The physical "profit" is 13 machines − 10 machines = 3 machines, while the profit in money terms is $13p$ dollars − $10p$ dollars = $3p$ dollars, if we value the input and output machines simultaneously.[9] Thus Dmitriev was right about the possibility of positive profit without surplus labor —*if* we accept any simultaneist interpretation's definition of profit.

Although these examples are highly unrealistic, they do refute the FMT. They also make it starkly clear that the performance of surplus labor and the production of physical surplus are two different things. The existence of one does not imply the existence of the other. This is one important reason why the FMT also fails in more complex, realistic cases.

10.4 Failure of the Simultaneous Dual-System FMT

Another key reason why the standard FMT fails is that "the" physical surplus is a meaningless concept once we take leave of the corn-model world. Not only is the physical surplus of each good different, but some physical surpluses are always *negative*. The economy-wide **physical surplus** of any good or service is the amount produced minus the amounts used up in production and consumed by workers:

physical surplus = total product − used-up input − workers' consumption

Thus, if the coal industry produces less coal today than the amount of coal that it and other industries use up and workers consume today (which is always possible if the coal they use up and consume comes partly or wholly from pre-existing stocks), today's physical surplus of coal is negative.[10]

It is fundamentally because of this simple fact that the standard (simultaneous dual-system) FMT fails. When surplus labor and profit are interpreted as "simply 'labour' and 'monetary' expressions of the [sic] physical surplus" (Steedman 1981: 17), then either can be positive while the other is negative, given that the physical surplus of at least one good is negative.

In order to see this, Steedman's terms need to be defined precisely. The simultaneous dual-system interpretation of Marx's theory maintains that total surplus labor is the total labor-time value of the physical surpluses,[11] and total profit is similarly the total price of the physical surpluses. (Note that these definitions are simultaneist: the same per-unit values and prices are attributed to coal used as an input at the start of a period and coal produced at the end.) Thus if we have a two-commodity economy in which the physical surpluses of the two goods are 1 and 10, while the labor-time values of the goods are 55 and 5, then total surplus labor is $(1 \times 55) + (10 \times 5) = 105$. And if the goods' money prices are 54 and 6, then total profit is $(1 \times 54) + (10 \times 6) = 114$.

Now imagine instead that the physical surplus of the first good is –1. Total surplus labor is $(-1 \times 55) + (10 \times 5) = -5$, but total profit is $(-1 \times 54) + (10 \times 6) = 6$. Since there is profit without surplus labor, it is clear that surplus labor is not the unique source of profit. If, on the other hand, the goods' values are 54 and 6 while their prices are 55 and 5, then total surplus labor is 6 but total profit is –5. Thus we have negative profit even though surplus labor was extracted. This likewise implies that surplus labor is not the unique source of profit: something more than surplus labor is needed in order for profit to exist, namely the "right" prices. The standard FMT has been disproved.

Physicalists instinctively respond to this refutation (and to the case of harvest failure above) by denying the relevance of economies in which some physical surplus is negative, on the ground that such economies cannot reproduce themselves. This objection is not well-founded.

In the first place, it has no bearing on the logical question at issue. If surplus labor and profit could fail to coexist in these economies, even in one period, before they run themselves into the ground—and we have seen that they could, given simultaneous dual-system definitions—that in itself proves that surplus labor is not the exclusive source of profit.

Secondly, such economies certainly can—and do—reproduce themselves. We live in them. There *are* harvest failures. There *are* days in which the coal industry produces less coal than other industries use up and workers consume. There are also commodities that get used up in production and consumed but *never* reproduced, because they are replaced by other commodities that serve similar purposes.[12] Indeed, these latter two phenomena are so common that there is undoubtedly a negative physical surplus of some commodity at every single instant.

Because the FMT is a claim about the real world, it would be illegitimate to assume these phenomena away when assessing whether the theorem is true or not. One would be assuming away the very conditions of the problem. It is certainly possible, on the other hand, to put forth a different theorem about hypothetical economies in which all physical surpluses are positive at every moment. Yet such a theorem would also fail to demonstrate that surplus labor is the unique source of profit, even in these hypothetical economies, because something in addition to surplus labor would be needed in order to guarantee that profit is positive—positive physical surpluses of everything, all of the time.

Some authors (Mohun 2003: 98, Veneziani 2004: 105–06) have objected to my use of "arbitrary" values and prices to disprove the FMT. This objection is likewise irrelevant to the logical question at issue. If there are any possible sets of values and prices at which surplus labor and profit would fail to coexist, then surplus labor is simply not the *exclusive* source of profit. Once again, something more—the "right" values and prices—is also needed in order to guarantee that there is both surplus labor and profit. Versions of the FMT which assume that all commodities are continually sold at their prices of production therefore fail to show that surplus labor, by itself, must always lead to positive profit—but that is exactly what must be shown.

10.5 Reasonable Prices Can Differ

In any case, if "arbitrary" is understood to mean unreasonable or freakish, rather than "not deduced from static equilibrium models," then it is easy to disprove the FMT without resorting to the use of arbitrary values and prices. The following two examples show that even the slightest deviation from equilibrium can cause the standard FMT to fail. (They also illustrate how reproduction occurs when there are negative physical surpluses.)

Consider a two-industry economy in which apples (good A) and broccoli (good B) grow on their own. Workers are needed to harvest the output, but no other inputs are needed. The physical data of Table 10.1 are based on the following assumptions. The daily real wage (physical wage) is one-half lb of apples and one-half lb of broccoli per worker. Workers are paid at the end of the day. One day of labor is needed to harvest one pound of each product, so the labor-time value of each product is one labor-day per pound. On Day 1, four workers pick apples and two workers harvest broccoli, while on Day 2 the figures are reversed. The capitalists, who own the land, have an initial stock of at least one lb of broccoli (acquired through their own labor); given this assumption, the necessary exchanges can take place.

Even though there is a negative surplus of one good in the economy as a whole on both days, the economy reproduces itself over the two-day period. The

Table 10.1. Failure of the Simultaneous Dual-System FMT

	Industry	Living Labor	Output	Real Wages	Physical Surpluses
Day 1	A	4	4A, 0B	2A, 2B	2A, −2B
	B	2	0A, 2B	1A, 1B	−1A, 1B
	Total	6	4A, 2B	3A, 3B	1A, −1B
Day 2	A	2	2A, 0B	1A, 1B	1A, −1B
	B	4	0A, 4B	2A, 2B	−2A, 2B
	Total	6	2A, 4B	3A, 3B	−1A, 1B
Days 1 + 2	A	6	6A, 0B	3A, 3B	3A, −3B
	B	6	0A, 6B	3A, 3B	−3A, 3B
	Total	12	6A, 6B	6A, 6B	0A, 0B

output of each good is exactly enough to allow the workers to obtain the apples and broccoli they need in order to return to work on Day 3.

Since the labor-time value of each product is 1, the value of the wages is exactly equal to the amount of labor performed, on both days and in both industries. (In Industry A on Day 1, for instance, the total value of wages is $(1 \times 2) + (1 \times 2) = 4$, and 4 days of labor are performed.) Surplus labor is therefore always 0 in each industry, and in the economy as a whole. But what about profit?

Recall that the simultaneous dual-system interpretation defines total profit as the total price of the physical surpluses. Thus total profit would equal 0, just like total surplus labor does, if the price of apples and the price of broccoli were exactly equal. However, even the *slightest* deviation from this equilibrium can cause total profit to be positive despite the lack of surplus labor. If, for instance, the prices of apples and broccoli are $100 and $99, then total profit on Day 1 is $(100 \times 1) + (99 \times -1) = \$1$, and if the prices are $99 and $100 on Day 2, then total profit is $(99 \times -1) + (100 \times 1) = \$1$ on that day, too. Over the entire two-day period, moreover, profit in each industry is $1. And since the economy reproduces itself, it would be possible to have positive profit without surplus labor *forever*—again, according to the dual-system definitions.

The second example is just like the first, except that workers in each industry have taken a very slight pay cut. Each worker's daily real wage is now 0.4999 units of each good, so the labor-time value of the daily wage is $(1 \times 0.4999) + (1 \times 0.4999) = 0.9998$. Thus each worker performs $1 - 0.9998 = 0.0002$ days of surplus labor each day.

The fall in the real wage also causes the physical surpluses to increase. Each day's total real wage is now $6 \times 0.4999 = 2.9994$ lbs of each good. Thus on Day 1, the total physical surplus of apples is $(4 - 2.9994) = 1.0006$ and the total physical surplus of broccoli is $(2 - 2.9994) = -0.9994$. If the prices of apples and broccoli are $99 and $100 on Day 1, then total profit is $(99 \times 1.0006) + (100 \times -0.9994) = -\$0.88$. Hence, we have surplus labor but negative profit, and this could likewise continue forever.[13]

There was nothing arbitrary—in the usual sense of the word—about either example. The assumptions were perfectly reasonable. The economy reproduced itself. Deviations of the prices from equilibrium were very small, as were the fluctuations in the prices. They were nonetheless sufficient to make profit positive when there was no surplus labor and negative when there was surplus labor—given the simultaneous dual-system definitions of these terms.

10.6 Failure of the NI-SSSI FMT

The New Interpretation (NI) and SSSI definitions of profit and surplus labor are only a bit less physicalist, and equally simultaneist. This is why these interpretations, too, imply that surplus labor is not the exclusive source of profit.

The concept of physical **net product** is crucial to the NI and SSSI definitions of profit and surplus labor (which are the same). The economy-wide net
product of any good or service is the amount produced minus the amount used
up in production:

$$\text{net product} = \text{total product} - \text{used-up input}$$

If, on a given day, the coal industry produces less coal than the amount of coal
that it and other industries use up, then the net product of coal is negative. When
typewriters were being used up in production but no longer being produced, the
net product of typewriters was also negative. So, just as in the case of physical
surpluses, it is clear that the net product of some commodity is always negative
—and that economies do reproduce themselves nonetheless.

And just as the total price of the physical surpluses can be negative, so can
the **price of the net product** (PNP), the economy-wide total price of all the net
products. The PNP is a simultaneist concept because, once again, a unit of coal
that enters production at the start of some period is valued at the same price as a
unit of coal produced at the end.

If there were negative net products of only a few goods, but their prices
were very high relative to other goods, then the PNP would be negative. Although this is unlikely, it is certainly possible in principle.

The possibility of a negative PNP is precisely what causes the NI-SSSI version of the FMT to fail. These interpretations maintain that the PNP is the monetary expression of the new value added by workers. And the labor-time measure
of the new value added by these workers is the total amount of labor they perform. The ratio of these two measures is thus held to express the relationship
between value in money terms and value in labor-time terms. In other words,
this ratio is the *simultaneist* monetary expression of labor-time (MELT):

$$\text{simultaneist MELT} = \frac{\text{PNP}}{\text{total labor performed}}$$

The simultaneist MELT is therefore negative whenever the PNP is negative.
A negative MELT in turn implies that whenever some monetary sum, like total
profit, is negative, its labor-time equivalent is positive. But the labor-time equivalent of total profit is total surplus labor,[14] and total profit must be negative
when the simultaneist MELT is negative, since the NI and SSSIs define it as:

$$\text{total profit} = \text{PNP} - \text{total money wages}$$

Thus total surplus labor is always positive, but total profit is always negative, when the PNP is negative. This proves that the NI and SSSIs imply that
surplus labor is not the sole source of profit. Something more than surplus labor

Table 10.2. A Negative Simultaneist MELT

Year	Good	Price (P)	Net Product (N)	P × N	Labor	Simultaneist MELT	Wages (W)	Profit = PNP – W, Surplus Labor
	A	$2	110	$220				
1	B	$10	–12	–$120				
	Total			$100 = PNP	5 hrs	$100 / 5 hrs = $20/hr	$60 = 3 hrs	$40 = 2 hrs
	A	$1	110	$110				
2	B	$10	–12	–$120				
	Total			–$ 10 = PNP	5 hrs	– $10 / 5 hrs = –$2/hr	$60 = –30 hrs	–$70 = 35 hrs

is needed in order for profit to exist—the "right" prices, prices that cause the PNP to be positive rather than negative.

Table 10.2 illustrates this phenomenon. The figures in boldface are data; all others are derived. In Year 1, when good A's price is $2 per unit, the PNP is positive, and thus the simultaneist MELT is also positive. And since total profit is positive, so is total surplus labor. In Year 2, however, the simultaneously determined price of good A drops to $1, causing the PNP to become negative. The simultaneist MELT is consequently negative as well. Because profit is now negative as a result of the fall in good A's price, and the MELT is negative, surplus labor is positive. This shows that, according to NI-SSSI definitions, surplus labor is not the exclusive source of profit. Another source is the high demand for good A in Year 1.

Attentive readers will have noted that surplus labor in Year 2, thirty-five hours, exceeds the *total* amount of labor performed, five hours. This is not an error on my part. Surplus labor is total labor performed minus variable capital in labor-time terms. Because the simultaneist MELT is negative, so is variable capital in labor-time terms—the workers produce an equivalent of their wages in less than no time! Thus surplus labor is greater than the total labor performed.

All of these problems disclose a serious conceptual flaw in the NI-SSSI view that the PNP is the monetary expression of the new value added by workers in production. On this view, workers' labor *subtracts* value if the PNP is negative.

10.7 Surplus Labor and Profit under the TSSI

In this section, I wish to show that the TSSI deduces Marx's conclusion that surplus labor is the exclusive source of profit—in every case, without exception. Some (fairly simple) algebra will be needed to demonstrate this, since numerical examples always leave open the possibility of exceptions. A numerical example, illustrating how the TSSI deduces Marx's conclusion when the PNP is negative, will follow in the next section.

The symbols used below stand for the following variables:

$L_{t,t+1}$	total labor performed (living labor)
$SL_{t,t+1}$	total surplus labor
$^{\$}C_t$	total constant capital (value transferred from used-up inputs)
$^{\$}V_t$	total variable capital
$^{\$}P_{t+1}$	price of total output
$^{\$}\pi_{t,t+1}^{NOM}$	nominal total profit
$^{\$}\pi_{t,t+1}^{REAL}$	real total profit
m_t	start-of-period temporalist MELT (input MELT)
m_{t+1}	end-of-period temporalist MELT (output MELT)
$i_{t,t+1}$	rate of change in the MELT; $i_{t,t+1} \equiv \dfrac{m_{t+1} - m_t}{m_t}$

Figures preceded by the $ superscript are measured in money terms, while L and SL are in units of labor-time. The production period begins at time t and concludes at time $t + 1$. I will assume that inputs enter production and wage contracts are finalized at time t, while output emerges at time $t + 1$.[15] Thus $^{\$}C$, $^{\$}V$, and the start-of-period MELT take the subscript t, while $^{\$}P$ and the end-of-period MELT take the subscript $t + 1$. The variables L, SL, $^{\$}\pi^{NOM}$, $^{\$}\pi^{REAL}$, and i take the subscript $t,t + 1$ in order to indicate that they refer to what transpires between the start and the end of the period.

According to the TSSI, the labor-time equivalent of the value transferred from inputs to output is the sum of value transferred divided by the MELT, $^{\$}C_t / m_t$. The total labor-time value of the output that emerges at time $t + 1$ is therefore $^{\$}C_t / m_t$ plus the living labor extracted, $L_{t,t+1}$. The total price of the output is the monetary expression of this total value—the total value times m_{t+1}. Thus total value equals total price divided by the output MELT, $^{\$}P_{t+1}/m_{t+1}$. Total value in labor-time terms is therefore

$$^{\$}P_{t+1}/m_{t+1} = {}^{\$}C_t/m_t + L_{t,t+1} \,.^{16} \qquad (10.1)$$

Also, surplus labor is the living labor extracted minus the labor-time equivalent of the variable capital,

$$SL_{t,t+1} = L_{t,t+1} - {}^\$V_t / m_t \qquad (10.2)$$

We have seen that Marx's exploitation theory of profit is incompatible with simultaneous valuation. Temporal valuation is required. Yet it is obvious that *nominal* profit can be positive even when surplus labor has not been extracted. If surplus labor and profit were both zero when the production process ended, but the nominal price of the output rose immediately thereafter, then nominal profit would be positive. Thus if we wish to make Marx's theory make sense, we must interpret the exploitation theory of profit as a theory of *real* profit.

Nominal profit is

$$ {}^\$\pi_{t,t+1}^{NOM} \equiv {}^\$P_{t+1} - {}^\$C_t - {}^\$V_t.{}^{17} \qquad (10.3)$$

Now, according to any definition of real profit, ${}^\$P_{t+1}$ must be "deflated" in order to adjust for inflation—that is, for the change during the period in the amount of money that represents one unit of real value. ${}^\$P_{t+1}$ is deflated by dividing it by "1 + the rate of inflation." For instance, if ${}^\$P_{t+1} = \$110$ and the rate of inflation has been $10\% = 0.1$, then ${}^\$P_{t+1}$ in real terms is $\$110/(1 + 0.1) = \$100$. Now the TSSI holds that the rate of inflation relevant to Marx's theory is $i_{t,t+1} \equiv \dfrac{m_{t+1} - m_t}{m_t}$, the rate of change in the MELT.[18] Thus "1 + the rate of inflation" is $1 + i_{t,t+1} = m_{t+1}/m_t$, so that total price in real terms is $\left(\dfrac{m_t}{m_{t+1}}\right){}^\$P_{t+1}$. Real profit is therefore

$$ {}^\$\pi_{t,t+1}^{REAL} = \left(\frac{m_t}{m_{t+1}}\right){}^\$P_{t+1} - {}^\$C_t - {}^\$V_t \qquad (10.4)$$

If we now multiply both sides of equation (10.1) by m_t and then subtract ${}^\$C_t$ from both sides, we get

$$ \left(\frac{m_t}{m_{t+1}}\right){}^\$P_{t+1} - {}^\$C_t = m_t(L_{t,t+1}) \qquad (10.1')$$

and substituting this result into equation (10.4) gives us

$$^{\$}\pi_{t,t+1}^{REAL} = m_t(L_{t,t+1}) - {}^{\$}V_t = m_t(L_{t,t+1} - {}^{\$}V_t/m_t). \qquad (10.4')$$

Using equation (10.2), we get, finally,

$$^{\$}\pi_{t,t+1}^{REAL} = m_t(SL_{t,t+1}). \qquad (10.4'')$$

Thus real profit is the monetary expression of surplus labor.

But we are not out of the woods just yet. As we saw above, the *simultaneist* MELT is negative whenever the PNP is negative. If the temporalist MELT could likewise be negative for this or any other reason, then real profit could be negative when surplus labor is positive and vice-versa.

Yet the temporalist MELT cannot be negative. Consider equation (10.1) once more:

$$^{\$}P_{t+1}/m_{t+1} = {}^{\$}C_t/m_t + L_{t,t+1}. \qquad (10.1)$$

$^{\$}P_{t+1}$ and $L_{t,t+1}$ are always positive[19] and $^{\$}C_t$ is always positive or zero. Thus if m_t is positive, then m_{t+1} must be positive as well. So if the "initial MELT" of time 0 is positive, then the MELT at time 1 is also positive. But if the MELT at time 1 is positive, then so is the MELT at time 2. And so forth and so on. *All* subsequent values of the MELT must be positive. Total real profit must therefore be positive if total surplus labor is positive.

Following Mohun's (2003: 99) and Veneziani's (2004: 106) objections to the "arbitrary assumption" that the MELT of time 0 is positive, Alan Freeman and I proved that this must be the case (Kliman and Freeman 2006). The crux of the proof is this. The temporalist MELT, usually defined as the ratio of total money price to total labor-time value, can also be defined, equivalently, as the ratio of a unit of money to the amount of labor commanded by a unit of money. Now, at whatever moment in the past that we arbitrarily designate as time 0, a unit of money commanded a positive amount of labor. Thus the MELT of time 0 was positive.

The temporalist MELT has therefore always been and must always be positive. Real profit as defined above has therefore always been and must always be positive when surplus labor is positive. If surplus labor were ever negative, moreover, then real profit would also be negative. Thus the TSSI, in contrast to all simultaneist interpretations of Marx's value theory, succeeds in deducing his conclusion that surplus labor is the exclusive source of profit.

10.8 TSSI Results in the Negative-PNP Case

I will now illustrate that the TSSI deduces Marx's conclusion even when the PNP is negative. Let us use the same data that we used in section 10.6 to construct Table 10.2, and assume that the temporalist MELT at the end of Year 1, when the PNP was positive, was equal to the simultaneist MELT, $20/hr. Thus living labor is $L_{t,t+1} = 5$ hrs and variable capital in money terms is $^\$V_t = \$60$. Since the end of Year 1 is the start of Year 2, the temporalist MELT at the start of Year 2 is likewise $m_t = \$20/hr$.

We also need figures for $^\$C_t$ and $^\$P_{t+1}$ in Year 2. Let us assume that $^\$C_t = \$500$ and $^\$P_{t+1} = \$450$. Thus $^\$P_{t+1} - ^\$C_t = -\$50$. This differs from Year 2's PNP, $-\$10$, because we are using the actual prices of the inputs at the start of Year 2, not the replacement cost of these inputs at the end of the year, to compute the sum of value transferred.[20]

Equation (10.2) tells us that surplus labor is $SL_{t,t+1} = L_{t,t+1} - ^\$V_t/m_t = 5 - 60/20 = 2$ hrs. Equation (10.3) tells us that nominal profit is

$$^\$\pi^{NOM}_{t,t+1} \equiv \, ^\$P_{t+1} - ^\$C_t - ^\$V_t = \$450 - \$500 - \$60 = -\$110.$$

This result appears to contradict Marx's theory. We shall see, however, that we *appear* to have surplus labor without profit only because the value created by an hour of labor is expressed as a smaller amount of money at the end of Year 2 than at the start—only because, in other words, the MELT has fallen in the meantime.

One way to find the end-of-year MELT is by means of equation (10.1): $^\$P_{t+1}/m_{t+1} = \, ^\$C_t/m_t + L_{t,t+1}$. Thus $450/m_{t+1} = 500/20 + 5 = 30$. But if $450/m_{t+1} = 30$, then $m_{t+1} = \$15/hr$. Since m_t was $20/hr, this means that the value created by an hour of labor is expressed as only 15/20ths (= 75%) as much money at the end of Year 2 as at the start; the rate of inflation of the MELT is -25%. Using equation (4), we find that

$$^\$\pi^{REAL}_{t,t+1} = \left(\frac{m_t}{m_{t+1}}\right)^\$P_{t+1} - ^\$C_t - ^\$V_t = \left(\frac{20}{15}\right)\$450 - \$500 - \$60 = \$40.$$

The real profit of $40 is exactly equal to the start-of-period MELT times the surplus labor, $20/hr × 2 hrs. We therefore see that a negative PNP does not cause the *temporalist* MELT to turn negative. Nor does it cause the TSSI's FMT to fail.

Once we have adjusted the nominal figures, both surplus labor and profit are the same in Years 1 and 2. This should not come as a surprise: in both years, workers work the same amount of time, and the labor-time value of their wages is the same, so they create the same amount of surplus-value. Thus, after we have adjusted for changes in the MELT, total surplus-value in money terms is the same in both years. And since total profit equals total surplus-value, total profit is also unchanged.

It might be claimed that the results exhibited in these last two sections prove nothing; they merely follow from the definitions. But that is *precisely* what needed to be proved here. The objective has been to make Marx's exploitation theory of profit make sense (not to prove that it is true). To make it make sense, one needs to find definitions—in other words, an interpretation of his terms and premises—from which his results do indeed follow. This is not a trivial task, as the failure of simultaneist interpretations to find the needed definitions makes clear. To *define* total surplus labor as the labor-time equivalent of total profit would indeed be trivial, tautological, and require no proof, but to *find* the definitions that lead to this result is quite a different matter.

10.9 Conclusions

Owing to their static character, simultaneist interpretations of Marx's value theory grant value no role in explaining the dynamics of capitalism. Although some proponents of simultaneist interpretations have acknowledged this fact, they seem untroubled by it. Duménil and Lévy (2000: 142), for instance, contend that "[t]he core of the explanatory power of the labor theory of value lies in the analysis of exploitation [. . . as] the origin of profit. . . . [O]ther theories also exist independently of labor value, such as the theory of crisis or of historical tendencies. In particular, the labor theory of value does not provide the framework to account for disequilibrium and dynamics in capitalism."

As this chapter has shown, however, the attempts to fragment Marx's value theory into static and dynamic aspects, and to embrace the former but jettison the latter, have not succeeded. When his value theory is interpreted in static terms, it is not only his explanations of dynamic issues, like the tendency of the rate of profit to fall, that seem false. His explanation of the origin of profit, a putatively static issue, seems false as well. Conversely, the TSSI, which vindicates the internal consistency of Marx's value theory in other respects, also vindicates the logical coherence of his exploitation theory of profit. His value theory is far more of a "package deal" than has hitherto been recognized.

Notes

1. Marx (1991a: 270) argued that surplus labor is "the exclusive source of profit."

2. I refer to Marx's "exploitation theory of profit" rather than his "theory of exploitation" because the former is only one facet of the latter. For a brief discussion of his overall theory of exploitation and its relation to other such theories, see Kliman (2006a).

3. Shortly after writing this, Roemer (1982, 1988) came out with models based on the FMT (but not value theory) that supposedly demonstrated an exact correspondence between how much wealth an individual has initially and her subsequent status as an exploiter or exploitee. He became rather famous for this work even outside of economics.

4. I say "stated above" because Okishio did prove something—just not anything like this claim. Using simultaneous dual-system definitions, he proved that (1) if workers perform surplus labor, then there are some *conceivable* sets of output levels at which total profit would be positive; and that (2) if profit could be positive in *every* industry at once, then surplus labor would also be positive. Clearly, the first proposition says nothing about the relationship between surplus labor and profit at actual output levels, while the second says nothing about their relationship when losses in some industries are needed in order for there to be profit in others.

5. The demonstrations in this chapter draw heavily on Kliman (2001) and Kliman and Freeman (2006).

6. In Marx's (1990a: 338–339) theory, surplus labor and the **surplus product** do correspond strictly, but the latter term means something very different from physical surplus as defined by physicalists. If 1000 tons of steel are produced today, and 20% of the labor needed to produce them is surplus labor, then the steel industry's surplus product, in Marx's sense, is 200 tons of steel (20% of the 1000 tons produced). But if the auto, construction, and other industries have used up 1200 tons of steel today, then the physical surplus of steel as defined by physicalists is 1000 tons − 1200 tons = −200 tons.

7. In other words, heart attack must be both a *necessary* condition and a *sufficient* condition for death. The usual way of putting the FMT is that surplus labor is both necessary and sufficient for profit.

8. The problem is even worse if we assume a positive corn-wage, say 1 bushel. This lowers the physical "profit" to −2, but surplus labor *increases* to 2. (If value is measured in terms of labor-time, the simultaneously determined per-bushel value of corn is the living labor divided by the net product: (1 worker-year)/(−1 bushel) = (−1 worker-year per bushel). Variable capital, the value of the corn-wage, is therefore the per-bushel value of corn times the amount of corn wages, (−1 worker-year per bushel) × (1 bushel) = (−1 worker-year), and surplus labor—the worker's labor minus variable capital—is (−1 worker-year) − (−1 worker-year) = (2 worker-years).

9. If p were zero, then profit would be zero, too, but I know of no simultaneist interpretation which holds that p must be zero in this case.

10. A negative physical surplus is the same thing as a depletion of stocks. Assume, for instance, that the initial stock of coal is twenty tons, that ten tons are used up as input and consumed by workers, and that eight tons of new coal are produced. Since the stock of coal at day's end is 20 tons − 10 tons + 8 tons = 18 tons, the change in the stock during the day is 18 tons − 20 tons = −2 tons, which is equal to the physical surplus (8 tons − 10 tons).

11. To get the total value of the physical surpluses, we multiply the physical surplus of each commodity by its per-unit value, and add up the results. But on this interpretation, the total value of the physical surpluses *is* total surplus-value, and total surplus-value measured in terms of labor-time *is* total surplus labor.

12. I am indebted to Alan Freeman for emphasizing this crucial point. It shows that economies cannot rigorously be theorized as systems in which inputs are reproduced as outputs.

13. In the first example, it is impossible for profit to be positive in both industries at once. In the second, total profit would be positive if equal amounts of apples and broccoli were produced every day. These examples are therefore perfectly compatible with what Okishio *actually* proved (see note 4 above).

14. Surplus labor is surplus-value in terms of labor-time, and these interpretations preserve the equality of total surplus-value and total profit in money terms. It follows that total surplus labor is the labor-time equivalent of total profit.

15. This is purely a simplifying assumption. All of the relations below can be stated in terms of continuous time without affecting the results (see Kliman 2001: 106–08).

16. This equation can be rewritten as a formula for the computation of the MELT,

$$m_{t+1} = \frac{^{\$}P_{t+1}}{^{\$}C_t / m_t + L_{t,t+1}}.$$ Since the total price of output ($^{\$}P_{t+1}$) equals the total value of

output in money terms, the right-hand side of the formula is in fact the ratio of the monetary and labor-time values of total output.

17. $^{\$}P_{t+1}$ depends upon end-of-period prices, while $^{\$}C_t$ depends upon start-of-period prices. Thus $^{\$}P_{t+1} - {}^{\$}C_t$ should not be confused with the PNP.

18. Orthodox economists, of course, define inflation as a rise in the price of a given set of goods and services rather than a given amount of labor-time value. Their definition does not work here; it takes us back to the conclusions of the corn model. If we were to use the orthodox rate of inflation, the real value of 99 bushels of corn harvested at the end of the year would always be only 99/100ths as much as the real value of 100 bushels planted at the start.

19. There is one exception to this: $L_{t,t+1}$ is zero in Dmitriev's case of fully automated production. But $SL_{t,t+1}$ is also zero in this case, so it follows from equation (10.4'') that *real* profit is zero, too, no matter what the value of the MELT might be. This resolves Dmitriev's paradox.

20. I am implicitly assuming that forty units of good A are used up during the year. Since good A's price falls by $1/unit during Year 2, the actual start-of-year cost of these forty units of good A is $40 more than their replacement cost. Thus $^{\$}C_t$ is $40 greater than its simultaneist counterpart and $^{\$}P_{t,t+1} - {}^{\$}C_t$ is $40 less than the PNP.

Chapter 11

An Empirical Defense of the Law of Value?

11.1 Introduction

The resurgence in the 1970s of the allegations that Marx's value theory is internally inconsistent was responded to in different ways. Proponents of the temporal single-system interpretation (TSSI), the simultaneous single-system interpretations, and the New Interpretation, which all emerged in the early 1980s, responded with new interpretations and conceptual approaches. Shortly thereafter, an attempt—initiated by Shaikh (1984) and Ochoa (1984)—got underway to sidestep the interpretive and conceptual problems, and instead defend "the labor theory of value" on empirical grounds. Until recently, this effort has been regarded as quite successful. During the next eighteen years, many additional studies replicated Shaikh and Ochoa's initial findings. The empirical defense also became rather popular outside this circle of researchers, evidently because it is easily and quickly understood and because it seemed to allow the interpretive and theoretical problems to be dismissed in four words: "Marx's theory holds empirically."

I wish to show in this chapter that the empirical defense is actually quite unsuccessful.[1] The statistical methods employed by its proponents are unsound, and new empirical results compel us to reject its version of "the" labor theory of value. Yet even if it were a success on its own terms, it would fail as a defense of Marx's value theory, contrary to what has sometimes been claimed. Our examination of the "value-form paradigm" (in section 2.2.5) and the "fundamental Marxian theorem" (in chapter 10) showed that Marx's theory cannot be rescued without directly confronting the allegations that it is internally inconsistent, and the point applies equally to the empirical defense. One must either reject Marx's theory or refute the allegations by means of an interpretation that eliminates the apparent inconsistencies.

11.2 The Labor Theory of Price

Shaikh at first attempted to solve the "transformation problem" by means of an iterative—step-by-step—version of the usual simultaneous, dual-system model. This allowed him to argue that Marx's own procedure was the correct first step. Yet once the process of iteration was completed, Shaikh's solution, like the others, failed to preserve two of Marx's three aggregate equalities (Shaikh 1977).

Still searching for a way to uphold "the labor theory of value," Shaikh turned to the data. He suggested that "variations in prices [across industries] are dominated by variations in values" (Shaikh 1984: 64). In other words, industry-level prices do not deviate *systematically* from values. If one industry's value is $x\%$ higher or lower than another's, its price will be approximately $x\%$ higher or lower as well. I shall call this the **labor theory of price** (LTP).

Shaikh and Ochoa's statistical results appeared to confirm the theory. Subsequent studies, using data from various countries and various years, seem to confirm it as well. The **correlation** between values and prices—a measure of the degree to which they vary together—has frequently been found to exceed 0.95, a figure quite close to the maximum value of 1. Moreover, deviations of prices from values have been found to be quite small; the average deviation is sometimes about $\pm20\%$ and often about $\pm10\%$ or even less. Scholars who have recently reviewed this literature have been impressed by the "strong evidence" (Foley 2000a: 19) and "robust empirical result[s]" (Desai 2002: 64) that have been obtained.

Some proponents of the LTP have used this evidence to suggest that criticisms of the received version of Marxian value theory are much ado about very little. For instance, Cockshott and Cottrell (1998: 70–71) argue that the reason why Marx cared about deviations of prices from values was that he mistakenly believed that seriously incorrect predictions would result if one assumed that prices of individual commodities equal their values. The clear implication is that, since prices do in fact tend to equal values, empirically oriented, scientific Marxist economists can get on with business as usual.

11.3 The LTP and Marx's Theory

It has also been thought that "the empirical results support Marx" (Desai 2002: 64). This is clearly incorrect. The LTP's proponents acknowledge that it differs from Marx's own value theory. "It is worth recalling that neither Marx nor Ricardo argue that cross-sectional variations are negligible. Indeed, they both emphasize that at any moment in time prices of production may significantly differ from values" (Shaikh 1984: 64; cf. Cockshott and Cottrell 1998: 70–71, Tsoul-fidis and Maniatis 2002: 360).

In fact, Marx explicitly rejected one of the LTP's key implications: if the amounts of capital advanced in two different industries are equal, then profit will tend to be lower in the industry in which less *variable* capital is advanced.[2] A rather well-known passage in volume I of *Capital* says the opposite: "Everyone knows that a cotton spinner, who, if we consider the percentage over the whole of his applied capital, employs much constant capital and little variable capital, does not, on account of this, pocket less profit or surplus-value than a baker, who sets in motion relatively much variable capital and little constant capital" (Marx 1990a: 421).

Thus evidence that supports the LTP does not serve to confirm Marx's value theory. Conversely, evidence that disconfirms the LTP—such as the evidence I will present below—does not serve to disconfirm Marx's theory. His defense of the law of value rests on the three *aggregate* price-value equalities, as we have seen, and he explicitly denied that price-value differences in *individual* industries have any bearing on the law's validity. "[T]he law of value [is not] affected by the fact that . . . governing average prices for commodities . . . differ from their individual values. This again affects only the addition of surplus-value to the various commodity prices; it does not abolish surplus-value itself, nor the total value of commodities as the source of these various price components" (Marx 1991a: 985).

A few years before he died, Marx wrote something similar in response to Adolph Wagner's critique of *Capital*. Wagner, a German economist, had pointed to the fact that prices depend on demand, and had construed this as evidence against Marx's value theory. Marx agreed with the first point but rejected the second:

> What has this to do with my theory of value? To the degree that corn is *sold* above its *value*, other commodities, whether in their natural form or in their money-form, are, to the same degree, sold *below their value*, and, to be sure, even if their own money price does *not* fall. The *sum of values* remains the same. . . . [I]t even remains the same in *monetary expression*, if money is reckoned among the commodities.[3]

11.4 The Spurious Correlation Problem

Freeman (1998) called attention to a fact that had not been sufficiently appreciated: strong price-value correlations may not be valid evidence, owing to a problem known as **spurious correlation**. If a correlation between two variables disappears or is lowered substantially once we control for the influence of a "hidden" third variable—that is, introduce it as a **control variable**—then the correlation is spurious. The word "spurious" is somewhat misleading, since the correlation is a statistical fact, but the point is that it cannot validly be used as evidence of a genuine relationship between the first two variables.

The strong correlation between the number of firefighters (F) at the scene of a fire and the dollar amount of damage (D) that is done is a well-known example of spurious correlation. The larger F is, the larger D is. Yet it is invalid to conclude that firefighters cause the damage (or vice-versa). What is actually going on, of course, is that a third variable, the size (S) of the fire, is the source of the relationship between F and D: larger fires cause more firefighters to come to the scene than small fires do, and larger fires cause more damage than small ones. *If we control for the differences in* S, *little if any correlation between* F *and* D *remains, so the original correlation was spurious.*

In precisely the same way, industry size (S) may be a third variable that causes industry-level values (W) and prices (P) to move together. *If we control for differences in* S, *and little or no correlation between* W *and* P *remains thereafter, then the original correlation was spurious.*[4]

Cockshott and Cottrell (2005) have argued that this is a false concern, because W and P are themselves measures of industry size. When we say that an industry is large or small, we may well mean that W and P are large or small.[5] "Size" is not some distinct third variable that causes them to vary together.

One problem with this argument is that empirical studies of the value-price relationship have necessarily used very aggregated government data, and gov-

Figure 11.1.

Aggregation Produces Spurious Value-Price Correlations

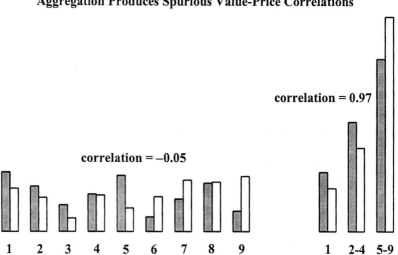

ernment statisticians *create* differences in industry size when they aggregate many industries into fewer ones. For instance, one aggregated industry may contain two "sub-industries," while another may contain twenty. Figure 11.1 shows how substantially aggregation may affect the measured price-value correlation. On the left are nine sub-industries. Prices (in grey) are on average no higher where the values (in white) are high than where the values are low; the correlation between their values and prices is a negligible –0.05. (A value of 0 would indicate that they do not move together at all.) On the right are three aggregated industries. They contain one, three, and five of the original sub-industries, respectively. Now the price is low when the value is low and high when the value is high. The price-value correlation has increased to 0.97.[6]

This example does not prove that the price-value correlations obtained from aggregated data are spurious. It could be the case that pre- as well as post-aggregation correlations are strong. The example does demonstrate, however, that the reported price-value correlations *may* be, partly or even entirely, mere by-products of the aggregation process. Lacking access to disaggregated data, we cannot know whether that is the case or not. It is therefore necessary to eliminate any possibility of spurious correlation arising from aggregation and—for this reason, if for no other—to control for differences in industry size.

11.5 The Tautological Correlation Problem

I believe that industry size needs to be introduced as a control variable for another reason as well: values and prices have a significant component in common, namely costs (Marx's "cost price," k). To see why this is a problem, consider an analogous case. Businesses' labor costs (LC) are the sum of workers' after-tax earnings (ATE) plus the taxes (T) that are deducted, while workers' incomes (I) are their after-tax earnings plus any non-labor income (NLI):

$$LC \equiv ATE + T$$
$$I \equiv ATE + NLI$$

The correlation between labor costs and workers' incomes is very strong. LC is large when I is large, and small when I is small. But this result is uninteresting and unimportant because it is obvious. It is obvious because LC and I are not two separate variables, but pretty much the same thing. And they are pretty much the same thing precisely because they have a significant component in common. In other words, ATE is a "third variable" that causes LC and I to move together, and it is necessary to control for its influence in order to guard against the possibility of spurious correlation. If the correlation between LC and I remains strong even after we have done so (which is highly unlikely), we then have an interesting and important empirical result. Somehow, the taxes that workers pay flow back to them in the form of non-labor income. We might wish to find out how this surprising phenomenon occurs.

As we saw in section 2.1.11, the case of values and prices is strictly analogous:

$$W \equiv k + s$$
$$P \equiv k + \pi$$

Thus k is a third variable that causes W and P to move together, and we must eliminate any possibility of spurious correlation by employing it as a control variable.[7] If a strong correlation remains after we have done so, we have discovered a very important fact: the amount of surplus-value an industry produces is the dominant determinant of the amount of profit it receives. Marx was wrong when he suggested that cotton spinners do not "pocket less profit" per dollar of capital advanced than bakers do, and the LTP is right.

We may find, however, that the correlation disappears or is substantially reduced after we control for variations in k. If that is so, we have learned that the initially strong relationship between W and P was merely a by-product of what I have called **tautological correlation**—in this case, the correlation of k with itself (Kliman 2005).

11.6 The Measure of Size Matters

Imagine that there is a strong correlation between the number of cars and the number of dogs in various cities, but only because the cities are of different sizes. There are large numbers of cars, and dogs, in large cities, and small numbers of cars, and dogs, in small cities. The correlation is spurious. Yet if we control for the influence of size by using the cities' areas as our measure, we may find that a strong correlation persists. Although area is certainly a measure of city size, it is a poor one in this context. Population is clearly the best measure to use.

This example shows three important things. First, the particular measure of size we choose matters, and we must try to find the best one. Second, the best measure of size is the one that eliminates the most spurious correlation. Finally, although the correlation between two variables may not decrease substantially when inferior control variables are used, this does not make the correlation a genuine one, and it should not prevent us from concluding that the correlation is spurious. If the introduction of *any* third variable substantially reduces the correlation between the first two, then the original correlation was spurious. (This follows from the definition of spurious correlation.)

The above discussion of tautological correlation indicates that industry cost (k) is the best measure of size to use in order to eliminate any possible spurious correlation between prices and values. By using it, we eliminate not only the problems caused by aggregation, but tautological correlation as well. Yet even if my analysis of the tautological correlation problem is not accepted, we have seen that cost may still be the best measure of size to use. That will be the case if we eliminate more of whatever spurious correlation may be present when we use cost than when we use other measures of industry size.

11.7 Data and Computations

In order to determine whether the LTP holds true once any possible spurious correlation has been eliminated, I first constructed price and value measures for industries in the U.S. during the 1977–1997 period, the years for which data were available. The raw data came from the U.S. National Income and Product Accounts (NIPA). In every respect but one, I followed Ochoa's (1984, 1989) methodology as closely as I could. Some industries in the NIPA data set were excluded in order to conform to his procedures. Owing to missing data, I had to aggregate some others. My final data set contains forty-two industries in each of the twenty-one years. The main difference between Ochoa's procedures and mine was that I used TSSI definitions when constructing my price and value measures, in order to simplify computations and increase the number of years for which data were available. Further details regarding the raw data, definitions, and methods used to compute the variables are provided in Kliman (2002) and Kliman (2004b).

11.8 Replication of Earlier Results

I first estimated the price-value relationship in the standard way—that is, without controlling for the influence of industry size. The correlation coefficients were larger than any previously reported. The average of the twenty-one years' price-value correlations was 0.991, and they ranged from 0.986 to 0.993. Similarly, the various measures of the average price-value deviation were smaller than any previously reported for the U.S. economy, and among the smallest reported for any country. The mean absolute (percentage) deviation, for example, ranged from 7.9% to 9.5%, and its average value was 8.6%. After pooling the twenty-one years of data, I ran the standard log-linear regression of the industries' aggregate prices ($\log(P)$) on their aggregate values ($\log(W)$). The results were remarkably close to those predicted by the LTP. For instance, each 1% difference between industries' aggregate values led to a 0.9996% difference between their aggregate prices, which is almost identical to the theory's prediction (1%). The value of the R^2 (the squared correlation coefficient) was 0.990, which means that variations in values accounted for 99% of the variations in prices.

One reason why these results are so "good" is that, in contrast to prior studies, I used TSSI definitions when computing my variables. In other studies, which employed dual-system definitions, "price" and "value" cost prices differ, and this difference increased the degree of deviation between prices and values of outputs.

11.9 Controlling for the Influence of Industry Size

I used cost as a control variable in two different ways. First, whereas prior tests of the LTP looked at the relationship between industries' aggregate prices and values, what I shall call Model 1 looked at the relationship between prices and values per dollar of cost. I demonstrated that this procedure was legitimate since, *if the LTP were "true," the price-value relationship would be exactly the same in the two cases* (see Kliman 2002: 303–304, and, for my response to Cockshott and Cottrell's critique of this demonstration, Kliman (2005)).

Model 2 introduced cost as a control variable in a more typical manner—by including it as a distinct variable in the regression equation. In this case, I looked at the relationship between industries' aggregate prices and values, but instead of treating aggregate value as a single variable, as prior studies had done, I decomposed it into cost and value per dollar of cost (Kliman 2004b).

The typical log-linear specification was used to estimate the models. In both cases, the LTP predicts that each 1% increase in "value per dollar of cost" (W/k) will result, *ceteris paribus*, in a 1% increase in "price per dollar of cost" (P/k). In other words, it predicts that the $\log(W/k)$ coefficient will equal 1.[8]

11.10 Regression Results

Table 11.1 summarizes the key results. The results from Model 1 indicate that the $\log(W/k)$ coefficient was a mere 0.05 on average and that it never exceeded 0.24. In seven of the twenty-one years, it was actually negative. These figures differ so greatly from the value of 1 predicted by the LTP that we can reject that prediction with a very high degree of confidence (at least 97.5%, using a one-tailed test) in every year. Moreover, the impact of cost-controlled values on cost-controlled prices was never statistically significant at any tolerable level (the largest t-value was 0.64). This means that we cannot reasonably reject the hypothesis that there is *no* relationship between industries' values and prices once we control for differences in costs.

Table 11.1. Log-linear Regression Results

Model		Constant	log(W/k)	log(k)	R^2
1	Average	0.13	0.05	—	0.00
	Low	0.11	−0.16	—	0.00
	High	0.16	0.24	—	0.01
2	Average	0.11	0.07	1.00	0.99
	Low	−0.14	−0.14	0.99	0.99
	High	0.27	0.24	1.02	0.99

Division of values and prices by costs necessarily lowers the price-value correlation, but the correlation coefficient would remain positive and statistically significant if the LTP were correct. However, whenever the log(W/k) coefficient is negative or statistically insignificant, so is the correlation coefficient. Thus it was negative one-third of the time and never significant. All R^2 figures were therefore insignificant as well, and very small; variations in cost-controlled values never accounted for more than 1% of the variations in cost-controlled prices.

In a recent dissertation that examined the price-value relationship in Spain's economy between 1986–1994, Osuna (2003) reported very similar results. Using a model much like Model 1, he found that industries' aggregate prices and values were very strongly correlated in every year, but that no statistically significant correlation remained after he controlled for differences in industry size. The nine estimated correlation coefficients were all small, and all but one was negative.

The results of Model 2 were also very similar to those of Model 1. The log(W/k) coefficient was negative in five of the twenty-one years and its highest value was again only 0.24. Its average value, 0.07, was so far below the value of 1 predicted by the LTP that we can again reject the prediction with at least 97.5% confidence in every year (using a one-tailed test). Since the largest t-value was 0.63, we are again unable to reasonably reject the hypothesis that, after the influence of differences in costs is removed, industry-level values have *no* remaining impact on industry-level prices.

The R^2 values of 0.99 indicate that Model 2 as a whole accounts for 99% of the variation among industries' aggregate prices in each year. This is solely because *costs* exert an extremely strong influence on the prices. Since the t-values associated with log(W/k) are all less than 1, inclusion of this variable actually reduces Model 2's explanatory power. We would obtain a better fit (i.e. a larger adjusted R^2) in every year if we were to account for variations in prices on the basis of costs alone.

Thus, contrary to the claim that industries' values are the dominant determinants of their prices, it is actually industries' costs, alone, that are the dominant determinants. Once cost is used as a control variable, there is no reliable evidence that industries' values have any influence on their prices whatsoever. The strong correlations between the prices and values are spurious, and the evidence compels us to reject the LTP.

11.11 The (In)significance of Small Price-Value Deviations

Measured price-value deviations remain small even after the spurious correlation between prices and values has been eliminated. In fact, the percentage deviation between an industry's aggregate value and price and between its value and price per dollar of cost is exactly the same. It might thus seem that, although strong price-value correlations do not constitute valid evidence in favor of the LTP, the fact that prices and values are close is indeed valid evidence.

This is not correct. First of all, measured price-value deviations are systematically reduced when industries are aggregated together. This is because positive and negative deviations tend to cancel one another out when many industries are aggregated into fewer ones. (For example, given that total price equals total value, we can completely eliminate the deviations by lumping all industries into one!) All measures of average deviation are affected by this problem and, since we lack disaggregated data, it is impossible to ascertain how serious the problem is. There is therefore no reason to believe that small average deviations reflect anything other than the fact that the data used to compute them are highly aggregated (see Kliman 2004b).

Secondly, once we have controlled for differences in costs, prices and values are no longer close in the specific sense that the LTP requires. The theory predicts that prices do not deviate systematically from values; prices will be high in industries in which values are high, and low in industries in which values are low. Both will indeed be high or low when we examine industries of different sizes, but it is conceivable that the relationship persists even after we have controlled for differences in size. The graph on the left side of Figure 11.2 depicts such a case. Prices per dollar of cost (P/k) are low, moderate, or high where values per dollar of cost (W/k) are low, moderate, or high.

There is, however, an entirely different sense in which prices and values might be close. After controlling for differences in cost, all industries' prices might be close to all industries' values, a situation depicted on the right side of Figure 11.2. In this case, P/k is no more likely to be high when W/k is high than when W/k is low, and P/k is no more likely to be low when W/k is low than when W/k is high. On average, in other words, the size of P/k bears no relationship to the size of W/k. Yet because the data points are all bunched closely together, all prices and values are "close." As measured by the mean absolute

Figure 11.2.

Two Sets of "Close" Prices and Values

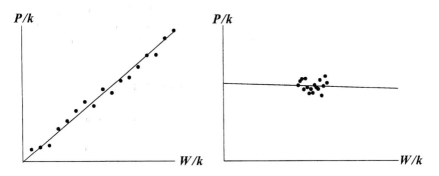

(percentage) deviation, they are just as "close" as the prices and values to their left. The mean absolute (percentage) deviation is 9.96% in both cases.

The *P/k* and *W/k* figures in my data set are like those on the right, not those on the left. If the correlation between the industries' aggregate prices and values is spurious, this will always be the case.

The fact that price-value deviations are small is therefore not valid evidence that the LTP is correct. All of the valid evidence suggests strongly that it is not correct. It is therefore not tenable to appeal to the data in order to sidestep either the allegations that Marx's value theory is internally inconsistent, or the failure of mainstream Marxian economics to make the theory make sense. The interpretive and theoretical issues need to be confronted squarely and resolved.

Notes

1. This discussion draws heavily on Kliman (2002, 2004b, and 2005).

2. Marx and the LTP both hold that (1) if the amounts of capital advanced in two different industries are equal, then surplus-value will tend to be lower in the industry in which less variable capital is advanced. (This is because the wages of the workers who produce all of the surplus-value are paid out of variable capital.) But the LTP holds, in addition, that (2) industry-level prices do not deviate systematically from values, which implies that (3) industry-level profits do not deviate systematically from surplus-values. Taken together, (1) and (3) imply that profit as well as surplus-value will tend to be lower in the industry with the smaller advance of variable capital.

3. Marx (1975: 187–88, emphases in original). The word "corn" is used in place of the original manuscript's "corn-price."

4. The fact that S is a cause of both W and P is *not* what makes a correlation between W and P spurious. If S is a cause of W, and W is a cause of P, then S is directly or indirectly a cause of both W and P. But if changes in W cause changes in P even when S does not change, then the W-P correlation is not spurious. In this case, when we control for the influence of S, the correlation will remain. Thus what makes a correlation between W and P spurious is the absence or near-absence of a relationship between them apart from the influence of S on both.

5. A different measure of size that naturally comes to mind is the physical output of the industry. As Ochoa pointed out, however, the industries in question all produce many different products, so their sizes cannot be measured in physical terms. Even if we had single-product industries, moreover, physical output would be a meaningless measure of size because the units in which it is measured are often arbitrary. For instance, we could increase the size of the coal industry 2000-fold by measuring the output of coal in pounds instead of tons. In light of these facts, it is impossible to measure the correlation between prices and values in the usual sense of these terms—prices and values per unit of output —and the correlation coefficient would be meaningless even if it were possible to compute it. See Ochoa (1984: 128–30).

6. See Kliman (2005) for my response to Cockshott and Cottrell. For additional discussion of the aggregation problem, see Kliman (2004b).

7. This conclusion also goes through if we employ dual-system definitions. In that case, if k is the value system's cost price, then an extra term d, the difference between the price system's cost price and k, must be added on to the definition of price. Because d is expected not to affect price in a systematic manner and it is rather small in reality, k is still a "third variable."

8. The explicit prediction of the LTP is $\log(P) = \log(W) + \varepsilon$, where ε is the error term. The theory therefore implicitly predicts that $\log(P/k) = \log(W/k) + \varepsilon$, and that $\log(P) = \log(W/k) + \log(k) + \varepsilon$, since the log of a ratio equals the log of its numerator minus the log of its denominator. My regression equations were therefore

Model 1: $\log(P/k) = \alpha_1 + \beta_1 \cdot \log(W/k) + \varepsilon_1$

Model 2: $\log(P) = \alpha_2 + \beta_2 \cdot \log(W/k) + \gamma_2 \cdot \log(k) + \varepsilon_2$

Thus the LTP predicts $\beta_1 = \beta_2 = 1$, as well as $\alpha_1 = \alpha_2 = 0$ and $\gamma_2 = 1$.

Chapter 12

Summary and Conclusions

12.1 General Summary and Main Results

For a full century, Marx's critics have alleged that his theories of value, profit, and economic crisis have been proven internally inconsistent. Drawing on a body of research that I and others have conducted since the 1980s, this book has challenged—and, I believe, disproved—these allegations. In doing so, it has removed the principal justification for the suppression of Marx's theories in their original form and for various efforts to "correct" *Capital,* fragment it, truncate it, or subsume it under one or another school of economics. Marx's critics are entitled to their theories, but Marx is equally entitled to his.

The main way in which this book has refuted the allegations of internal inconsistency is by showing that there exists an interpretation of Marx's value theory, the temporal single-system interpretation (TSSI), that eliminates the appearance of internal inconsistency in every case. The very fact that Marx's arguments *can* be interpreted as internally consistent demonstrates that inconsistency has not been proved. This fact also suggests strongly that the allegations of inconsistency are implausible, because the interpretations of Marx's texts that generate the appearance of inconsistency are implausible. When one interpretation makes a text make sense, while others repeatedly give rise to inconsistencies, it is not plausible that the latter interpretations are correct.

I have also endeavored to explain why Marx's theories have appeared for so long to be internally inconsistent. The alleged proofs of Marx's inconsistencies and errors all depend crucially upon one key, but little-recognized and little-understood, interpretive error—the notion that inputs and outputs are valued simultaneously in Marx's theory. We have seen throughout this book that simultaneous valuation is incompatible with the fundamental principle of Marx's value theory: the notion that value is determined by labor-time. In case after case, internal inconsistencies have been shown to appear when his theory is construed as simultaneist and to disappear when it is construed as non-simultaneist (temporalist). Temporal valuation is necessary, and temporal valuation com-

205

bined with a single-system interpretation of Marx's value theory is sufficient, to eliminate all of the apparent inconsistencies.

In order to facilitate a more careful and rigorous evaluation of my claims and demonstrations, I shall now briefly summarize the main results of this book's analysis:

1. The "physical quantities approach" (physicalism) is necessarily incompatible with Marx's theory that value is determined by labor-time. Simultaneous valuation necessarily leads to physicalist conclusions. Hence, a host of internal inconsistencies in Marx's theory arise when he is construed as a simultaneist.

2. Direct textual evidence also suggests that Marx was a temporalist. A great deal of evidence clearly favors this interpretation. The evidence that supposedly disconfirms it admits of a plausible and, in some cases, a more plausible, temporalist reading.

3. Direct textual evidence suggests that Marx was a single-system theorist. A good deal of evidence clearly favors this interpretation. Evidence adduced on behalf of the dual-system interpretation is equally compatible with the single-system interpretation.

4. The proofs of the Okishio theorem are logically invalid.

5. The Okishio theorem does not disprove Marx's law of the tendential fall in the rate of profit (LTFRP). Its conclusions hold true only when input and output prices are assumed *a priori* to be equal.

6. The LTFRP becomes logically valid once the *a priori* assumption that input and output prices are equal is jettisoned. If faster productivity growth tends to lower prices, the (temporally determined) rate of profit:

   (a) can fall under conditions in which the Okishio theorem says that it must rise;

   (b) *necessarily* tends to fall in relation to the theorem's simultaneist-physicalist rate of profit; and

   (c) can fall forever even if the simultaneist-physicalist rate of profit rises forever.

7. All results in point 6 hold true whether or not the faster productivity growth actually causes prices to fall. It only needs to lower the rate of inflation.

8. Bortkiewicz did not prove that Marx's account of the value-price transformation is internally contradictory; (simple) reproduction can occur when input and output prices differ. Hence, there was no logical need to correct Marx's account; the so-called "correct solutions" are actually alternatives to his.

9. When Marx is interpreted as a single-system theorist, all three of his aggregate value-price equalities are obtained.

10. However, when Marx is interpreted as a *simultaneous* single-system theorist, the rate of profit is physically determined, contrary to what he concluded. Hence, the logical validity of his account of the transformation is fully confirmed only when he is also interpreted as a temporalist.

11. The "Fundamental Marxian Theorem" does not prove that surplus labor is either necessary or sufficient for the existence of profit. On all simultaneist interpretations, Marx's theory implies that there can be profit without surplus labor, and vice-versa.

12. When Marx is read as a temporal single-system theorist, his theory implies that (real) profit exists when, but only when, surplus labor has been performed.

13. Even if evidence that values and prices are strongly correlated and "close" were valid, it would not tend to support Marx's value theory. Owing to a "spurious correlation" problem, the evidence is invalid. Recent studies have found that no statistically significant correlation remains after this problem is corrected. This also implies that values and prices are not "close" in the relevant sense.

One other conclusion is also worth highlighting:

14. Böhm-Bawerk's critique of Marx's account of the value-price transformation is insupportable. His key claim—namely, that Marx denied that it was self-contradictory to hold that prices *do and do not* tend to equal values—is implausible and unsubstantiated. Also, Böhm-Bawerk's conclusion that Marx's account is tautological rests on a very controversial premise.

Most of these results, particularly the most important ones, are no longer seriously disputed. Critics of Marx's value theory and other critics of the TSSI have acknowledged, however grudgingly and implicitly, that point 1 and points 5–11 are correct.[1] Thus it has been acknowledged that the LTFRP and Marx's account of the value-price transformation have *not* been shown to be logically invalid, and that his "metaphysical" value theory has *not* been shown to be superfluous to his conclusion that surplus labor is the exclusive source of profit.

Of the remaining six points, refutations of points 4, 12, and 13 would not imply that Marx's theories are logically invalid, and Böhm-Bawerk's critique (point 14) has not been a significant factor in the controversy for decades. This leaves only points 2 and 3, which pertain to contested readings of the direct textual evidence.

Thus the *proofs* of inconsistency are no longer defended; the entire case against Marx has been reduced to the *interpretive* issue. Specifically, it reduces to the critics' preference for highly implausible interpretations of his texts. What makes their interpretations implausible, I repeat, is that they fail to make Marx's texts make sense, even though it possible to do so (see point 1 and points 5–12). When an interpretation is available that eliminates the appearance of inconsistency, interpretations that produce these apparent inconsistencies are not credible. In short, the case against Marx is no case at all.

12.2 Why Does the Myth of Inconsistency Persist?

The most important of the above results (5, 6(a), 8, 9, and 10) have been in the public domain for more than fifteen years. Yet the myth of Marx's inconsistency is almost as ubiquitous as before. Why is this so?

The current ideological and political climate, in general and on the left, is certainly a factor. Interest in Marx's thought is far less widespread and less intense than when the value theory controversy was rekindled in the early 1970s. Yet this does not explain why the myth of inconsistency persists among those who should know better. To take the examples of section 1.4, why has this myth been repeated in recent years by respected academics—Brewer and his interlocutors, Brenner, and Sørensen and his interlocutors—and a respected journalist like Cassidy?

The major reason is undoubtedly that the gatekeepers to the broader public —the specialists in the field, mainly Marxist and Sraffian economists—have not done their part to set the record straight. Their acknowledgements that the proofs of inconsistency are invalid, and that Marx can be read in a way that makes his contested arguments logically valid, have come quite late in the day. As we have seen above (especially in sections 7.5 and 9.6), moreover, in almost every case these acknowledgements are buried in discussions that divert attention from the question of internal inconsistency, and they are stated in ways that make it nearly impossible to recognize that the author is indeed acknowledging error.[2] With the exception of an acknowledgement by Foley (2000b: 282), none of them has even come close to the explicitness of, say, the opening sentences of points 5 and 8 above. Most importantly, any *effort* to set the record straight has been negligible, especially in comparison with the time and energy that has been spent rehearsing and correcting Marx's alleged inconsistencies and errors. This phenomenon is perhaps surprising. Since almost all of these economists view themselves as working in the tradition of Marx, it might be expected that they would jump at the chance to dispel the myth of inconsistency. Indeed, this is what I initially expected. So why have these economists responded in the opposite manner? In light of their gatekeeping function, this is the key question that must be answered in order to explain why the myth persists. What I offer here are only some provisional and conjectural beginnings of an answer. The present case might be a fruitful one for historians of economic thought and sociologists and philosophers of social science to explore further.

To some extent, the present case seems to be an instance of a broader problem noted by the physicist Max Planck (1949: 33–34): "A new scientific truth does not triumph by convincing its opponents and making them see the light, but rather because its opponents eventually die and a new generation grows up that is familiar with it." This phenomenon is apparently common in many fields. For example, Darwin suffered from it, Wegener's now-accepted "continental drift hypothesis" was resisted by geologists for several decades, and Kline (1985: 74) observed that "[t]he history of mathematics illustrates . . . that it is more difficult to get a truth accepted than to discover it."

Yet failure to *accept* new ideas is not the main issue here. One need not accept that Marx's disputed conclusions are true in order to acknowledge that they are logically valid. One need not accept that they are logically valid in order to acknowledge that there exists an interpretation according to which they are valid. One can even continue to believe that Marx's conclusions are logically invalid while acknowledging that the proofs of inconsistency have been decisively refuted. And one can do all this clearly and forthrightly, without trying to divert readers' attention or change the subject. Thus the key question is not why the new findings that vindicate Marx have failed to gain acceptance, but why they have been *suppressed*.

Suppression of dissident ideas seems to be a very common phenomenon. Drawing on his very extensive study and documentation of such suppression in the physical sciences and elsewhere,[3] Brian Martin (1998: 609) concludes, "A person who challenges the conventional wisdom is likely first to be ignored, then dismissed, and finally, if these responses are inadequate, attacked." The present case clearly conforms to this pattern with respect to the first two stages.[4]

To explain why suppression of dissident ideas takes place in science, Martin (1998: 606–608) suggests that we consider a scientific community in terms of its interests. One example is a group's interest in "maintaining control over an occupation." If we replace "occupation" with "field," it is plausible that some suppression may have occurred for this reason in the present case.

Martin (1998: 607) also notes that dissident ideas are ignored and dismissed because "scientists . . . can develop a psychological interest in particular theories and methods. If a challenger comes along with a simple alternative to the theory on which they have built their careers, most scientists are not likely to be receptive, since their status will be undermined and their lifelong commitment apparently wasted."[5] *I believe this to be the dominant factor behind the suppression of the new findings in value theory.*

This might seem implausible. Again, it is reasonable to expect that economists working in the tradition of Marx would be quite receptive to findings that vindicate the logical validity of his value theory. Aren't these economists in fact committed to what Martin calls the "simple alternative"—the theory of Marx?

They are not. The Marxist and Sraffian economists are committed to the so-called corrections of Marx, while the "simple alternative" is his original theory (understood in a way that eliminates the logical imperative to correct it). Much effort has been put into correcting Marx and to pursuing research programs founded on "correct" versions of his work. Indeed, Marxian and Sraffian economics have consisted of little else, at least in the English-speaking world, since Sweezy wrote *The Theory of Capitalist Development* six decades ago. Thus, much research will have been in vain, and several research programs will lose their foundation, if the allegations of internal inconsistency and the consequent need to correct Marx go away.

This would not be such a problem if, as has so often been claimed, the "corrections" were mere technical revisions. Were that the case, it would be easy for the Marxian and Sraffian economists to reconstitute their research programs on the basis of Marx's own theory. Yet we have seen that the revisions are far from mere technicalities; the original and the revised versions of his theory lead to conflicting conclusions in many important respects. The most obvious and politically important case is that Marx's original theory and the physicalist revisions arrive at diametrically opposite conclusions regarding the effect of labor-saving technological change on the rate of profit. Thus, if the myth of internal inconsistency were to disappear, the Marxist and Sraffian economists would first have to abandon their current theoretical perspectives, perspectives to which almost all of them seem deeply committed, before they could reconstitute their research programs on the basis of Marx's theory.

Yet there is another option as well. They could remain fully committed to their current perspectives and research programs, while happily accepting that Marx's value theory is logically valid and doing their part to set the record straight. They would simply need to acknowledge that their theories are *alternatives* to Marx's and to represent them as such.

Why has this simple solution not been embraced? I suspect that there are two main reasons. First, the Marxist and Sraffian economists want to have their cake and eat it too. On the one hand, they disagree with at least a large part of Marx's critique of political economy (when it is understood in a way that makes it logically valid). On the other hand, they regard themselves as Marx's successors. The myth of inconsistency allows them to have it both ways, since they can claim to have eliminated "Marx's errors . . . without undermining his basic account of how capitalism functions" (Mongiovi 2002: 395; cf. Bellofiore 2002: 104, Laibman 2004: 16). If the myth of inconsistency were to disappear, they would need to choose between having their cake and eating it.

Second, I suspect that their research programs are not compelling enough to stand on their own, uncoupled from the supposed need to correct Marx that gave rise to them. Even Sraffianism, the strongest and least traditionally Marxist of these research programs, would have little appeal, and its key theorems would have much less significance, if it could no longer be portrayed as the sole rigorous formulation of "the" surplus approach founded by Ricardo and Marx.

Thus the Marxist and Sraffian economists cannot reclaim Marx's value theory in its original form without abandoning their physicalist perspective. But neither can they accept it as a viable alternative to their own theories without relinquishing their claim to be Marx's successors and jeopardizing their research programs. Both options are very unattractive. The only option that remains is to try to disqualify Marx's original theory. To accomplish this task, the "well-established proofs" of inconsistency are just what are needed. They allow Marx's original theory to be disqualified effortlessly, decisively, and on seemingly neutral, scientific grounds.

Hence, given the alternatives they face, the Marxist and Sraffian economists have a clear and strong interest in preserving the myth of inconsistency. I believe that they are acting in their own interests, and that this is the main reason why the new findings in value theory have been suppressed and why so little has been done to set the record straight.

12.3 The Task Ahead

As we have seen, Planck suggested that a new idea generally triumphs because its opponents eventually die out and a new generation comes along that is familiar with it. Yet we cannot sit back and wait for the next generation of scholars to recognize that the charges of inconsistency are mythical, and then to give Marx's *Capital* the reconsideration it deserves. At this moment, there seems to be no new generation able to replace the old one.

I am not suggesting that "Marx is dead," or that the younger generation is uninterested in his thought. On the contrary, there seems to be more interest among youth today in Marx and Marxism, especially outside of the United States, than there was a decade ago, and there are some signs of a revival of Marxian scholarship. But general interest in Marx is one thing; renewed development of his *critique of political economy* is another. Owing to the disintegration of Marxian economics and the strong barriers that exist between academic disciplines, the institutional resources and the depth of knowledge that would be needed to reclaim *Capital* as a totality—not merely to use one or another particular aspect of it—appear to be lacking at present. If the myth of inconsistency persists much longer, it is far from certain that this situation will improve. People will go on believing that *Capital* cannot be reclaimed as a totality, and the resources needed to reclaim it will not be forthcoming.

Yet the refutations of the inconsistency allegations give us an excellent opportunity to help turn things around, provided that we shine a bright spotlight upon these refutations and keep it focused upon them, shining brightly, until the myth of inconsistency is eliminated. It is up to the present generation to set the record straight—big time.

Notes

1. To the best of my knowledge, only a few authors continue to challenge any of these points. Loranger (2004) challenges point 1; Moseley (2000a, 2000b), points 1 and 10; Screpanti (2003, 2005), points 8 and 11; Veneziani (2004), point 7; and Mongiovi (2002) seems to challenge point 11. Refutations of points 1, 7, 10, and 11 would not imply that Marx's theories are logically invalid. Only a refutation of point 8, challenged by Screpanti alone, would do so. But Screpanti's (2005) rejection of point 8 fails to take account of Kliman and McGlone (1988) and subsequent works in which this point is demonstrated (see Carchedi 2005).

2. By way of contrast, Levhari and Samuelson's retraction of their "nonswitching theorem" during a debate with Sraffa's followers (the "capital controversies") is a model of honesty and clarity. Their paper, "The Nonswitching Theorem is False," begins as follows: "We wish to make clear for the record that the nonswitching theorem associated with us is definitely false. We are grateful to Dr. Pasinetti for first giving examples that raise legitimate doubts about the theorem's truth . . . . And we are grateful to Professor Morishima, Professor Garegnani and Mr. Sheshinski for independent counterexamples that settle this matter definitively" (Levhari and Samuelson 1966: 518).

3. See the materials archived on his "Suppression of Dissent" website, www.uow. edu.au/arts/sts/bmartin/dissent (Dec. 19, 2005).

4. I shall not try to answer whether it has progressed to the third stage, attack. As Martin (1988: 610) notes, "only some types of attacks are easy to document," and "[a]ttacks on dissidents are never admitted as such. They are always justified as being due to the inadequacies on the part of the dissident, such as low quality work or inappropriate behavior." Let me simply call readers' attention to a statement issued by the parent body, managing editor, and editorial board of the *Review of Radical Political Economics,* which states in part: "the Editorial Board has removed the sanction denying Dr. Kliman the right to submit articles to *RRPE* for publication. There was no intention to inflict harm on Dr. Kliman." (*Review of Radical Political Economics* 34:1, Winter 2002, page facing inside back cover.)

5. Similarly, Dunbar (1995: 161) observes that sometimes "[m]istakes of logic are made [by scientists], the evidence fudged and the results of tests fiddled, all in a desperate effort to preserve a theory that an individual has committed most of his or her life to. Who amongst us wants to end a lifetime that has been devoted to the pursuit of a theory with nothing but failure to show for it?"

Bibliography

Alberro, José and Joseph Persky. 1981. The Dynamics of Fixed Capital Revaluation and Scrapping, *Review of Radical Political Economics* 13:2, 21–37.

Arthur, Christopher J. 2001. Value, Labour and Negativity, *Capital and Class* 73, 15–39.

Baggini, Julian and Peter S. Fosl. 2003. *The Philosopher's Toolkit: A compendium of philosophical concepts and methods*. Malden, Mass. and Oxford: Blackwell.

Barkai, Haim. 1965. Ricardo's Static Equilibrium, *Economica* 32, no. 125, 15–31.

————. 1967. A Note on Ricardo's Notions of Demand, *Economica* 34, no. 133, 75–79.

Baumol, William J. 1974. The Transformation of Values: What Marx "really" meant (an interpretation), *Journal of Economic Literature* 12:1, 51–62.

Bellofiore, Riccardo (ed.). 1998. *Marxian Economics. A reappraisal. Vol. 2: Essays on volume III of "Capital": profit, prices and dynamics*. London: Macmillan.

————. 2002. "Transformation" and the Monetary Circuit: Marx as a monetary theorist of production. In Campbell, Martha and Geert Reuten (eds.), *The Culmination of Capital: Essays on volume III of Marx's "Capital."* Houndmills, UK: Palgrave Macmillan, 102–27.

————. 2005. A Ghost Turning into a Vampire: The concept of capital and living labour. Presented at *Historical Materialism* conference, Univ. of London, Nov. 5.

Böhm-Bawerk, Eugen von. 1984 (1896). *Karl Marx and the Close of his System*.

Bortkiewicz, Ladislaus von. 1952 (1906–1907). Value and Price in the Marxian System, *International Economic Papers* 2, 5–60.

————. 1984 (1907). On the Correction of Marx's Fundamental Theoretical Construction in the Third Volume of *Capital*. In Böhm-Bawerk 1984, 197–221.

Brenner, Robert. 1998. The Economics of Global Turbulence, *New Left Review* 229, 1–265.

Brewer, Anthony. 1995. A Minor Post-Ricardian?: Marx as an economist, *History of Political Economy* 27:1, 111–45.

Butterfield, Herbert. 1965 (1931). *The Whig Interpretation of History*. New York: W. W. Norton.

Carchedi, Guglielmo. 1984. The Logic of Prices as Values, *Economy and Society* 13:4, 431–55.

————. 2002. The Art of Fudging. In Vasapollo, Luciano (ed.), *Un Vecchio Falso Problema/An Old Myth*. Rome: Laboratorio per la Critica Sociale, 157–90.

————. 2005. Sapiens Nihil Affirmat Quod Non Probat, *Review of Political Economy* 17:1, 127–39.

Cassidy, John. 1997. The Return of Karl Marx, *The New Yorker*, Oct. 20 & 27, 248ff.

Chalmers, Alan. 1990. *Science and Its Fabrication*. Minneapolis: University of Minnesota Press.

Charasoff, Georg von. 1910. *Das System des Marxismus: Darstellung und kritik*. Berlin: Hans Bondy.

Cockshott, Paul and Allin Cottrell. 1998. Does Marx Need to Transform? In Bellofiore (ed.) 1998, 70–85.

————. 2005. Robust correlations between sectoral prices and labour values: a comment, *Cambridge Journal of Economics* 29:2, 309–16.

Connolly, John M. and Thomas Keutner. 1988. Introduction: Interpretation, Decidability, and Meaning. In Connolly and Keutner (eds.), *Hermeneutics versus Science?: Three German views*. Notre Dame: Univ. of Notre Dame Press, 1–67.

Croce, Benedetto. 1914. *Historical Materialism and the Economics of Karl Marx*. London: Allen & Unwin.

Cullenberg, Stephen. 1994. The Falling Rate of Profit: Recasting the Marxian debate. London: Pluto.

Darwin, Charles. 1872 (1859). *The Origin of Species*, 6th ed. London: John Murray.

Desai, Meghnad. 1988. The Transformation Problem, *Journal of Economic Surveys* 2:4, 295–333.

————. 2002. *Marx's Revenge: The resurgence of capitalism and the death of statist socialism*. London and New York, Verso.

Dmitriev, V. K. 1974 (1898). *Economic Essays on Value, Competition and Utility*. Cambridge: Cambridge Univ. Press.

Dobb, Maurice. 1972. The Sraffa System and Critique of the Neo-Classical Theory of Distribution. In Hunt and Schwartz (eds.) 1972, 205–21.

Duménil, Gérard. 1980. *De la Valeur aux Prix de Production: Une réinterprétation de la transformation*. Paris: Economica.

————. 1983. Beyond the Transformation Riddle: A labor theory of value, *Science & Society* 47:4, 427–50.

Duménil, Gérard and Dominique Lévy. 2000. The Conservation of Value: A rejoinder to Alan Freeman, *Review of Radical Political Economics* 32.1, 119–46.

Dunayevskaya, Raya. 1991 (1982). *Rosa Luxemburg, Women's Liberation, and Marx's Philosophy of Revolution*, 2nd ed. Urbana, IL and Chicago: Univ. of Illinois Press.

————. 2000 (1958). Marxism and Freedom: From 1776 until today, 6th ed. Amherst, NY: Humanity Books.

————. 2003 (1973). *Philosophy and Revolution: From Hegel to Sartre, and from Marx to Mao*, 4th ed. Lanham, Md.: Lexington Books.

Dunbar, Robin. 1995. *The Trouble with Science*, Cambridge: Harvard Univ. Press.

Ernst, John R. 1982. Simultaneous Valuation Extirpated: A contribution to the critique of the neo-Ricardian concept of value, *Review of Radical Political Economics* 14:2, 85–94.

Farjoun, Emmanuel and Moshé Machover. 1983. *Laws of Chaos*. London: Verso.

Feyerabend, Paul. 1988 (1975). *Against Method*, revised ed. London and New York: Verso.

————. 2002 (1987). *Farewell to Reason.* London and New York: Verso.

Fish, Stanley. 1980. What Makes an Interpretation Acceptable?. In Fish, Stanley, *Is There a Text in This Class?: The authority of interpretive communities.* Cambridge: Harvard Univ. Press, 338–55.

Foley, Duncan K. 1982. The Value of Money, the Value of Labor Power and the Marxian Transformation Problem, *Review of Radical Political Economics* 14:2, 37–47.

————. 1986. *Understanding Capital: Marx's economic theory.* Cambridge: Harvard Univ. Press.

————. 1997. Review of *Marx and Non-Equilibrium Economics, Eastern Economic Journal* 23:4, 493–96.

————. 1999. Response to David Laibman, *Research in Political Economy* 17, 229–33.

————. 2000a. Recent Developments in the Labor Theory of Value, *Review of Radical Political Economics* 32:1, 1–39.

————. 2000b. Response to Freeman and Kliman, *Research in Political Economy* 18, 279–83.

Freeman, Alan. 1984. The Logic of the Transformation Problem. In Mandel and Freeman (eds.) 1984, 221–64.

————. 1996. Price, Value and Profit—a continuous, general, treatment. In Freeman and Carchedi (eds.) 1996b, 225–79.

————. 1997. If They're So Rich, Why Ain't They Smart?: Another prelude to the critique of economic theory. Unpublished paper, Univ. of Greenwich, UK. www.gre. ac.uk/~fa03/research/7a-eaepe97.rtf (Dec. 19, 2005).

————. 1998. The Transformation of Prices into Values: Comment on the chapters by Simon Mohun and Anwar M. Shaikh. In Bellofiore (ed.) 1998, 270–75.

————. 1999. Between Two World Systems: A response to David Laibman, *Research in Political Economy* 17, 241–48.

————. 2004. The Case for Simplicity: A paradigm for the political economy of the 21st century. In Freeman, Kliman, and Wells 2004, 55–66.

Freeman, Alan and Guglielmo Carchedi. 1996a. Foreword. In Freeman and Carchedi (eds.) 1996b, vii–xx.

———— (eds.). 1996b. *Marx and Non-equilibrium Economics,* Cheltenham, UK: Edward Elgar.

Freeman, Alan and Andrew Kliman. 2000. Two Concepts of Value, Two Rates of Profit, Two Laws of Motion, *Research in Political Economy* 18, 243–67.

Freeman, Alan, Andrew Kliman, and Julian Wells (eds.). 2004. *The New Value Controversy and the Foundations of Economics,* Cheltenham, UK: Edward Elgar.

Freudenthal, Gideon. 1986 (1982). *Atom and Individual in the Age of Newton: On the genesis of the mechanistic world view.* Dordrecht: Reidel.

Graça Moura, M. da. 2000. Metatheory as the Key to Understanding: Schumpeter after Shionoya. Presented at Cambridge Realist Workshop Conference, Cambridge Univ., May 7. www.econ.cam.ac.uk/seminars/realist/events/conf2000/papers/download/ moura.rtf (Dec. 19, 2005).

Greenspan, Alan. 2000. Technology and the Economy. Speech at the Economic Club of New York, Jan. 13. www.federalreserve.gov/boarddocs/speeches/2000/200001132. htm (Dec. 19, 2005).

Hahnel, Robin. 2005. *Economic Justice and Democracy: From competition to cooperation.* New York and London: Routledge.

Harcourt, G. C. 1969. Some Cambridge Controversies in the Theory of Capital, *Journal of Economic Literature* 7:2, 369–405.

Hilferding, Rudolph. 1984 (1904). Böhm-Bawerk's Criticism of Marx. In Böhm-Bawerk 1984, 119–96.

Hirsch, E. D. 1967. *Validity in Interpretation*. New Haven: Yale Univ. Press.

Hodgson, Geoffrey M. 2001. *How Economics Forgot History: The problem of historical specificity in social science*. London: Routledge.

Hogan, Patrick Colm. 1996. *On Interpretation: Meaning and inference in law, psychoanalysis, and literature*. Athens, Ga. and London: Univ. of Georgia Press.

Hollander, Samuel. 1990. Ricardian Growth Theory: A resolution of some problems in textual interpretation, *Oxford Economic Papers* 42:4, 730–50.

Howard, M. C. and J. E. King. 1992. *A History of Marxian Economics: Volume II, 1929–1990*. Princeton, NJ: Princeton Univ. Press.

Hudis, Peter. 2000. Can Capital Be Controlled?, *News & Letters*, April. www.newsandletters.org/Issues/2000/April/4.00_essay.htm (Dec. 19, 2005).

Hunt, E. K. and Jesse G. Schwartz (eds.). 1972. *A Critique of Economic Theory*. Harmondsworth, UK: Penguin.

Kliman, Andrew J. 1988. The Profit Rate Under Continuous Technological Change, *Review of Radical Political Economics* 20:2–3, 283–89.

———. 1996. A Value-theoretic Critique of the Okishio Theorem. In Freeman and Carchedi (eds.) 1996b, 206–24.

———. 1999a. Internal Inconsistencies of the Physical Quantities Approach, *Political Economy* 4, 57–76.

———. 1999b. Sell Dear, Buy Cheap?: A reply to Laibman, *Research in Political Economy* 17, 235–40.

———. 2000a. Marx's Concept of Intrinsic Value, *Historical Materialism* 6:1, 89–113.

———. 2000b. The Need for a Genuinely Empirical Criterion of Decidability among Interpretations: Comments on a paper of Fred Moseley's. www.akliman.squarespace.com/writings (Dec. 19, 2005).

———. 2001. Simultaneous Valuation vs. the Exploitation Theory of Profit, *Capital and Class* 73, 97–112.

———. 2002. The law of value and laws of statistics: sectoral values and prices in the US economy, 1977–97, *Cambridge Journal of Economics* 26:3, 299–311.

———. 2003. Value Production and Economic Crisis: A temporal analysis. In Westra, Richard and Alan Zuege (eds.), *Value and the World Economy Today*. London and New York: Palgrave Macmillan, 119–36.

———. 2004a. Marx vs. the "20th-Century Marxists": A reply to Laibman. In Freeman, Kliman, and Wells (eds.) 2004, 19–35.

———. 2004b. Spurious Value-Price Correlations: Some additional evidence and arguments, *Research in Political Economy* 21, 223–38.

———. 2005. Reply to Cockshott and Cottrell, *Cambridge Journal of Economics* 29:2, 317–23.

———. 2006a. Exploitation. In Ritzer, George (ed.), *Blackwell Encyclopedia of Sociology*. Oxford: Blackwell (forthcoming).

———. 2006b. Screpanti vs. Marx on Exploitation, *Review of Political Economy* 18:2, 265–69.

Kliman, Andrew and Alan Freeman. 2000. Rejoinder to Duncan Foley and David Laibman, *Research in Political Economy* 18, 285–93.

————. 2006. Replicating Marx: A reply to Mohun, *Capital and Class* 88, 117–26.

Kliman, Andrew and Ted McGlone. 1988. The Transformation non-Problem and the non-Transformation Problem, *Capital and Class* 35, 56–83.

————. 1999. A Temporal Single-System Interpretation of Marx's Value Theory, *Review of Political Economy* 11:1, 33–59.

Kline, Morris. 1985 (1967). *Mathematics for the Nonmathematician*, New York: Dover Publications.

Komorzynsky, J. V. 1897, 'Der dritte Band von Carl Marx "Das Kapital"': eine Kritische Abhandlung über die Arbeitswerttheorie und die Socialistische Lehre vom Capitalsertrage', *Zeitschrift für Volkswirtschaft, Socialpolitik und Verwaltung*, 6:2, 242–99.

Kosík, Karel. 1976. *Dialectics of the Concrete: A study on problems of man and the world*. Dordrecht-Holland and Boston: D. Reidel Publishing.

Krause, Ulrich. 1982. *Money and Abstract Labour*. London and New York: Verso.

Kuhn, Thomas S. 1970 (1962). *The Structure of Scientific Revolutions*, 2nd ed., enlarged. Chicago and London: Univ. of Chicago Press.

————. 2000. What are Scientific Revolutions? In Kuhn, Thomas S., *The Road since "Structure": Philosophical essays, 1970–1993, with an autobiographical interview*, Conant, James and John Haugeland (eds.). Chicago and London: Univ. of Chicago Press, 17–36.

Laibman, David. 1982. Technical Change, the Real Wage and the Rate of Exploitation: The falling rate of profit reconsidered, *Review of Radical Political Economics* 14:2, 95–105.

————. 1997. *Capitalist Macrodynamics: A systematic introduction*. Houndmills, UK: Macmillan.

————. 1999a. Okishio and His Critics: Historical cost versus replacement cost, *Research in Political Economy* 17, 207–27.

————. 1999b. The Profit Rate and Reproduction of Capital: A rejoinder. *Research in Political Economy* 17, 249–54.

————. 2000. Two of Everything: A response, *Research in Political Economy* 18, 269–78.

————. 2004. Rhetoric and Substance in Value Theory: An appraisal of the new orthodox Marxism. In Freeman, Kliman, and Wells 2004, 1–17.

Lee, Chai-On. 1993. Marx's Labour Theory of Value Revisited, *Cambridge Journal of Economics* 17:4, 463–78.

Levhari, David and Paul A. Samuelson. 1966. The Nonswitching Theorem is False, *The Quarterly Journal of Economics* 80:4, 518–19.

Levine, A. L. 1974. This Age of Leontief . . . and Who?: An interpretation. *Journal of Economic Literature* 12:3, 872–81.

Lipietz, Alain. 1986. Behind the Crisis: The exhaustion of a regime of accumulation. A "Regulation School" perspective on some French empirical works, *Review of Radical Political Economics* 18:1–2, 13–32.

Loranger, Jean-Guy. 2004. A profit-rate invariant solution to the Marxian transformation problem, *Capital and Class* 82, 23–58.

Lorde, Audre. 1984. The Master's Tools Will Never Dismantle the Master's House. In Lorde, Audre, *Sister Outsider: Essays and Speeches*. Freedom, CA: The Crossing Press, 110–13.

McConnell, Campbell R. and Brue, Stanley L. 2005. *Economics: Principles, Problems, and Policies*, 16th ed. Boston: McGraw-Hill/Irwin.

McGlone, Ted and Andrew Kliman. 2004. The Duality of Labor. In Freeman, Kliman, and Wells 2004, 135–50.

Maldonado-Filho, Eduardo. 1997. Release and Tying up of Productive Capital and the "Transformation Problem." Presented at Eastern Economic Association conference, Boston, March.

Malinowski, B. 1921. The Primitive Economics of the Trobriand Islanders, *Economic Journal* 31, no. 121, 1–16.

Mandel, Ernest. 1991. Introduction. In Marx 1991a, 9–90.

Mandel, Ernest and Alan Freeman. 1984. *Ricardo, Marx and Sraffa: The Langston memorial volume*. London: Verso.

Martin, Brian. 1998. Strategies for Dissenting Scientists, *Journal of Scientific Exploration* 12:4, 605–16.

Marx, Karl. 1971 (1889). *Value, Price and Profit*. New York: International Publishers. (Written in 1865.)

————. 1973 (1939). *Grundrisse: Foundations of the critique of political economy*. London: Penguin. (Written in 1857–1858.)

————. 1975a (1930). Marx's *Notes* (1879–1880) *on Adolph Wagner*. In Carver, Terrell (ed.), *Karl Marx: Texts on method*. Oxford: Blackwell, 179–219. (Written in 1879–1880.)

————. 1988. *Karl Marx, Frederick Engels: Collected Works*, Vol. 30. New York: International Publishers. (Notebooks I–VII of the 1861–1863 Economic Manuscript.)

————. 1989a. *Karl Marx, Frederick Engels: Collected Works*, Vol. 31. New York: International Publishers. (Notebooks VII–XII of the 1861–1863 Economic Manuscript.)

————. 1989b. *Karl Marx, Frederick Engels: Collected Works*, Vol. 32. New York: International Publishers. (Notebooks XII–XV of the 1861–1863 Economic Manuscript.)

————. 1990a (1890). *Capital: A critique of political economy*, Vol. I. London: Penguin. (This and other English-language editions are based on the 4th German edition of 1890, edited by Frederick Engels. Between 1867 and 1875, Marx oversaw the publication of the first two German editions and the original French edition.)

————. 1990b (1933). Results of the Immediate Process of Production. In Marx 1990a, 948–1084. (Written in 1863 and/or 1864.)

————. 1991a (1894). *Capital: A critique of political economy*, Vol. III . London: Penguin. (Written between 1863 and 1880.)

————. 1991b. *Karl Marx, Frederick Engels: Collected Works*, Vol. 33. New York: International Publishers. (Notebooks XV–XX, plus closing part of Notebook V, of the 1861–1863 Economic Manuscript.)

————. 1992 (1885). *Capital: A critique of political economy*, Vol. II. London: Penguin. (Written between 1863 and 1881.)

————. 1994. *Karl Marx, Frederick Engels: Collected Works*, Vol. 34. New York: International Publishers. (Manuscripts written between 1861 and 1864, incl. Notebooks XX–XXIII of the 1861–1863 Economic Manuscript.)

Medio, Alfredo. 1972. Profits and Surplus Value: Appearance and reality in capitalist production. In Hunt and Schwartz (eds.) 1972, 312–46.

Milios, John, Dimitri Dimoulis, and George Economakis. 2002. *Karl Marx and the Classics: An essay on value, crises and the capitalist mode of production.* Aldershot, UK and Burlington, Vt.: Ashgate.

Mirowski, Philip. 1988. *Against Mechanism: Protecting economics from science.* Lanham, Md.: Rowman & Littlefield.

————. 1989. *More Heat than Light: Economics as social physics, physics as nature's economics.* Cambridge: Cambridge Univ. Press.

Mohun, Simon. 1984–1985. Abstract Labor and its Value Form. *Science & Society* 48:4, 388–406.

————. 2003. On the TSSI and the Exploitation Theory of Profit, *Capital and Class* 81, 85–102.

Mongiovi, Gary. 2002. Vulgar Economy in Marxian Garb: A critique of temporal single-system Marxism, *Review of Radical Political Economics* 34:4, 393–416.

Morishima, Michio. 1973. *Marx's Economics: A Dual Theory of Value and Growth.* Cambridge: Cambridge Univ. Press.

Moseley, Fred. 1993a. Marx's Logical Method and the "Transformation Problem." In Moseley (ed.) 1993b, 157–83.

———— (ed.). 1993b. *Marx's Method in Capital: a reexamination.* Atlantic Highlands, NJ: Humanities Press.

————. 1999. Marx's Concept of Prices of Production: Long-run center-of-gravity prices. Presented at Eastern Economic Association conference, Boston, March.

————. 2000a. The Determination of Constant Capital in the Case of a Change in the Value of the Means of Production. Presented at Eastern Economic Association conference, Washington, DC, March. www.mtholyoke.edu/~fmoseley/CONCP.htm (Dec. 19, 2005).

————. 2000b. The "New Solution" to the Transformation Problem: A sympathetic critique, *Review of Radical Political Economics* 32:2, 282–316.

Moszkowska, Natalie. 1929. *Das Marxsche System: Ein Beitrag Zu Dessen Aufbau.* Berlin: Verlag Hans Robert Engelmann.

Mühlpfort, Wolfgang. 1895. Karl Marx und die Durchschnittsprofitrate, *Jahrbücher für Nationalökonomie* 65, 92–99.

Nakatani, Takeshi. 1979, Price Competition and Technical Choice, *Kobe University Economic Review* 25, 67–77.

Naples, Michele I. 1989. A Radical Economic Revision of the Transformation Problem, *Review of Radical Political Economics* 21:1–2, 137–58.

————. 1993. Unperceived Inflation in Shaikh, and Kliman and McGlone: Equilibrium, disequilibrium, or nonequilibrium?, *Capital and Class* 51:1, 119–37.

New Left Review editors. 1998. Themes, *New Left Review* 229, i–v.

Nuti, D. M. 1974. Introduction. In Dmitriev 1974, 7–28.

Ochoa, Edward M. 1984. *Labor-Values and Prices of Production: An interindustry study of the United States economy, 1947–1972.* Ph.D. dissertation, Department of Economics, New School for Social Research, New York.

Ochoa, Eduardo M. 1989. Values, Prices, and Wage-Profit Curves in the US Economy, *Cambridge Journal of Economics* 13:3, 413–29.

Okishio, Nobuo. 1961. Technical Changes and the Rate of Profit, *Kobe University Economic Review* 7, 85–99.

————. 1993a. *Nobuo Okishio—Essays on Political Economy: Collected papers.* Frankfurt am Main: Peter Lang.

————. 1993b. A Mathematical Note on Marxian Theorems. In Okishio 1993a, 27–39.

————. 1993c. Three Topics on Marxian Fundamental Theorem. In Okishio 1993a, 77–94.

————. 1993d. Value and Production Price. In Okishio 1993a, 41–59.

Osuna Guerrero, Rubén. 2003. *Un Modelo Secuencial para el Cálculo de Precios. El caso Español 1986–1994.* Ph.D. dissertation, Facultad de Ciencias Económicas y Empresariales. Universidad Nacional de Educación a Distancia UNED, Spain.

Perez, Manuel. 1980. Valeur et Prix: Un essai de critique des propositions néoricardiennes, *Critiques de l'Economie Politique*, Nouvelle Série No. 10, 122–49.

Petry, Franz. 1916. *Der Soziale Gehalt der Marxschen Werttheorie.* Jena: G. Fischer.

Planck, Max. 1949. *Scientific Autobiography, and Other Papers; with a memorial address on Max Planck.* New York: Philosophical Library.

Plotnitsky, Arkady. 1997. "But It Is Above All Not True": Derrida, relativity, and the "science wars," *Postmodern Culture* 7:2, www3.iath.virginia.edu/pmc/text-only/issue.197/plotnitsky.197 (Dec. 19, 2005).

————. 1998. On Derrida and Relativity: A reply to Richard Crew. *Postmodern Culture* 8:2, www3.iath.virginia.edu/pmc/text-only/issue.198/8.2exchange (Dec. 19, 2005).

Polya, G. 1988 (1945). *How to Solve It: A new aspect of mathematical method,* 2nd ed. Princeton: Princeton University Press.

Postone, Moishe. 1993. *Time, Labor, and Social Domination: A reinterpretation of Marx's critical theory.* Cambridge: Cambridge Univ. Press.

Quine, W. V. O. 1960. *Word and Object*, Cambridge and London: MIT Press.

————. 1980. *From a Logical Point of View: Nine Logico-Philosophical Essays*, 2nd edition, revised, Cambridge and London: Harvard Univ. Press.

Ramos-Martínez, Alejandro. 1991. Competencia y Reproducción Capitalista: Una Interpretación de la Transformación de Valores en Precios de Producción, *Ciencias Económicas*, 11:1–2, Costa Rica, 53-79. Reprinted, with some changes, in *Realidad Económica*, nos. 105–106, Buenos Aires 1992, 191–212.

————. 1998-1999, Value and Price of Production: New evidence on Marx's tranformation procedure, *International Journal of Political Economy* 28:4, 55–81.

————. 2004. Labour, Money, Labour-Saving Innovation, and the Falling Rate of Profit. In Freeman, Kliman, and Wells (eds.) 2004, 67–84.

Rescher, Nicolas. 2001. *Philosophical Reasoning.* Malden, Mass. and Oxford: Blackwell.

Reuten, Geert. 1993. The Difficult Labor of a Theory of Social Value: Metaphors and systematic dialectics at the beginning of Marx's "Capital." In Moseley (ed.) 1993, 89–113.

Robinson, Joan. 1941. Marx on Unemployment, *Economic Journal* 51, 234–48.

————. 1967. *An Essay on Marxian Economics,* 2nd ed. London: Macmillan.

Roemer, John. 1981. *Analytical Foundations of Marxian Economic Theory.* Cambridge: Cambridge Univ. Press.

————. 1982. *A General Theory of Exploitation and Class.* Cambridge: Harvard Univ. Press.

————. 1988. *Free to Lose: An Introduction to Marxist Economic Philosophy.* London: Radius.

Rorty, Richard. 1991. Texts and Lumps. In Rorty, Richard, *Objectivity, Relativism, and Truth: Philosophical papers,* Vol. 1. Cambridge: Cambridge Univ. Press, 78–92.

Rosenberg, Jay F. 1984. *The Practice of Philosophy: A handbook for beginners,* 2nd ed. Englewood Cliffs, NJ: Prentice-Hall.

Saad-Filho, Alfredo. 2001. *The Value of Marx: Political economy for contemporary capitalism.* London: Routledge.

Salvadori, Neri. 1981. Falling Rate of Profit with a Constant Real Wage. An example, *Cambridge Journal of Economics* 5:1, 59–66.

Samuelson, Paul A. 1957. Wages and Interest: A modern dissection of Marxian exploitation models, *American Economic Review* 47:6, 884–912.

———. 1971. Understanding the Marxian Notion of Exploitation: A summary of the so-called "transformation problem" between Marxian values and competitive prices, *Journal of Economic Literature* 9:2, 399–431.

———. 1973. Samuelson's "Reply on Marxian Matters," *Journal of Economic Literature* 11:1, 64–68.

———. 1974a. Insight and Detour in the Theory of Exploitation: A reply to Baumol, *Journal of Economic Literature* 12:1, 62–70.

———. 1974b. Rejoinder: Merlin unclothed, a final word, *Journal of Economic Literature* 12:1, 75–77.

Screpanti, Ernesto. 2003. Value and exploitation: a counterfactual approach, *Review of Political Economy* 15:2, 155–71.

———. 2005. Guglielmo Carchedi's "Art of Fudging" Explained to the People, *Review of Political Economy* 17:1, 115–26.

Seton, Francis. 1957. The "Transformation Problem," *Review of Economic Studies* 24, 149–60.

Shaikh, Anwar M. 1977. Marx's Theory of Value and the "Transformation Problem." In Schwartz, Jesse, *The Subtle Anatomy of Capitalism.* Santa Monica: Goodyear Publishing, 106–39.

———. 1978. Political Economy and Capitalism: Notes on Dobb's theory of crisis, *Cambridge Journal of Economics* 2:2, 233–51.

———. 1982. Neoricardian Economics: A wealth of algebra, a poverty of theory, *Review of Radical Political Economics* 14:2, 67–82.

———. 1984. The Transformation from Marx to Sraffa. In Mandel and Freeman (eds.) 1984, 43–84.

Sharrock, Wes, and Rupert Read. 2002. *Kuhn: Philosopher of Scientific Revolution,* Cambridge, UK: Polity Press.

Shibata, Kei. 1934. On the Law of Decline in the Rate of Profit, *Kyoto University Economic Review* 9:1, 61–75.

Sørensen, Aase B. 2000. Toward a Sounder Basis for Class Analysis, *American Journal of Sociology* 105:6, 1523–58.

Sperber, Dan. 1982. Apparently Irrational Beliefs. In Hollis, Martin and Steven Lukes, *Rationality and Relativism.* Cambridge: MIT Press, 149–80.

Sraffa, Piero. 1951. Introduction. In Ricardo, David, *On the Principles of Political Economy and Taxation.* Cambridge: Cambridge Univ. Press, pp. xiii–lxii.

———. 1960. *Production of Commodities By Means Of Commodities: Prelude to a critique of economic theory.* Cambridge and New York: Cambridge Univ. Press.

Steedman, Ian. 1977. *Marx after Sraffa.* London: New Left Books.

———. 1981. Ricardo, Marx, Sraffa. In Steedman, Ian, et al. 1981, 11–19.

Steedman, Ian, et al. 1981. *The Value Controversy.* London: Verso.

Stigler, George J. 1965. Textual Exegesis as a Scientific Problem, *Economica* 32, no. 128, 447–50.

———. 1990. Ricardo or Hollander?, *Oxford Economic Papers* 42:4, 765–68.

Sweezy, Paul M. 1970 (1942). *The Theory of Capitalist Development: Principles of Marxian political economy*. New York: Modern Reader Paperbacks.

Tugan-Baranowsky, Michael I. 1901, *Studien zur Theorie und Geschichte der Handelkrisen in England*. Jena: Fischer.

Tsoulfidis, Lefteris, and Thanasis Maniatis. 2002. Value, prices of production and market prices: Some more evidence from the Greek economy, *Cambridge Journal of Economics* 26:3, 359–69.

URPE Steering Committee, Hazel Dayton Gunn, and the Editorial Board of *RRPE*. 2002. Statement by URPE Steering Committee, Hazel Dayton Gunn, Managing Editor of *RRPE*, and the Editorial Board of *RRPE*, *Review of Radical Political Economics* 34.1, 114 (page facing inside back cover).

Veneziani, Roberto. 2004. The Temporal Single-System Interpretation of Marx's Economics: A critical evaluation, *Metroeconomica* 55:1, 96–114.

Warnke, Georgia. 1993. *Justice and Interpretation*. Cambridge: MIT Press.

Wilson, N. L. 1959. Substances Without Substrata, *Review of Metaphysics* 12:4, no. 48, 521–39.

Winternitz, J. 1948. Values and Prices: A Solution of So-Called Transformation Problem, *Economic Journal* 58, no. 230, 276–80.

Wolff, Richard, Bruce Roberts, and Antonino Callari. 1982. Marx's (not Ricardo's) "Transformation Problem": A radical reconceptualization, *History of Political Economy* 14:4, 564–82.

Wolff, Richard, Antonino Callari, and Bruce Roberts. 1984. A Marxian Alternative to the Traditional "Transformation Problem," *Review of Radical Political Economics* 16: 2–3, 115–35.

Wright, Erik Olin. 1981. The Value Controversy and Social Research. In Steedman, I. et al. 1981, 36–74.

———. 2000. Class, Exploitation, and Economic Rents: Reflections on Sørensen's "Sounder Basis." *American Journal of Sociology* 105:6, 1559–71.

Index

Note: technical terms are defined on page numbers set in boldface.

About the Author

Andrew Kliman is professor of economics at Pace University in Pleasantville, New York. A member of Phi Beta Kappa, he holds B.A. and Ph.D. degrees in economics from the University of Maryland and the University of Utah, respectively. Co-editor of *Critique of Political Economy,* a new pluralistic and interdisciplinary scholarly journal, he has served as co-organizer of the International Working Group on Value Theory since 1993. He is also a co-founder of and teacher at The New SPACE (The New School for Pluralistic Anti-Capitalist Education) in New York City, where he and his wife reside.

Professor Kliman is a co-editor of and contributor to *The New Value Controversy and the Foundations of Economics.* Other edited collections to which he has contributed include *Marx and Non-equilibrium Economics, Un Vecchio Falso Problema / An Old Myth,* and *Value and the World Economy Today.* His work has also appeared in numerous scholarly journals, including *Beiträge zur Marx-Engels-Forschung,* the *Cambridge Journal of Economics, Capital and Class, Historical Materialism, Political Economy, Research in Political Economy,* and *Review of Political Economy.* He is currently working on a study guide and commentary to volumes II and III of *Capital.*